Adoption and Adaption in Digital Business

Adoption and Adaption in Digital Business

Keith Sherringham and Bhuvan Unhelkar

BEP
BUSINESS EXPERT PRESS
Leader in applied, concise business books

Adoption and Adaption in Digital Business

First published in 2021 by
Business Expert Press, LLC
222 East 46th Street, New York, NY 10017
www.businessexpertpress.com

ISBN-13: 978-1-63742-024-9 (paperback)
ISBN-13: 978-1-63742-025-6 (e-book)

Business Expert Press Service Systems and Innovations in Business and Society Collection

Collection ISSN: 2326-2664 (print)
Collection ISSN: 2326-2699 (electronic)

First edition: 2021

10 9 8 7 6 5 4 3 2 1

Description

Bringing sustainable change is part of our lives and occurs because we decide to do things differently. To become a winning sports team, the consistent and persistent application of proven principles is pragmatically and incrementally used with adoption and adaption to circumstance. The sports team undertakes campaigns or programs to address emergent behaviors while delivering specific outcomes through its people. The team trains differently, skills up, varies the plays and nurtures the players, brings new leadership, and takes time to resolve issues. The wining team comes from the emergent behavior of empowered emotional individuals who have ownership. They have pride in who they are, what they do, and who are prepared to do things differently, because their interests and values are aligned. The leadership works best when they are the change they wished to see and treat others as they themselves would be treated.

Similarly, with COVID-19. The environment was changed, behaviors were instilled, people were supported, and outcomes were achieved. Having people want to do things differently was key to containing and living with COVID-19. This also applies to a business being transformed or undergoing digital transformation. Sustainable change comes through having people do things differently. An emergent behavior of empowered individuals with an emotional response having ownership with pride in who we are and what we do. We make change because interests and values are aligned, we understand the need, and we have trust in the process. When we are supported and provided with the skilling (the ability to do) and training (the how to do), we make changes and an emergent behavior is formed. We respond to a change in our environment, we exhibit revised behaviors, and we achieve an outcome.

Change requires ambiguity management, messaging with the emotional bond to create empowered emotional ownership which requires decision making, leadership being the change they wish to see and treating others as they themselves would wish to be treated to enable interests and values to be aligned. A hands-on approach to "fixing the pipes and helping people" for sustainable change is provided within this book to enable the emotional empowered ownership with interests and values alignment required for change to support "I do good work, change is coming, help me with the change, and I can do more".

Keywords

ambiguity management; behaviors management; business transformation; change leadership; change management; COVID-19; decision making; digital transformation; interests & values; leadership; operational change; organizational change; process improvement; project management; risk management; service management; strategy

Contents

Foreword

Grant me the serenity to accept the things

I cannot change,

courage to change the things I can,

and wisdom to know the difference

Serenity Prayer
Reinhold Niebuhr

Preface

From coaching a children's sports team, to lifting people out of poverty across a country, to transforming a company, through digital transformation, to making the work environment better for a group within an organization, change is part of our lives. Change is how we better ourselves, achieve our goals and dreams, or improve the lives of those around us. Change does not occur by some magic wand or silver bullet or panacea that just works and produces results quickly with minimal issues. You only have to look at the varying successes in business transformation to see this. Yet, the sports team becomes a winning championship team through the consistent and persistent application of proven practices. The winning sports team forms an emergent behavior to make the changes necessary. Amongst others, the winning sports team manages ambiguity, provides support and messaging with an emotional bond, brings empowered emotional ownership, makes decisions, provides leadership, and aligns interests and values through skilling and training and other supporting activities.

Change is about people and getting us to do things in another way, like eating differently for better health. We understand the issue, the impacts, what we should do, and where to get help and support. The actions then come from empowered individuals with ownership, pride in who they are and what they do, who are responding emotionally, because interests and values are aligned. With help and support provided, an emergent behavior is formed, and change occurs: *"I do good work, change is coming, help me with the change, and I can do more."*

Whether it is a business attempting digital transformation or our experience from a winning sports team, we see that crafting and shaping change is about working with the nuances and complexities of people as well as getting the best from them to do things differently. By being the change we wish to see and treating others as we ourselves would wish to be treated, we form an emotional bond to align interests and values in those around us who we then influence. The environment for the team is changed, the behaviors are instilled, and the results achieved. The change to a winning team has come from an emergent behavior by the actions of empowered individuals who have ownership with the alignment of interests and values.

The global response to the COVID-19 pandemic saw people from around the world stand up and help each other in an emergent behavior. The emergent behavior included the sharing of time, goods, and skills and expertise. A change in the environment occurred, behaviors were shaped, and an outcome of responding to COVID-19 and the new normal was seen. This emergent behavior was crafted and shaped through the actions of empowered individuals having ownership with pride in who they are and what they did. Knowing the issue, the importance to them, what was needed to be done, and where to get help enabled people to better themselves and those around them.

Whether you are leading transformation in a country, or coaching and mentoring a business through change, or wanting to influence your team, this book provides a hands-on approach to bringing real and sustainable change through the betterment of people. A range of pragmatic and practical experience and advice is brought together in a series of chapters to form some self-contained guidelines within an overall approach to successfully achieving change. Please feel free to mix and match what you need for your circumstance to help you to help those around you.

We hope this book has grabbed your attention and that it will resonate with your views, experiences, and goals and aspirations. Thank you for your most valued gift, your time, and we hope to repay your investment for you and those you help.

Perspective

We live with change. A sports team becomes a winning team through the consistent and persistent application of proven principles applied pragmatically. The sports team trains differently, skills up, varies the plays and nurtures the players, brings new leadership, and takes time to resolve, rather than the magic wand or panacea or the one size fits all approach. The wining team comes from the emergent behavior of empowered emotional individuals who have ownership. They have pride in who they are and what they do and do things differently because the interests and values are aligned. The leadership works best when they were the change they wished to see and treated others as they themselves would be treated. The environment was changed, behaviors were instilled, and outcomes are achieved.

Managing the COVID-19 global pandemic showed similar patterns. The importance of crafting and shaping emergent behaviors in bringing the change was seen. It was the actions of empowered individuals with ownership which was required to contain the spread of the virus (individuals washed hands, social distanced, wore a mask, and volunteered for testing). The response was emotional, but people changed what they did because interests and values were aligned. People responded to leadership which guided and made decisions, especially when the leaders were the change they wished to see and treated others as they themselves would be treated. The efforts of people were recognized, issues were explained, the impacts understood, and help and support were provided. People responded and helped those around them. People were taken on a journey of change; efforts were made to get the best from people, with adoption and adaption to circumstance.

In COVID-19, the environment was changed, behaviors were instilled, and outcomes were achieved through the emergent behavior of individuals over time. We responded differently according to our experiences and views, but overall, we responded when our interests and values were aligned. We were accepting when mistakes were made, because we saw the adoption and adaption to circumstance. Budgets and resources were required. The impacts had to be managed and a multitude of approaches, which varied according to circumstance, were used. The combination of Ambiguity Management, Messaging, Empowered Emotional Ownership, Decision Making, Leadership, and Interests and Values alignment (AMEDLI) was seen to bring the change and sustain the change for responding to COVID-19.

Both the sports team and COVID-19 show how change is achieved. These same principles applied pragmatically bring changes to teams, organizations, or countries. From the transformation of business, to making changes in response to costs or regulatory changes, or a business trying to undergo digital transformation, bringing change requires people to do things differently. We know how to do this, and the change is enabled through supporting "I do good work, change is coming, help me with the change, and i can do more." The next step is with us. Do we want to fix the pipes and help people (make the decisions necessary and take the required actions)?

Getting the Most from This Book

This book is about a real-world approach to having us do things differently. Pragmatically and practically bringing change in us or those around us, a range of text, images, and videos are provided for the consistent and persistent application of proven principles and practices (www.amedli. biz). It is often best to just start and bring those around you on the journey, because any time is a good time to start with a real-world approach to having us do things differently.

Helping the reader to bring empowered emotional ownership, be the change they wish to see, and to treat others as we ourselves would be treated. The intent of the book is to shape actions on what is required and how to go about bringing sustainable change. What an individual reader gets from this book is up to us as individuals and what we elect to do. Read as standalone sections, end-to-end, incrementally, or sequentially to develop an overall picture. Choose to read selected sections, in parts or entirety, and/or referenced back, as well as mixing and matching according to needs with the videos (www.amedli.biz). For ease of access and use, chapters include:

QR Code for
www.amedli.biz

- Summary—A summary for prioritization of reading.
- Key learnings—As bullet points, key learnings from the chapter are also included.
- Next steps—Action items on how to implement the main points from the chapter.

Most of the chapters provide sections around the themes, how to set the example, what to do to make it happen, and then links to the supporting materials (often linking to supporting videos).

Beyond the direct business and management use of this book, the book can also be used to assist in the setting of policies, governance, and management of transitions and services across industry sectors as well as within government. Applicable on both the business and the technology sides, the book brings value within business management and operations, as well as skilling and training within business. Also suited for educational purposes, this book can also play a role within undergraduate and post-graduate teaching forming the basis for lectures, discussions, and practical projects. Example audiences include:

- Executive Level: From the role of leadership in organizational change management to the business impacts of technology at the board level, this book provides insights to make transformation real.
- Senior Management Level: To those faced with maintaining operations whilst making strategic and operational changes, the realities of achieving change and the forming of emergent behaviors are laid out.
- Technologist: From the ICT operations management to those who love to develop the technology, the realities of adoption and adaption around technology are explored.
- Business Operations Manager: For those faced with pragmatic adoption and integration, this book provides an approach for making it happen.
- Postgraduate Researcher: Opportunities and areas for research are hinted at throughout the book.
- Masters Student (Technology or Business or Both): This book provides a valuable teaching aid around achieving change as this is the environment in which they will live and work.
- Lecturer: For those teaching and preparing lectures, ample material is furnished that can be used alongside industry and course-specific teaching.
- Trainers: A range of course material is provided to those writing and providing training whether it is for operational change, technology adoption, or specific capacity and capability building.

- Management Consultants: The consultants advising businesses on transformation and the adoption of technology and for those implementing, the book provides valuable insights and guidance as well as how cloud-based knowledge worker services are changing the business model of the consultants.
- Accreditors and Certifiers: Use of the material within other offerings, or within modules, as part of accreditation and certification across a range of industries with focus on the professional skills.

Change is part of our lives and is about getting people to do things differently. Change the environment, instill the behaviors, to achieve the outcomes. It is the actions of empowered emotional individuals with ownership and pride in who they are and what they do that brings change. Change comes from the alignment of interests and values and having leadership that is the change they wish to see and treat others as they themselves would be treated. Change is about working with what you have, crafting and shaping the emergent behaviors, to get the best from people. Change takes time and comes from the consistent and persistent application of proven principles implemented pragmatically.

Whether you are a leader shaping the future, aspiring to make a better future, wishing to further an education, or just seeking to help the people around you, please enjoy the read and the videos (www.amedli.biz) as best suits and may the rewards come your way.

CHAPTER 1

Taking What Works and Learning from Mistakes

Change succeeds when we resolve our need and trust in the change

Summary

"I do good work, change is coming, help me with the change, and I can do more." Change is part of our lives, like our desire to better ourselves and those around us to changing the form of a sports team. Technology and automation have transformed agriculture and food production, as well as mining and extractive industries. Manufacturing and logistics have also been transformed and technology is transforming the services sector. Change is brought by people, and success is seen when we can resolve our needs and trust in the change is seen. Change comes through the consistent and persistent application of proven practices, learning from mistakes, and adopting and adapting. This chapter provides the context for achieving organizational change management that works because of the valuing of people.

Core Concepts

A series of core concepts (Weekly Mirror Message—Concepts in the Management of Change—https://youtu.be/8uCQuChnjug) around change are presented, which are addressed throughout this book including:

- We must be the change we wish to see.
- We need to treat others as we ourselves would wish to be treated.
- Change is about people and getting people to do things differently. This takes time. There needs to be an emotional bond and an alignment of interests and values.

- Change comes from the emergent behavior with the actions of empowered individuals having ownership and pride in who they are and what they do.
- Change the environment, instill the behavior, and achieve the outcomes.
- "I do Good Work, Change is Coming, Help Me with the Change, and I can do More" is the mantra.
- Tell me the issue, the importance to me, what I need to do, where I can get help and support, and what you are doing to help me.
- Change is the consistent and persistent application of proven principles applied pragmatically rather than the magic wand or the panacea or the silver bullet.
- Trust in leadership with trust in the process is required for sustainable change.
- Take what works and make it better, but change is sustained and ongoing.
- Provide the recipes to enable us to follow, as well as to customize to meet their needs.
- Change is incremental which adopts and adapts to circumstance rather than the one size fits all approach.
- Decision making is part of change. A decision is only as good as its implementation and the response to varying circumstances.
- Sustainable change requires ambiguity management, messaging for the emotional bond, empowered emotional ownership, decision making, leadership, and interests and values aligned.

Key Learnings

Key learnings from this chapter include:

- Change and transformation is part of our lives. We live the experience as we try to improve the results of a sports team or community group.

- Bringing change is about people and what they do. Success comes when we work to get the best from people. Change is nuanced and requires the emotional response from people. It also takes time to bring sustainable change.
- Change succeeds when you can answer questions like "what makes you think you can get people to change what they do?" or "Do I understand what is being asked and why?" or "What do I need to make the change?" or "Would I make this change?"
- Change comes through the consistent and persistent application of proven business principles pragmatically applied.
- Alongside other frameworks for delivery like service management or project management, change management needs to address the complexities and nuances of managing people. This includes Ambiguity Management, Messaging, Empowered Emotional Ownership, Decision Making, Leadership, and Interests and Values aligned (AMEDLI).

Introduction

Whether you coach a sports team, are a player in a team, are the leader of an organization, are guiding a business through digital transformation, or are the leader of a country, we are faced with managing change. As much as we may wish for things to slow down and remain steady, change is with us and is ongoing. If there was no change, the performance of the sports team would remain with championships lost. Change is about people doing things differently because it is in their interest to do so and the change is aligned with their values. Look no further than the new plays and the practicing drills to be a better player or musician or artist. To make change, we need to know "what is the issue?," "what we need to do?," "why we need to do it?," and "where to get help and support?" We value knowing that support is around us and that assistance is there to help us. We know that things are complex and nuanced, and we may need help in making decisions. We value leadership and respond to messaging that forms an emotional bond with us. We respond with emotion to many things. We tend to do things when our Interests and Values are aligned, and we have empowerment and ownership. If we have trust in the change, we are prepared to make them.

Bringing change to the sports team or having a society respond to a global pandemic is about the emergent behavior from the actions of empowered individuals with ownership of their actions and pride in who they are and what they do. This requires the crafting and shaping of the emergent behaviors with the capacities and capabilities to hand. It is about how we get the best from people and take them on a journey (the Journey Model). By changing the environment, behaviors are instilled, and outcomes achieved.

At the heart of realizing the results from change is *"I do good work, change is coming, help me with the change, and I can do more."* An example is the player in a team who wants to do better using the guidance of the coach to do different drills, team exercises, and a different diet. This is where this book can be of value. This book is given so that it may help you and those you help by sharing skills and expertise that are proven in working with change. We ask you compare your lived experience and see if this book is of help.

This chapter provides some context and background and introduces some concepts that underpin successful change and transformation with other concepts being introduced in subsequent chapters. After discussing aspects of change, the consistent and persistent application of proven practices is addressed. An overarching approach to working with the nuances and complexities of people in change is introduced. This overall approach addresses the people and emotional issues in sustainable change of Ambiguity Management, Messaging, Empowered Emotional Ownership, Decision Making, Leadership, and Interests and Values alignment (AMEDLI) in forming the emergent behaviors required. An outline of the chapters in this book is also presented, together with suggested next steps.

Aspects of Change Transformation

Change Is Part of Our Lives

From coaching a children's sports team, to lifting people out of poverty across a country, to transforming a company or a group within an organization, change is all around us. With rapid changes in technology, the pace of transformation is increasing and is penetrating all aspects of life. When agricultural production was automated, jobs were transferred to manufacturing and brought changes to the industry. Opportunities were made, livelihoods changed, people felt uncertainty, and a change management process was followed to bring the transformation. Further transformation in agriculture is occurring with the use of high-intensity indoor food production and with the use of robots for planting, weeding, caring, and picking. Automation is being used in food processing plants and hi-tech jobs are increasing in agriculture as more technology is used. Other primary industries like mining have also been automated and technologies like automated trucks and trains are being adopted by the industry, which bring changes to the numbers employed, the skill sets used, and the technical expertise required.

With the move of jobs from agriculture to manufacturing and the use of the assembly line, new roles were created for which skilling (the ability to do) and training (the how to do) were required. The automation of manufacturing has changed the skills and expertise mix, as well as the number of jobs in manufacturing. Some manufacturing in low labor cost countries remains manually intensive, while other high-end specialist and custom manufacturing using advanced technologies requires skilled manual labor, but with fewer people employed. Similarly, other industries like transport and logistics make greater use of technology and automation such as the automation of ports and computerized inventories. Less people are employed, having different skill sets, and are often working in different roles.

Automation is also transforming the jobs in the service sector. Jobs that require complex people management like the changing of bed sheets and the administering of healthcare use technology and are likely to remain labor intensive. Roles requiring complex stakeholder management are likely to remain labor intensive but with technology use. Other parts of the service industry such as retail with online shopping and automated fulfillment are being transformed through technology. Again, the types of jobs, the numbers employed, and the skills and expertise required are changing. Through digital transformation and automation, impacts to roles within knowledge worker services and business operations like loan approvals or routine legal advice or insurance applications are being seen because of automation and the use of artificial intelligence and machine-to-machine learning. More sophisticated knowledge worker services like tax or audit or software development are also being automated, and at a faster rate. Consider a career in tax where the emerging career paths are:

- Specialist high-end advice and services, which remain mainly labor intensive but with use of technology and high-end skills.
- Running routine operations that are highly automated. This requires less people who use increasing levels of technology with a proactive "exceptions management" skill set. The example of the checking of format and data validation to the tax office now requires less people than several years ago because of automation, even though more data are being checked.
- Bringing automated operations and its products and services to clients. This requires highly skilled resources with excellent industry experience as well as technology application.

Like it was for agriculture and manufacturing, the automation of knowledge worker services brings changes in roles, skills, expertise, and numbers employed. Similarly, for the companies specializing in tax or legal services, the threat from digital transformation is the technology company that automates their services with fewer people being employed in routine operations with major changes in revenue and service models. While these changes bring opportunities, the sentiments of uncertainty, resistance to rapid change, and fear about livelihoods can often prevail. For many of us, including the routine knowledge workers:

- With services being the final people-intensive sector and the other sectors being automated, where are the opportunities emerging, and what are the numbers of people required with what skill sets?
- Different skills and expertise are needed in the high-end services, but can people make the transition?
- Even with the right skill sets and expertise, lesser numbers of people are needed for automated operations, but are there enough opportunities in the high-end manual services?

- For the low-end operations and services at minimal wage, will they be able to flourish and grow in an automated society?

While we may not have all the answers or know how things will play out, history has shown us how and our lived experience tells us what we need to do (Adoption and Adaption to Automation—https://youtu.be/dQJ8UbyN0d4).

Our Feelings Toward Change

Our feelings toward change and business transformation are nuanced and are an emotional response from people.

About People

Achieving success in transformation or change is realized by the actions of people. It is we as people who put the artificial intelligence software onto a computer and establish a database or configure data feeds. It is we who run and maintain the technology and provide services, and it is we who use the results to deliver products and services. Recognizing the role of people in transformation is key because if the right people are motivated with right skills and expertise, then the implementation of the change has a better chance of succeeding.

Recognition of Nuanced Emotions in Change

Where we have trust in the process and the outcomes are aligned with our values and interests, we are more accepting of change, even when it is difficult. Making the decisions and undergoing the process to build a winning sports team may be difficult, but we are accepting. The business transformation that sees us being laid off and with no certainty for our livelihoods or the poorly led project that just increases our workload for little value to us sees a different emotional response in us. It is this recognition of nuanced emotions which forms part of the success in bringing change.

Getting the Best from What We Have

With recognition of the importance of people and their nuanced emotions forming the basis for successful change implementation and adoption comes the acceptance that to achieve the outcomes, it is about getting the best from the resources we have. Rather than "if we had this" or "if only they did this," the effort is on working with what is to hand and how to build the emotional nuanced response to get the best from the resources we have. The sports team analogy again prevails. A coach has a set number of players they can use and in a winning week the coach brings out the best in the cohesive and motivated team for a win. The next week, the team may lose because their performance is below par. Either way, the coach works with what they have and strives to bring out the best in the team.

Acceptance of Time

Triggering the right emotional response is only part of the success in achieving change. Change takes time to achieve. Training is the how to and skilling is the ability to do. Training can be achieved quicker if the skill base exists, while building skills takes longer. Since people take time to respond and do things differently, bringing transformation or change takes time to implement and time for the results to be seen. Part of effective organizational change management is acceptance that transformation takes time to implement and for the results to be achieved.

The Basic Questions

From influencing the behaviors of children as they grow, to economic transformation of a country, bringing change is about having us do things differently. For change to occur, the basic questions need to be asked by those seeking to make changes: "what makes you think you can get people to change what they do?" or at the least answer "why do you think your change will work?" Other questions that need to be answered include:

• Do I understand what is being asked and why?—As a leader
  of change and asking people to do things, we need to be able

to answer this question. As a participant in the change, if we can answer this, then we will know what to do.

- What do I need to make the change?—As a leader of change we need to know this so that we can judge if the change will succeed and we will need to be able to answer questions from those around us seeking guidance and advice on what to do. As a participant in the change, if I can answer this, then I can get help and support.
- Does this make sense and is there a benefit?— As a leader of change we need to know this so that we can communicate the change. Where the benefit is missing the personal emotional bond, the change is harder to achieve. As a participant in the change, my motivation is reduced when I do not see its value and it does not make sense.
- Can I sustain it?—As a leader of change we need to know whether the change implementation can be sustained and, once implemented, will the change continue because of the new or revised habits. As a participant, I need the motivation and capacities and capabilities to continue the new or revised habits, otherwise it is just resorting to existing practices.
- Would I make this change?— If you yourself are not prepared to make the change, then why are others?
- What makes you think you can get people to change what they do?— Whether you are a leader of change or a participant in the process, if you are not able to answer all of the former questions in the affirmative, then why will the change occur?

Being able to answer these questions is a requisite for change being successful.

Making Change and Transformation Work

This short introduction shows us the need for understanding the role of people, the nuanced emotional response, acceptance of time, and working to get the best from what we have. Some of the most elementary questions integral to success have been posed. Already we are starting to see the picture of the components that need to come together. Combine this emerging view with our lived experience of bringing change and transformation being nuanced, requiring a multitude of approaches which are sustained over time. Simply, managing people is complex. Triggering and sustaining the right emotional response is also difficult.

Therefore, transformation does not occur by some magic wand or silver bullet or panacea that will just work and produce results quickly with minimal issues. While the one size fits all approach with all the buzz words has appeal, we know better. Transformation is not some quick training session on a new process and being left on your own after that point. Whether it is building up our sports team, a community group, motivating colleagues at work, or bringing organizational change management across a business, it is the consistent and persistent application of proven principles and practices that yields results. It is about taking the proven practices of what works, learning from mistakes, and adopting and adapting to the changing environment.

Applying Proven Principles

To Get the Most

Getting the most from change management comes from the consistent and persistent application of proven principles (Weekly Mirror Message— Pragmatics and Realities of Change—https://youtu.be/jnsF_nf2piY): building the capacities and capabilities, adopting and adapting to the situation to hand, learning the lessons from mistakes, and sustaining the effort. Change is about working with what we have and to get the best from it.

Setting the Example

Pragmatic business experience shows a tendency for unrealistic expectations, a desire to have one size fits all, and the use of the "silver bullet" or "magic wand" or "panacea" approach which will just bring transformation and realize results. The reality is that making change, bringing business transformation, and realizing sustained outcomes is complex, takes time, and can be frustrating because it is about the actions of multiple people. Successful business transformation shows us that it is the consistent and persistent application of proven principles that brings results. Looking at examples where change has been less successful, the lack of the pragmatic consistent and persistent application of proven principles is seen.

Like the functioning of a successful sports team, it is an emergent behavior from the actions of individuals in response to a series of drivers through which change and business transformation occurs (Figure 1.1). The business drivers (e.g., markets, customers, costs, regulatory) with the availability of resources and funds, combined with the emotional bond formed, all drives the shaping of the emergent behavior. The emergent behavior comes through the leadership, the enablement of people, the facilitation of the process, and the communication of the change.

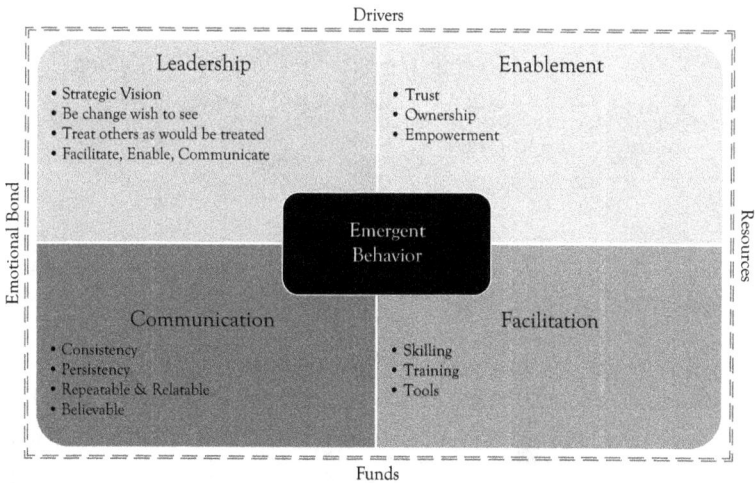

Drivers

Leadership	Enablement
• Strategic Vision	• Trust
• Be change wish to see	• Ownership
• Treat others as would be treated	• Empowerment
• Facilitate, Enable, Communicate	

Emergent
Behavior

Communication	Facilitation
• Consistency	• Skilling
• Persistency	• Training
• Repeatable & Relatable	• Tools
• Believable	

Emotional Bond

Resources

Funds

Figure 1.1 Those bringing success have pragmatically applied proven business practices and principles

Making It Real

The consistent and persistent pragmatic application of proven business practices is required for the realization of benefits from and for sustainable business transformation and change. Like a change in habits, good habits require effort to be ongoing, and it is easy to resort to bad habits without the incentives and drivers. Making it real is a leadership decision to use the proven practices rather than the silver bullet or the magic wand approach. It is then about leadership staying the course and following through. The communication which was used to bring the change is used to sustain the effort together with the facilitation and ownership. A review mechanism and improvement process is part of the ongoing sustaining of effort.

Further Details

- Forming the Emotional Bond—People bring change in response to an emotional bond (see Chapter 4, Section "Having Empowered Emotional Ownership").
- Basic Questions—Change comes when the basic questions are asked and resolved (see Chapter 6, Section "Why and How Are We Going to Change What We Do?").
- Video—Problem Solving Together for Our Future: Sharing Skills and Expertise—Applying Proven Principles (https://youtu.be/4Ti9pqilS-k).

AMEDLI

To Get the Most

Change Management can be achieved through a variety of frameworks of which ADKAR (Awareness, Desire, Knowledge, Ability, Reinforcement) is one example. Like any framework, these frameworks have their advantages and short comings and are only as good as their usage. A mixture of frameworks (e.g., project management, vendor management, financial management, as well as change management) with pragmatic and practical application which are "fit for purpose" is how change returns results (see Chapter 8, Section "Frameworks"). The area of emergent behaviors for change with their crafting and shaping, the people aspects, and the emotional needs of change (e.g., a resistance to change may be accumulative from a series of previous changes) are part of the leadership of change and are to be managed. To help with the layout of this book and to reinforce the elements required for managing people and emergent behavior in successful change, the mnemonic of AMEDLI is used (Figure 1.2).

A Ambiguity Management

M Messaging

E Empowered Emotional Ownership

D Decision Making

L Leadership

I   Interests and Values

Figure 1.2 AMEDLI is an overall or overarching approach alongside other frameworks for managing nuances and complexities of people in change management

AMEDLI (www.amedli.biz) provides an overall or overarching approach to the crafting and shaping of emergent behaviors. AMEDLI brings together all of the people factors, dependencies, and interrelationships of change management into a coherent approach. AMEDLI can be used alongside other change management frameworks or others for project management or service management that are required to deliver sustainable transformation.

Setting the Example

Whether it is change management within a business group, for the organization, or for a country, as well as at the individual level, we are faced with addressing (Figure 1.3):

- *Ambiguity Management*—The management of ambiguity that comes in the implementation and ongoing. This results from the differences in people, their capacities, capabilities, skills, expertise, and motivations. The business environment is subjected to ongoing variations as well. Adoption of the response and adaption to revised circumstances are all part of ambiguity management along with risk management.
- *Messaging*—The communication of all aspects of the change, from what is happening and why, to who is doing it, to the impacts, motivations, and leadership decisions, as well as

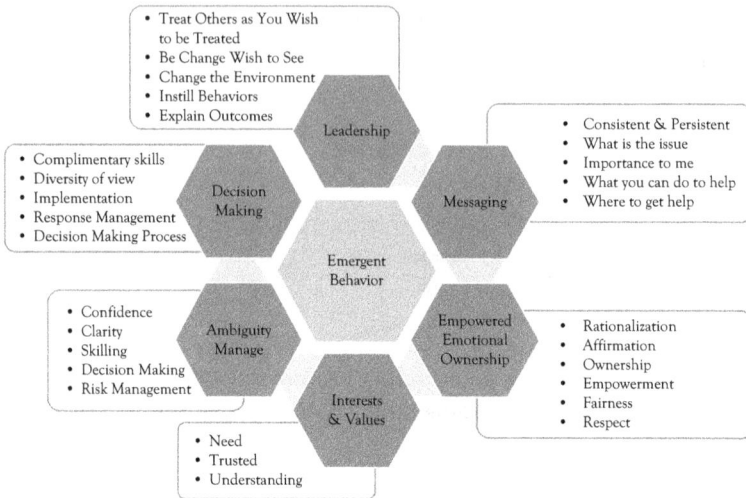

Figure 1.3 AMEDLI—Ambiguity Management, Messaging, Empowered Emotional Ownership, Decision Making, Leadership, Interests and Values

reporting and performance. The correct messaging with the emotional bond is required.

- *Empowered Emotional Ownership*—The effectiveness, efficiency, and excellence of emergent behavior come from the actions of individuals who are empowered and have ownership. This is an emotional response. Forming this emotional response, creating ownership, and empowering are an integral leadership function.

- *Decision Making*—At all levels, decisions need to be made and then implemented. It is the implementation of the decisions and the revised response to varying conditions that make the decisions successful.

- *Leadership*—Leaders need to be the change they wish to see and to treat others as they themselves would be treated. With the required leadership having vision, direction, strategy, and showing what is required and instilling the required behaviors, the required response is invoked, and change is realized.

- *Interests and Values*—When interests and values are aligned with the change, the required motivation can be achieved.

Ambiguity Management, Messaging with the emotional bond to create Empowered Emotional Ownership which requires Decision Making, Leadership being the change they wish to see and treating others as they themselves would wish to be treated to enable Interests and Values to be aligned. When all of these elements come together the emergent behavior can be formed.

Consider the coach of a sports team. The coach is seeking the emergent behavior for the team of a cohesive unit of individuals working together. The players are seeking similarly. Collectively they address:

- Ambiguity Management—Varying the game plan and responding to specific plays as the game evolves. The mistakes of the opposing team are exploited, and the team tries to cover for its mistakes.
- Messaging—Communication between the team of the game plays, the motivations, and tactics to name a few.
- Empowered Emotional Ownership—It is the actions of the individuals in the team working together that brings success. The players are Empowered and are expected to perform. The players have an emotional bond to the outcomes. The players take Ownership for their roles and responsibilities and help cover for teammates.
- Decision Making—Across the team, decisions of all types are made, but they look to the captain and the coach for direction, intent, and strategy.
- Leadership—Captains and coaches are expected to lead the teams. Teams lacking leadership underperform.
- Interests and Values—When the interests and values of the team with those of the managers, coaches, support staff, and owners are aligned, a successful team is seen. When there is division within the group and/or the interests and values are not aligned, weaker performance results.

AMEDLI is aimed at forming the emergent behavior for managing change. AMEDLI is an overarching approach that addresses the nuances and realities of working with people which can be pragmatically applied.

AMEDLI is aligned to proven real-world experiences for ease of use and adoption. AMEDLI still uses frameworks like project management or service management or vendor management and other proven business practices as needed within the implementation and operations. With an acceptance of the factors mentioned previously (see Section "Our Feelings toward Change" of this chapter), AMEDLI becomes a logical overarching approach to refer back to because it also addresses the basic questions of change (see Section "The Basic Questions" of this chapter) as given in Table 1.1.

Table 1.1 AMEDLI provides a framework for answering key questions that lead to successful change management

Example questions	AMEDLI example
What makes you think you can get people to change what they do?	• Ambiguity Management: Management of nuances and uncertainty is included which is missing in many other change frameworks • Messaging: The importance of messaging is accommodated • Decision Making: Supported • Empowered Emotional Ownership: The personal motivational factors are provisioned for • Leadership: The need for leadership is a critical part of the solution • Interest and Values: Recognize the importance and alignment of interests and values in forming the emotional bond
Do I understand what is being asked and why?	• Messaging: The messaging to meet this is included • Empowered Emotional Ownership: The personal motivational factors are provisioned for • Interest and Values: Alignment of interests and values
What do I need to make the change?	• All of the required elements are provided from which the details can be determined
Does this make sense and is there a benefit?	• Messaging: Provides the details so that it makes sense • Interest and Values: Alignment of interests and values for the benefit
Can I sustain it?	• Messaging: The messaging to meet this is included • Empowered Emotional Ownership: The personal motivational factors are provisioned for • Interest and Values: Alignment of interests and values
Would I make this change?	• All of the required elements are provided from which the details can be determined

Making It Real

Forming and management of the emergent behaviors is often a requisite for the delivery and for achieving sustainable change. Beyond addressing the basic questions of change, AMEDLI provides a complimentary framework for managing the nuances, complexities, and interdependencies of people factors. AMEDLI can then be used as an overall and overarching approach for achieving and sustaining change. With the use of AMEDLI, the making it real is then about:

- Skilling and training on AMEDLI as part of the capacity and capability for change management.
- Use of AMEDLI as the overall and overarching approach and managing ambiguity.
- Messaging AMEDLI and use of AMEDLI.
- Decision is made to use AMEDLI and it forms part of the decision-making process.
- Empowered Emotional Ownership uses AMEDLI principles.
- Leadership uses AMEDLI.
- Interests and Values are aligned by using AMEDLI within the change management approach.

Making it real requires the consistent and persistent pragmatic application of AMEDLI as part of the proven business practices required.

Further Details

- Video—AMEDLI—Ambiguity Management, Messaging, Empowered Emotional Ownership, Decision Making, Leadership, Interests and Values (https://youtube. com/playlist?list=PL_oMn8eF6JVgUtZgfFT6PAao7- H0ADyWb).
- Video—Problem Solving Together for Our Future: Sharing Skills and Expertise—AMEDLI (https://youtu.be/ V3TkCBDOwtQ).

- Video—Weekly Mirror Message—The Story of an Individual (https://youtu.be/xxHgmdiQmjg).
- Video—AMEDLI—Deciding to Make Use of AMEDLI (https://youtu.be/tbxxYcM3lcU).

COVID-19

At the time of writing of this book, the COVID-19 pandemic was impacting the world. With all of the complex and the varying responses and ongoing measures, the commonality of the importance of people and having people change what they do is seen within managing COVID-19 (Weekly Mirror Message—Transformation Lessons from COVID-19— https://youtu.be/YqLFAEFCyeM). Common themes in managing the response occurred including:

- *People*—Change is achieved by people. Realizing change requires people to do things differently. "*I do good work, change is coming, help me with the change, and I can do more*" helps people and was part of the COVID-19 response:
  - *I do good work*—Recognizes the work so far. Shows what works. We like to be recognized for what we have done. Leaders praised their staff or citizens within COVID-19 to reassure them, to encourage them, and to aspire to do better and keep up the efforts.
  - *Change is coming*—Advising what is happening, why, and the impacts to align interests and values. Leaders messaged what is happening and why. From encouragement to social distance, to wearing masks, or to prepare populations for loss of life, good leadership messaged emotionally what is coming.
  - *Help me with the change*—Creates the confidence, provides assurance, and strengthens the engagement. Leaders advised people where to get help support from testing to counseling to receipt of support and payments. Leaders also provided training, skilling, and messaging.

    ◦ *I can do more*—Influence those around and reinforce the motivation to do more. People took the initiative to help others and this was supported and encouraged by leadership.

- *Consistent and Persistent Application of Proven Principles*—There was no one size fits all solution for managing COVID-19. There was no magic wand, no panacea, and no silver bullet. According to the situation in hand, it was the consistent and persistent application of proven principles applied pragmatically that mattered. Social distancing was more effective in first-world economies where the infrastructure and support enabled it and social factors like different generations living in different households helped.

- *AMEDLI*—The overarching approach of AMEDLI was seen within the COVID-19 response:

    ◦ Ambiguity Management—Managing the response to COVID-19 is nuanced and complex. First-world economies responded differently between themselves and to developing economies.

    ◦ Messaging—Messaging around the impacts, what was needed to be done, and where you could get help and support was required. Messaging from leadership on what was happening was needed and had the best impact where the emotional bond was formed. Messaging was needed to advise guidelines changes and encourage compliance.

    ◦ Empowered Emotional Ownership—The empowerment was seen through communities helping each other such as emergence of local food banks and manufacturers switching to supply equipment needed (even for no profit). The ownership is seen in the action people did to protect themselves, their families, and loved ones, as well as in the actions undertaken. The emotional response was seen where people assisted strangers or made masks at home and sent the masks to impacted areas at their own expense.

    ◦ Decision Making—Decision making was required at all levels, from the actions of individuals to governments and

businesses. The success of the implementation was critical
to the decisions made as well as responses as the situation
changed (e.g., people not isolating and spreading the virus
or people electing not to follow guidelines).

   ○ Leadership—From the actions of political leaders in
   coordinating efforts to high-profile people providing
   support, to voluntary converts online to assist in morale.
   Effective leadership led the response.

   ○ Interests and Values—COVID-19 aligned interests and
   values in the response, so change was seen. For some,
   the social distancing restrictions were seen as a violation
   of rights, and the nonalignment of interests and values
   impacted the spread of the virus.

• *Environment, Behaviors, Outcomes*—COVID-19 also showed
the importance of:

   ○ Change the Environment—To bring change, you change
   the environment. COVID-19 was a massive change in the
   environment in a short period of time. Emergent behaviors
   resulted.

   ○ Instill the Behaviors—To manage COVID-19, people
   needed to wear masks, maintain social distance (isolate),
   and wash hands to control the spread. Leadership that
   instilled these behaviors achieved better outcomes.

   ○ Manage the Outcomes—COVID-19 was a major change
   that occurred quickly and the impacts like depression and
   unemployment needed to be managed.

• *Leadership*—The role of leadership was highlighted in
COVID-19 and success was seen where leadership:

   ○ Was the change we wish to see—This shows people what is
   needed, forms the emotional bond, and crafts and shapes
   the emergent behaviors.

   ○ Treated others as they themselves would wish to be
   treated—This forms the emotional bond and aligns
   interests and values. People feel that they were being
   supported in a difficult time.

These same themes are required going forward to manage the response and the adoption and adaption to the emerging COVID-19 environment. These same themes apply to the sports team seeking to turn around their performance or to a financial services organization making changes in responses to regulatory breaches or automating roles and adopting artificial intelligence (Strategy and Leadership to Influence Environment & Behaviours to Realise Operations—https://youtu.be/eoCa20XRIwg).

Chapters in This Book

The following chapters occur within this book with a range of styles and approaches to try and "paint the picture" of how to make business transformation and organizational change real through the actions of people.

- *Chapter 1—Taking What Works and Learning from Mistakes.* This is the introductory chapter and is the overview and background to set perspective. The AMEDLI overarching approach (Ambiguity Management, Messaging, Empowered Emotional Ownership, Decision Making, Leadership, Interest and Values alignment) is introduced as a tool in managing change. Also use this chapter as a guide to using other areas of this book.
- *Chapter 2—Ambiguity Management.* Using the AMEDLI overarching approach, this chapter looks at how to manage ambiguity, including risk management, a nuanced approach, and working with gray.
- *Chapter 3—Messaging.* The role and importance of Messaging within change management and business transformation as part of the AMEDLI overarching approach context is explored. The significance of the emotional bond is emphasized.
- *Chapter 4—Empowered Emotional Ownership.* Continuing the AMEDLI overarching approach, the role of the individual in delivering change through ownership, empowerment, and the emotional response required is discussed in this chapter.

- *Chapter 5—Decision Making.* The need for decision making and the importance of implementation and adoption and adaption to variations in the environment are considered in this chapter as part of the AMEDLI overarching approach.
- *Chapter 6—Leadership.* Leadership being the change they wish to see and treating others as they themselves would wish to be treated is part of the success in business transformation and change management. Other aspects impacting leadership are considered in this chapter using the AMEDLI overarching approach as context.
- *Chapter 7—Interests and Values alignment.* Building upon the importance of the emotional bond within change management, this chapter reviews the alignment of interests and values in forming the emergent behavior. Again, the AMEDLI overall and overarching approach is part of the solution.
- *Chapter 8—On the Ground.* Provides a series of operational principles and guidance to compliment the other chapters.
- *Chapter 9—Bringing It Together.* Leveraging the lessons from each of the chapters, a consolidated picture of the adoption and adaption of change and transformation is presented through examples and the context of AMEDLI.
- *Appendix A—Suggested Change Leadership Courses.* By crafting and shaping the leadership, the emergent behaviors are induced. Some suggested courses on leadership in change are presented.

Next Steps

The next steps can be summarized as follows:

- Selecting the parts of the experience and expertise—Using AMEDLI as a guide for prioritization, use the required sections of this book to help you lead, implement, manage, or respond to change and transformation that is impacting you.
- Deciding to use—This is one of the most difficult steps— deciding to apply and use some or all of the expertise within

this book to meet your needs. It is ok to make mistakes and it may take time, but start small with one area, pragmatically apply to meet your needs. For example, as a leader of change, answer the basic questions before you start or be the change you wish to see and treat others as you would wish to be treated. Learn from the experiences and then extend out to others and apply more experience incrementally.

- Consistency of application—Using the expertise you develop through incremental pragmatic use, build capacity and capability within those around you through your influence. Continue to adopt and adapt the experience to your needs.
- Being the change—With best efforts, be the change you wish to see and treat others as you would wish to be treated.

It is in the proven business practices, pragmatically applied, with consistency and persistency in which the future is shaped. It is the capacity and capability building for adaptiveness and responsiveness that see success in transformation. The future lies in your hands and the pride you have in who you are and what you do. Thank you for your time. We hope that the investment is being returned.

CHAPTER 2

Ambiguity Management

*Successful change comes from managing
ambiguity and working with gray*

Summary

Uncertainty, risk, nuance, and shades of gray are part of the ambiguity of
our lived experience and are present within change. Whether we recognize and elect to manage ambiguity and respond or not, the impacts are
there. Success in managing change and business transformation comes
through the proactive management of ambiguity and when the ambiguity
management skill is used across the implementation. Having ambiguity
management developed for use in ongoing operations and services is also
of benefit. This chapter aims to provide an overall approach to the adoption and adaption of ambiguity management within transformation and
organizational change management because of the value it brings to those
leading and undergoing change.

Key Learnings

Key learnings from this chapter include:

- Managing ambiguity is part of bringing and leading change
  and transformation and enables adoption and adaption.
- Ambiguity management is an emergent behavior required at
  all levels and includes managing gray, working the unplanned,
  having a nuanced approach, and management of risk and
  Project Risk (Impact Risk, Outcomes Risk, Delivery Risk,
  External Risk).

- Working with what you have and bringing out the best in them, learning the lessons, and building capacities and capabilities lead to the crafting and shaping of the emergent behavior.
- The emergent behavior is often developed over time based on skills and expertise with leadership being the change they wish to see and treating others as they would be treated.
- Managing ambiguity is used in the crafting and shaping of the emergent behavior and the emergent behavior is used to manage ambiguity.

Introduction

Bringing change requires the management of ambiguity. Within an implementation, nuanced situations occur, people respond differently, and what works for one group in one location may not work for another group in a different area. Our lived experience is that we know that the one size fits all approach seldom works. Whether it is a revised response to implementation as circumstances change or we find our skills and expertise vary with additional support needed, we live in a world of gray and nuance. It is the ability to manage ambiguity that is integral to managing both change and ongoing business operations. Look no further than the ambiguity or the unknown in decision making with corresponding impacts.

The management of nuances, ambiguity, and gray is seen within digital transformation, where the need to respond to technology exists, balanced by the uncertainty of outcomes with the need to pragmatically keep the business operating, including managing the risk associated with the transformation. After all, things will go wrong, and the unplanned will need to be managed.

Ambiguity Management (the A in AMEDLI) is first because we need this ability from the moment we decide to start planning or making change, through to the last minute of implementation, and ongoing operations and services. Look no further than the community group or sports team where running the operation has a range of situations for which ambiguity needs to be managed, for example, rescheduling of venues or changes in attendance. Also, in its simplest terms, change is about getting people to do things different and any transition will proceed differently from person to person. Therefore, ambiguity management is needed, and if the capacity and capability to manage ambiguity exists, a better outcome is likely.

Working with ambiguity (Figure 2.1) requires diversity of skills with respect and confidence within each other. Handling of the unknown is managed through decision-making capacities and capabilities and the ability to respond as required. Ambiguity and unknown requires the working with incomplete information and there needs to be a process for assessment to know what is working and what needs to be addressed.

When implementing a new technology solution or replacing a legacy system, the following are required:

- Managing Gray—From estimating the business case to managing vendors to scope creep in requirements or changing deadlines, managing gray is part of the work.
- Managing the Unplanned—Changes in the business environment during the time of implementation bring changes to what is required. These are unplanned and need to be managed.
- Nuance—Many of the decisions and trade-offs are nuanced. It is not known how things will unfold.

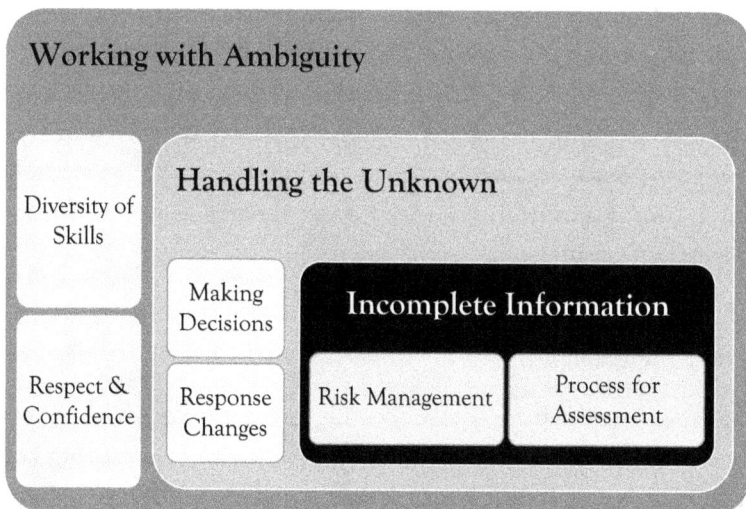

Figure 2.1 *Ambiguity, the unknown, and the incomplete is the norm and not the exception*

- Risk Management—The risk to the business of making the change needs to be managed. Risk management skills and frameworks are part of bringing the change.
- Project Risk—Most new technology solutions or legacy system replacements are managed as projects, requiring the management of Project Risk.

Such nuance is needed in many other areas of managing change. This chapter seeks to help build these capacities and capabilities within leaders, groups, and participants in change and transformation so that they can adopt and adapt better to the circumstances impacting. The topics covered include the managing of gray, managing the unplanned, use of nuance in delivering change, and managing risk and the risk in projects (after all, bringing change is a project). Some next steps are also included.

Managing Gray

To Get the Most

Within our lives we may seek to look at things in terms of black and white. Yet, when it comes to people and what they do and how they do it, many things are not a simple binary option or black and white. The many competing factors and interdependencies come to the fore and life is about managing multiple shades of gray. This is also the case with change management, the decisions made, the implementation, and the responses needed. Have the capacity and capability to work with gray, manage the outcomes, and be able to support others within a world of gray is part of successful change and transformation as well as ongoing support and operations.

Setting the Example

The capacity and capability to work with and manage gray comes from the emergent behavior of empowered individuals with ownership and pride in who they are and what they do. Building, managing, and sustaining (crafting and shaping) an emergent behavior for managing gray requires various skills and expertise from leadership and those around us as well as within us (Figure 2.2).

The emergent behavior for managing gray requires all of the elements (Figure 2.2) to create, sustain, and manage. What varies is the comparative amount at different stages which differs with people and circumstance as well as their skills and expertise. Forming the emergent behavior for managing gray requires the management of ambiguity and uses the skills of working with gray. This requires:

- *Confidence*—For the leaders crafting and shaping the emergent behavior through the actions of empowered individuals, confidence is needed. Leaders need to have confidence in those undergoing the change just as much as those experiencing the change need confidence in leadership. Confidence between colleagues is also required. Confidence comes where there is credibility (mutual respect) as well as an understanding of what is happening and why. Confidence requires the management of complexity across multiple stakeholders. By showing a caring for the needs of others, confidence is instilled (a confident team is part of success).
- *Clarity*—We seek clarity as this helps with uncertainty and ambiguity which serve to bring confidence. Where we see

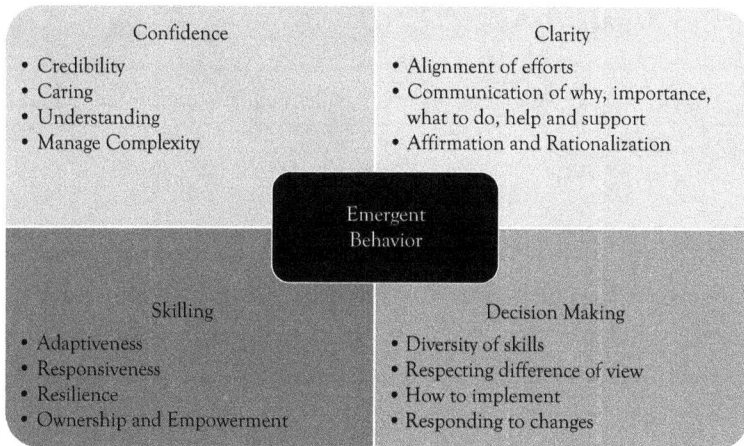

Confidence
- Credibility
- Caring
- Understanding
- Manage Complexity

Clarity
- Alignment of efforts
- Communication of why, importance, what to do, help and support
- Affirmation and Rationalization

Emergent Behavior

Skilling
- Adaptiveness
- Responsiveness
- Resilience
- Ownership and Empowerment

Decision Making
- Diversity of skills
- Respecting difference of view
- How to implement
- Responding to changes

Figure 2.2 Emergent behavior to manage gray

an alignment of efforts and a fair contribution, it helps
with clarity. Clear communication of why, the importance,
what to do, and where to get help and support also serve to
clarify the actions. With affirmation of our efforts and the
ability to rationalize, a sense of clarity is seen. Across the
leadership, colleagues, and within individuals, success comes
from a clarity of purpose (e.g., the sports team winning a
championship).

- *Skilling*—People are of different personalities, skills and
expertise, and experience. Across the team or group, a mixture
of complementary abilities is required. Part of successful
change is building the required capacities and capabilities.
Skills required include Adaptiveness, Responsiveness,
Resilience, and the forging of Ownership and Empowerment
(e.g., team building for a sports team). It is the skilling that
lifts the capacities and capabilities for adaptiveness and
responsiveness in the emergent behavior for managing gray.

- *Decision Making*—Having clear decision-making
responsibilities and the ability to make decisions across
the group or team are required. Good decision making
comes from having a diversity of skills and respecting and
inclusion of different views. Decisions are only as good as the
implementation which depends upon responses required as
circumstances change.

Collectively an emergent behavior is formed to support the management of gray.

Making It Real

Building the required emergent behavior can take time, and once
developed, it needs to be sustained and strengthened. At the leadership
level, the focus is on the overall capacities and capabilities across the
emergent behavior. Bringing out the best in individuals through the sense
of ownership and empowerment is how the emergent behavior is built
and sustained. The role of leadership is to craft and shape to enable the
individuals. Making it real may include:

- Defining what is required to form the emergent for managing gray.
- Distinguishing the behaviors required and how to instill through skilling.
- Identifying the complimentary skills and expertise across the group or team.
- Recognition of strengths and needs for development.
- Start small and develop over time. Be the change you wish to see and treat others as you would wish to be treated. Take advantage of opportunities to build support and structures to adopt and adapt.

Further Details

- Emergent Behavior—Change comes through the emergent behaviors that crafted and shaped (see Chapter 4 Section "Having Empowered Emotional Ownership").
- Actions of Individuals–Leadership is needed to craft and shape emergent behaviors, but it is the actions of empowered individuals with ownership and the emotional bond that delivers the emergent behavior (see Chapter 7 Section "Relate to Me").
- Video—Weekly Mirror Message—Managing People Shutdown (https://youtu.be/m_PsC1gObd8).
- Video—Problem Solving Together for Our Future: Sharing Skills and Expertise—Managing Grey (https://youtu.be/92mmJSxhbNs).

Managing the Unplanned

To Get the Most

We know that the unexpected occurs, that things can go wrong even with the best laid plans. Situations vary over time and revised responses are required and mistakes are made. The unplanned is the norm rather than the exception. Managing the unplanned is working with the unexpected and seeking to gain from it to make the most with what we have. Provisioning for managing and responding to the unplanned is part of Ambiguity Management and compliments the management of gray. Managing the unplanned is also an emergent behavior requiring many of the elements of managing gray, but also has its own elements (Figure 2.3).

Managing and working with the unplanned requires:

- *Understanding*—Difference in understanding occurs which brings out the unplanned. By changing the environment, to instill the behaviors required to influence the outcomes in response to needs, we create an understanding for working with the unplanned.
- *Expertise*—Variations in expertise of those involved with differing motivations, experience, and skill levels occur, which impact the unplanned. Through skilling, shared experience, and motivation with shared Interests and Values of empowered ownership, the expertise is built and strengthened to work with the unplanned.
- *View*—A variety of views occur based on shared interests and values as well as experiences based on past outcomes achieved or what has been seen. By aligning interests and values and using the past outcomes experience, the diversity of view can

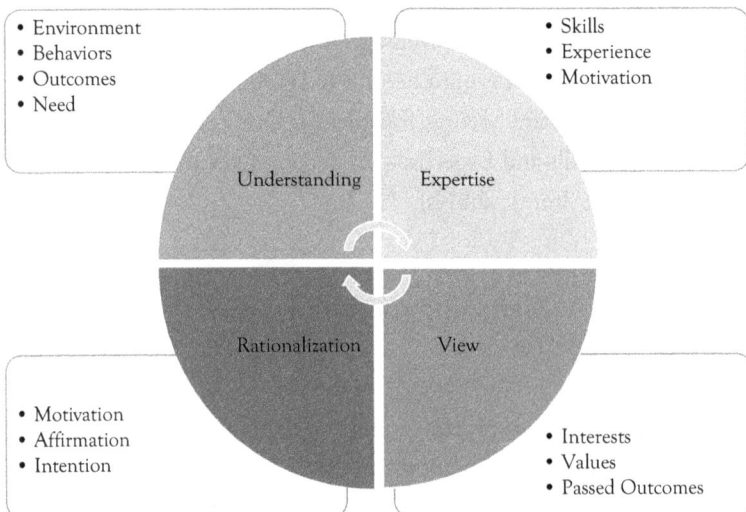

Figure 2.3 Understanding the unexpected response

be included within the emergent behavior for managing the unplanned.

- *Rationalization*—With the unplanned, we need to rationalize. Our rationalization helps us manage mistakes, prepare for avoiding future mistakes, and provides a framework for our understanding and actions. The rationalization includes our motivation, our intentions, and affirmation of our actions. Including rationalization within managing the unplanned is a tool for managing and working with the unplanned as well as a way to strengthen capacities and capabilities for future adoption and adaption.

Collectively the working with the unplanned is accommodated within ambiguity management and forms the basis for making the most of the unplanned to better our people and what we do.

Setting the Example

Working with the unplanned requires the incorporation of the advantageous and beneficial. Where the unplanned is disadvantageous, there is a reason, with opportunities for lessons learned and reshaping the emergent behavior. Working with and managing the unplanned (Figure 2.4) requires making use of AMEDLI through:

- *Enablers*—By changing the environment, to instill the behaviors required to influence the outcomes, the emergent behavior is crafted and shaped.
- *Aligning the Achievers*—The enablers are used collectively to align the achievement through alignment of effort, providing rails for operation, and building momentum.
- *Use of the Assurers*—These assure the overall outcomes in forming the emergent behavior and from the emergent behavior to work with the unplanned.

It is the combination of strategy and leadership, strengthened with skilling, to influence the environment, to instill the behaviors, which gives the

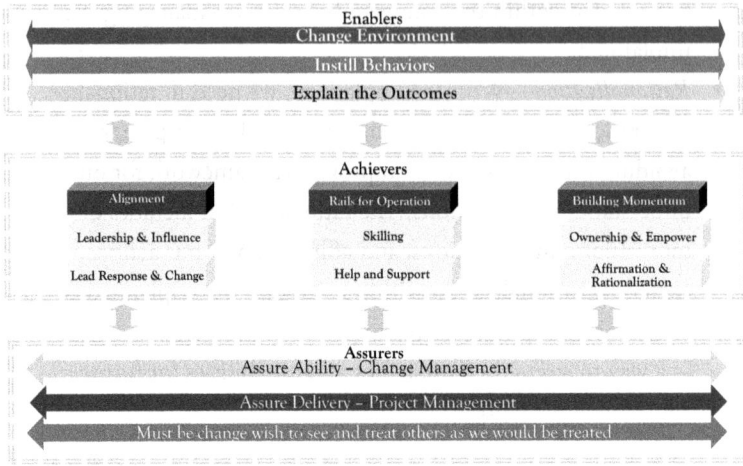

Figure 2.4 Leveraging the unexpected response

capacity and capability to form the emergent behavior through adaptiveness, responsiveness, and resilience. It is our response as individuals with empowerment and ownership with the required affirmation and rationalization that forms the emergent behavior and provides the help and support to others. We know how to form, manage, shape, and influence the emergent behavior. We work with the unexpected. We make the most of what we have. We bring forth the best from us. Through this we manage the unplanned responses.

Making It Real

Working with the unplanned is characterized by:

- Accepting that the unplanned is the norm and planning and working on this basis rather than assuming things will go well.
- Learning the lessons when the unplanned occurs.
- Heading the warnings from the unplanned rather than ignoring, especially repeat occurrences.
- Admitting errors and mistakes or changes in circumstances to adapt and adopt.

The emergent behavior for managing the unplanned is developed similar to that for managing gray (see Section "Managing Gray" of this chapter), but with a focus on the inclusion of experience.

Further Details

- Emotional Rationalization—Part of managing the unplanned and gaining from it is the emotional rationalization (see Chapter 4 Section "Emotional Rationalization")
- Forming the Emotional Bond—The messaging from leadership and people of influence is important in managing the unplanned (see Chapter 3 Section "Communicating to Form Bonds").
- Video—Weekly Mirror Message—Starting the Change Journey Using Opportunities to Build Along the Way (https://youtu.be/4WjqIzbHpew).
- Video—Problem Solving Together for Our Future: Sharing Skills and Expertise—Managing the Unplanned (https://youtu.be/lBIp0PWVvFY).

Nuanced Approach

To Get the Most

Pragmatic experience shows us that business is nuanced. Situations are often complex. Interdependencies exist. Logistics need to be worked through and expectations managed. Despite our desire for simplicity, we know that there is no one size fits all, no panacea, no silver bullet, and no magic wand. The path we take has lots of detours, dead ends occur, we double back, and progress is not always incremental. We don't always say the right thing. Our actions do not always work as planned. Others respond differently than expected and events change. While we simplify and prioritize so that the complexities can be managed, it is our management of nuance and our responses to nuance that delivers.

Setting the Example

Nuance is about working with what we have to manage the changing situations we experience. Managing nuance is also an emergent behavior with a strong experience-based aspect to it. Managing nuance requires a series of elements (Figure 2.5) that are consistently and persistently applied.

Nuance is developed through the lessons learned in mistakes. Nuance includes:

- *Management of Mistakes*—Acceptance of mistakes, adopting and adapting to mistakes, learning from mistakes, but also trying to head off and minimize mistakes. It is important to support people when mistakes occur because this is how they recover and improve. The supporting and nurturing sports team is a better environment and often more successful than the negative one.
- *Adapting to the Unexpected*—The unplanned and the unexpected occurs. The issue is how we respond and the change in approach for adoption and adaption to the situation at hand.
- *Accepting the Complexity*—Managing the complexity is in itself nuanced. Yet it is often the simple that works in resolving the complexity. Breaking complexity down into component parts, addressing root causes (not just the symptoms), consistent application of what we know that works, and working with rather than fighting the complexity are required.
- *Expecting the Unknown*—Even with the best planning and the best people and processes, there is always the unknown. Like adapting to the unexpected, it is preparation for responding to the unknown and capacity and capability building for the unknown that is required. When the unknown occurs, it is about expectation management to work through the situations that occur.
- *Different Approaches*—Working with nuance requires the use of different approaches according to the varying circumstances. Local factors come into play for which a customized response is required. While the response may be based on the proven recipes (people, processes, tools, information) for implementation, the ability to adapt and adopt is also required.
- *Combining Solutions*—The one size fits all approach seldom works, and situations vary over time. A multitude of

approaches used in different ways, at different times, and
varying over time are necessary. Aspects need to be included
and other areas wound back as the response matures.

Nuance is managing the reality we have with the resources we have and
working to get the best from them. Crafting and shaping the emergent
behavior for nuance is part of the skilling for change and is a valuable tool
within realizing change and transformations.

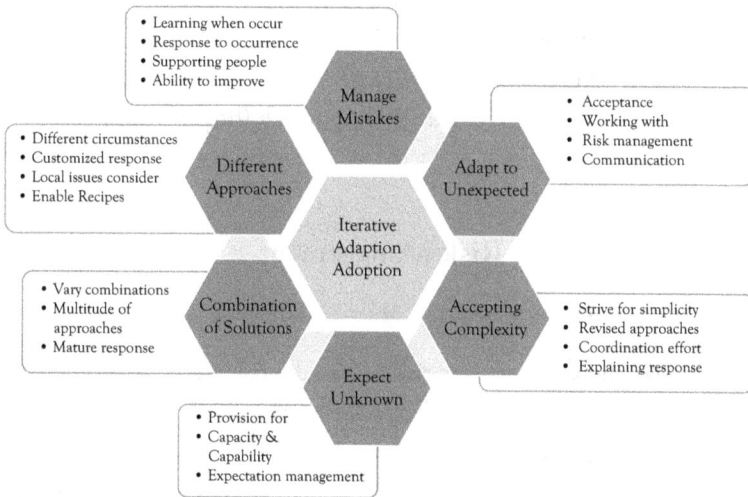

Figure 2.5 Nuance is about managing the reality with what we have

Making It Real

Taking a nuanced approach and working with nuance is developed,
managed, and sustained in a similar way to managing gray (see Section
"Managing Gray" of this chapter) and managing the unplanned (see
Section "Managing the Unplanned" of this chapter). Managing nuance
is ongoing and is developed over time with experience. Leaders need to
trust the team and provide support. Leaders work with what they have to
build the behaviors to get what they seek to achieve. Managing nuance
does require accountability and responsibility which come from the
Empowered Emotional Ownership.

Further Details

- Iterative Adoption and Adaption—Nuance requires decision making (see Chapter 5) and a sustained approach to keep people motivated (see Chapter 7 Section "Adoption and Adaption").
- Nuance Is Managing Risk—Managing risk is part of achieving change (see Section "Risk Management" of this chapter).
- Leadership Influences the Emergent Behavior—Leaders work with what they have to build the behaviors to get what they seek to achieve (see Chapter 6).
- Video—Problem Solving Together for Our Future: Sharing Skills and Expertise—Nuanced Approach (https://youtu.be/nTJiHobefLs).

Risk Management

To Get the Most

Whether we choose to manage risk or not, the risk is still there, and Risk Management is part of our lived experience. Managing risk is often emotionally driven by personalities, experience, and skills. Look no further than the extreme sports person alongside the person with an extended family and heavy financial commitments or the trader on a trading floor alongside the audit and regulatory team. From the risk of the change implementation being unsuccessful or overrunning the cost, through to the risk of people resisting change, to risk of loss of promotion or job, risk is inherent in our lives. Whether consciously or not, we adopt a risk-based approach to business (Figure 2.6) and to our activities. The capacity and capability to manage risk is part of change management or transformation and is required at all levels and by all those involved in the activity.

Setting the Example

Risk Management has a particular use in realizing change or transformation through its use in expectation management. Risk is

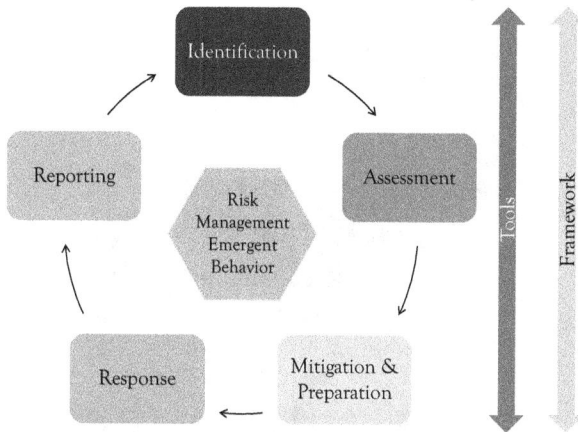

Figure 2.6 Risk management-based approach in business

used to shape messaging by advising and reinforcing and is a tool for alignment of Interests and Values. Risk management comes from an emergent behavior of the actions of people where the right environment brings the behaviors to result in the outcome of an emergent behavior to manage risk including:

- Understanding—Where we understand the risk and the impacts, for example, preparing a bushfire survival plan.
- Relevance and Importance—When the risk is seen to be relevant and important. Those living in areas hit by cyclones are motivated to have a plan, especially as the cyclone season approaches.
- Emotions—Through responding to our emotions. Fear can see us clean gutters and trim trees from around the house in the bushfire season. Greed can see us take chances like the responding e-mails that offer us money for no reason. Our risk management can see us Move Toward safety and Move Away from the hazard by preparing for a cyclone.
- Having Ownership—If we feel in control, we get ownership.

Crafting and shaping the capacity and capability for risk management requires a motivation (Figure 2.7) and includes:

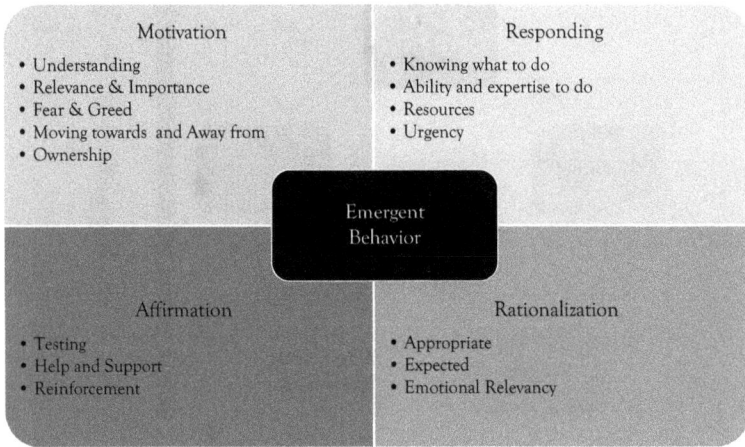

Figure 2.7 Managing risk through the emergent behavior of people

- A Motivation:
  - ○ Understanding what is required.
  - ○ It is relevant and important to those involved.
  - ○ The sense of ownership exists.
  - ○ The emotions of fear and greed are addressed.
  - ○ The move away from and the move toward emotions are resolved.
- Respond to risk through:
  - ○ Knowing what to do.
  - ○ Having the ability and expertise to respond.
  - ○ Having the resources to respond, for example, time and people.
  - ○ An urgency to respond.
- Our ability to Rationalize is part of our management of risk because it strengthens the emotional bond of Motivation:
  - ○ We need to feel our actions are appropriate.
  - ○ Where we feel that our efforts and responses are expected, we respond accordingly. Knowing that colleagues at work approve of our measures to help protect them is part of our rationalization and achieves better risk management outcomes.

○ We need to feel that what we are doing is relevant to us and those we care about. This Emotional Relevancy is part of the rationalization and helps with the emergent behavior.

• When we receive Affirmation for our efforts, better risk management is seen. Affirmation can come from:

○ Testing. We can test our emergency evacuation plans, for example, at a set time we can grab the agreed emergency packs and the family and drive to a location and assess the results. Through testing we know that our responses are fit for purpose and we can affirm our actions.

○ Help and support. We can get help and guidelines to know what an emergency plan should contain. We can work with family and friends and neighbors and through these, we get affirmation of our efforts.

○ The views of experts and people we respect around us confirming our risk management provides Reinforcement.

By providing the Motivation, by Responding, and with Rationalization and Affirmation, the emergent behavior of people managing their risk can be achieved. This emergent behavior applies to management of risk in business or to emergency responses or to the daily management of risk in our lives. This also gives us our ability to manage gray (see Section "Managing Gray" of this chapter) and the unplanned (see Section "Managing the Unplanned" of this chapter).

Making It Real

Achieving and sustaining the emergent behavior of risk management is a collective response from us as empowered individual with a sense of ownership, because we are motivated, can Rationalize, and are supported with the right Affirmation (Figure 2.8). Incumbency and Vested Interest impact our actions. By Providing us with Support and Guidance, showing Empathy, assisting with Skilling, and given a Purpose, we can then manage risk. Our risk management is impacted by our Peers. We are motivated by shared Interests and Values, and we Influence those

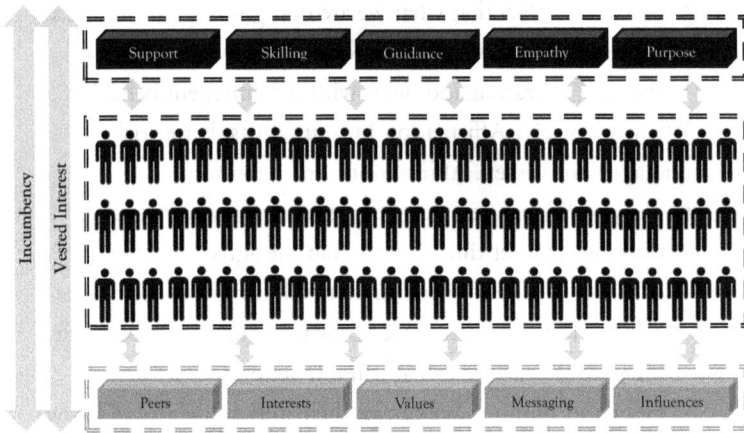

Figure 2.8 Behavioral response to a risk for emergent behavior

around us, as they Influence us. Consistency and clarity of motivational messaging also helps us.

Further Details

- Reference—Sherringham, K. & Unhelkar, B., (2010). Achieving Business Benefits by Implementing Enterprise Risk Management. Cutter Consortium Enterprise Risk Management & Governance Executive Report 7(3).
- Video—Weekly Mirror Message—Risk Management within the Change Stacks (https://youtu.be/mIqLs3N7A7g).
- Video—Problem Solving Together for Our Future: Sharing Skills and Expertise—Managing Risk (https://youtu.be/J97ah30XrjE).

Project Risk

To Get the Most

Related to Ambiguity Management, and to the overall management of risk, is the management of risk from projects (programs or portfolios, see Figure 2.9) of work. Implementing change or transformation is a series of projects, programs, or portfolios (e.g., process changes or a new system

Project	Manage a series of activities requiring coordination with multiple parties to deliver agreed outcome

- Requires someone to coordinate activities across multiple stakeholders to ensure alignment of effort
- Dependencies and impacts upon each other are clearly understood and aligned
- Progress details are shared so that actions can be accommodated and resources allocated
- Alignment of understanding as to what is required

Program	Manage a series of Projects to deliver agreed outcome

- Requires multiple projects with managers to deliver
- Alignment of understanding as to what is required, whether across dependent projects, or independent projects, to ensure alignment of effort
- Dependencies and impacts between projects, as required, are clearly understood and aligned
- Progress details are shared so that actions can be accommodated and resources allocated

Portfolio	Manage a series of Programs and/or Projects to deliver agreed outcome

- Requires multiple project and/or program with managers to deliver
- Alignment of understanding as to what is required across the portfolio to ensure alignment of effort
- Dependencies and impacts across and between portfolios, as required, are clearly understood and aligned
- Progress details are shared so that actions can be accommodated and resources allocated

Figure 2.9 Summary of projects, programs, and portfolios

or the implementation of awareness courses within sports teams) that are established, managed, and transitioned to ongoing activities. Each one has its own risks and risks to the overall business. This makes managing Project Risk a skill and an expertise to have when implementing change with capacities and capabilities across those involved (i.e., another emergent behavior).

Setting the Example

A risk-based approach and the management of risk are integral to the delivery of change, but the risk management of projects is more than the routine tracking of a risk impacting the delivery of a project. Project Risk (Figure 2.10) includes:

- *Impact Risk*—This is the risk to the business from the project. Considerations include a lower risk profile to the business from a proactive project, whilst a reactive project may have greater impact, especially when the project is late or not integrated into the business properly.

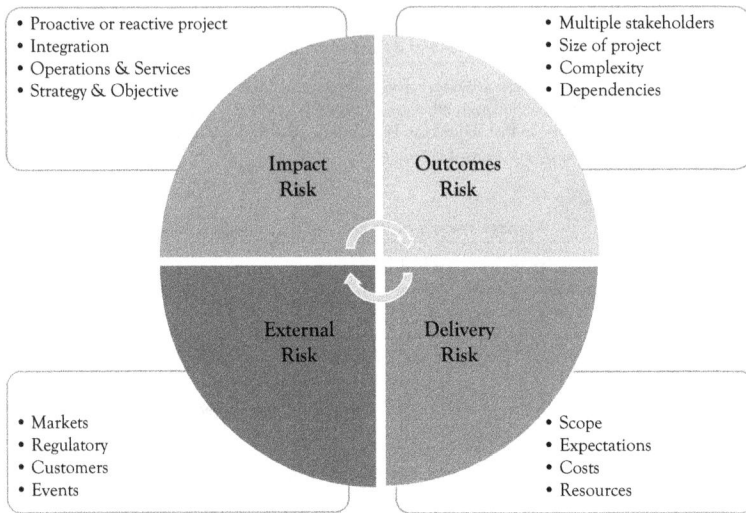

Figure 2.10 Managing project risk

- *Outcomes Risk*—This is the risk of the project delivering the required outcomes. The more complex the project, the more stakeholders, the more dependencies, and the larger the size, the higher the risk (i.e., less chance of delivering).
- *Delivery Risk*—The risk in delivering the project. This is the most often tracked risk by project managers, as these are the risks impacting schedule or cost.
- *External Risk*—These are the external factors, often beyond the control of the business, impacting a project.

Irrespective of the size, type, or sector of a business, Project Risk management experience alongside project management skills and expertise is required for managing change and transformations as well as part of Ambiguity Management.

The importance of project risk is often within digital transformation, where the technology leads the business integration and the technology is deployed followed by remediations.

Making It Real

The management of Project Risk changes the focus of Program Management and Portfolio Management (Figure 2.11) as follows:

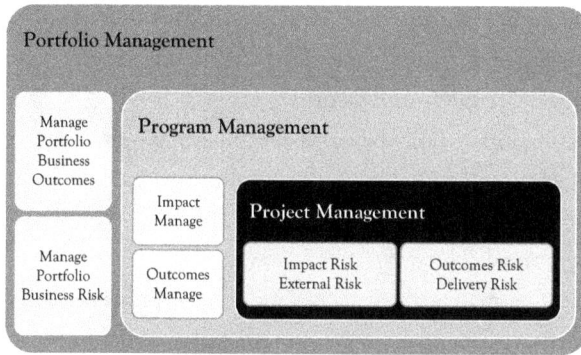

Figure 2.11 Business risk from project risk

- *Projects*—Project Risk management is more than the traditional delivery risk management. Project risk management becomes focused on assurance to the needs of the portfolio and the business outcomes.
- *Programs*—Although Project Risk is managed at the Project level, Project Risk still occurs at the Program level. The focus of the Program is on the management of the outcomes from the projects to meet those of the portfolio as well as the impact management from the Projects to the Program.
- *Portfolios*—At the Portfolio level, the risk from projects and programs still occurs, but with a change in focus. Portfolio management is about managing a series of business risks as a coherent portfolio and the business outcomes to meet the risks.

This change of focus is included within the capacity and capability building for the change or transformation as an emergent behavior similar to that of managing gray (see Section "Managing Gray" of this chapter), managing the unplanned (see Section "Managing the Unplanned" of this chapter), managing nuance (see Section "Nuanced Approach" of this chapter), as well as being part of overall risk management (see Section "Risk Management" of this chapter).

Consider a business responding to a large economic downturn; a portfolio of work may be needed with programs and projects to address:

- Facilities management changes including revised accommodation.

- Finance and treasury to address liquidity, cash-flow management, and revenue adoption and adaption.
- Revisions to safety and security.
- Meeting legal, regulatory, and compliance requirements.
- ICT infrastructure and operations and services.
- Managing the risk to people.
- Operational changes.
- Customer management including revenue preservation, retention, sales, and marketing in the new constrained markets.

Irrespective of the size, type, or sector of a business, Project Risk management experience alongside project management skills and expertise in true costed projects is required by a business undergoing transformation.

Further Details

- Project Risk is Part of Business Risk—Project Risk impacts a business and is part of business risk and the risk-based approach to business (see Section "Risk Management" of this chapter).
- Project Risk in Project Management—Change is a series of projects which need to manage Project Risk (see Chapter 8 Section "Project Management").
- Video—Problem Solving Together for Our Future: Sharing Skills and Expertise—Project Risk (https://youtu.be/HeWR1__3grQ).

Next Steps

The next steps can be summarized as follows:

- Recognizing the significance of ambiguity management within the change or transformation and its role in ongoing operations and services.
- Working with the need for managing ambiguity, what is the role and need for managing gray, working the unplanned,

having a nuanced approach, management of risk and Project Risk (Impact Risk, Outcomes Risk, Delivery Risk, External Risk) across the activities.

- Based on those involved, deciding the comparative skills and expertise for the management of ambiguity, then working to integrate the respective skilling to craft and shape the overall capacities and capabilities for ambiguity management.

- Start to form the emergent behavior in a staged and iterative approach, accepting that it is nuanced, and it will take time. Build the capacity and capability and strengthen with expertise.

CHAPTER 3

Messaging

Message the emotional bond as to what
I need to do, why, and where to get help

Summary

Messaging that forms the emotional bond to create a response is part of getting us to do things differently and is therefore part of successful change management. Where the message is credible, is relevant, is of benefit, aligns with interests and values, and is respectful, the engagement and response can be seen. The consistency and persistency of the messaging is also important, together with messaging that advises what is the issue, the impact, what we need to do, and where we can get help and support. This chapter looks at aspects of messaging for successful change and transformation based on the importance of people and their emotional response.

Key Learnings

Key learnings from this chapter include:

- Messaging that is credible, is relevant, is of benefit, aligns with interests and values, and is respectful is engaging and forms an emotional bond for a response.
- Consistency and persistency of the messaging is important, together with messaging that advises what is the issue, the impact, what we need to do, and where we can get help and support.
- Either extreme with contrary views can lack credibility with each other. An extreme draws support and reinforcement from those around. To influence, there needs to be a sharing

of expertise and guidance so that those in the middle, who
can be convinced, can respond.
• To change minds, leadership is needed. Communication
needs to avoid the sense of isolation and alienation of those
with a different view or who are still to be convinced.
• The same drivers and influencers of an emergent behavior
and messaging that are used to craft and shape supportive and
nurturing can be used for the nefarious. Turning around the
nefarious is the use of the same drivers and influencers.

Introduction

With bringing change being about getting people to do things differently
and it is people who realize change, it therefore follows that change and
transformation is an emotionally driven activity. Therefore, the messaging
around the change needs to form emotional bonds (Figure 3.1). When
we are engaged, understand what is being asked and why, know where
to get support and be motivated, the emotional bond can be formed. It
is the showing of care, the credible source, and the ongoing engagement
that forms and strengthens the emotional bond. Once the bond is made,
a response can be realized. Consistency and persistency of targeted messages also attracts attention. If the right emotional bond is formed, the
messages convey important information within a change. It is not enough

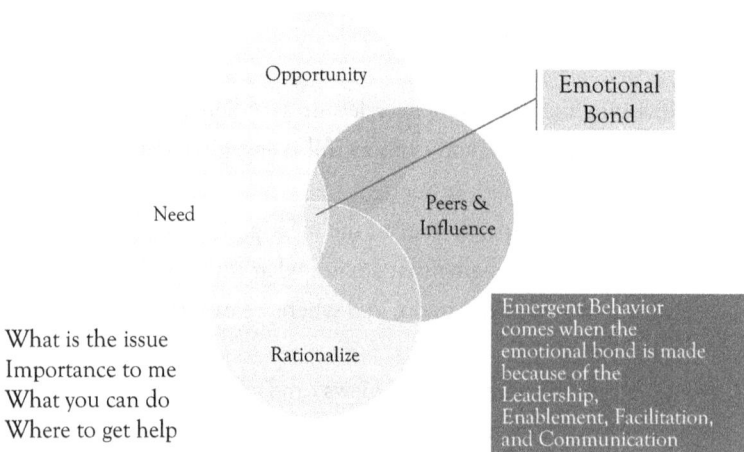

Figure 3.1 The message is about the emotional bond

to message, but to message in the right way, at the right time, with the right information, to the right parties for effect.

Messaging (the M in AMEDLI) comes next because of the need to consistently and persistently communicate throughout the change. From the initial ideas and planning, during preparation and implementation, in the revised responses, and across the diversity of stakeholders, messaging is crucial. Explaining what is happening, why, what to do to help yourself and those around you, and where to get help and support are all important. The affirmation, the rationalization, the emotional support, the confirmation, and the validation are all part of the messaging. Messaging is part of the capacity and capability of ambiguity management, but nuance and other ambiguity management skills are needed in the personalization of messaging and in forming the emotional bond.

COVID-19 has challenged societies and how they operate. With all of the complexity and diversity of people and their views and expectations in a time of stress, messaging has been important including:

- Communicating in Times of Change—COVID-19 required skills in communication at difficult times to a diverse group.
- Communicating to Form Bonds—COVID-19 had the emotional element included by default (how to stay safe) in the messaging to gain attention, create desire, and invoke actions.
- Working with Nefarious—COVID-19 saw leadership having to communicate with audiences who were unengaged or seeking to exploit opportunities for their own interests.
- *"I do good work, change is coming, help me with the change, and I can do more"*—This underpinned how people responded to COVID-19 to form the emergent behavior to help contain the spread.

Whether it is the sports team, politicians seeking votes, or working through the changes of roles in a business, messaging which forms the emotional bond is required. This same emotional messaging is part of digital transformation, whether it is the glamor of "leading edge technology" or assuring people about their jobs. This chapter looks at aspects of messaging and its role within change and transformation. The topics covered include forming the emotional bond when communicating in times of change. Working with the nefarious and some next steps are also included.

Communicating in Times of Change

To Get the Most

In seeking to improve the performance of a sports team, preparing for an emergency like a bushfire or messaging changes to operations around technology, the challenge is to communicate in a time of change which is also bringing change. The engagement and communication needs to show caring, come from a credible source, and bring ongoing engagement so that an emotional bond can be created.

Setting the Example

Realizing change often requires engaging a contrary audience with multiple approaches for gaining the attention of the unengaged. Those seeking the change may be considered as one extreme and those reluctant to make a change (for whatever the reason) as another extreme with those in the middle open to and accepting, but needing understanding, help, and support.

Now, having one extreme telling the other extreme that their view is wrong or that they should change their view is often unproductive (Figure 3.2). All this does is to entrench the extremes. Either extreme lacks credibility with each other, and an extreme draws support and reinforcement from those around. The early adopters, those that share a view they are seeking others to adopt, need to share expertise and guidance so that those in the middle, who can be convinced, can respond. The early adopters need to welcome people who have changed their views. The early adopters empower them to make changes, and work to create a sense of pride and ownership. To change minds, leadership is needed. Communication needs to avoid the sense of isolation and alienation of those with a different view or who are still to be convinced.

While either extreme often makes the most noise and is reinforcing to those with the same view, it is by convincing those in the middle to move

Ongoing engagement
of the contrary without
isolating or alienating

Convince the middle to move with reinforcement from
those around. Leadership to advise why, impact, how to
help themselves, and where to get help

Early adopters share
expertise, guidance,
and welcome others

Caring and Credible communication to influence

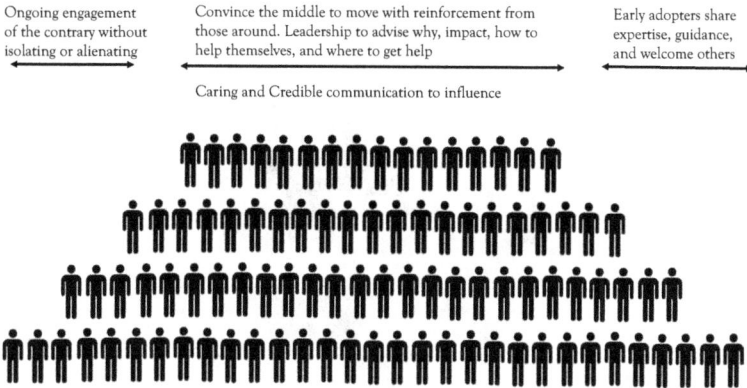

Figure 3.2 Communicating the message

that change is achieved. It is those in the middle that can influence and reshape the extremes. When the communication is credible and shows caring, the middle influences the extremes. When the middle feels isolated or alienated, the extremes influence the middle. By explaining why, the impact, what they can do so that they feel empowered, and where they can get help, the middle can be moved.

Those with a contrary view can be influenced to feel engaged and by becoming part of the solution. A sense of isolation and alienation reinforces views and can increase resistance. Those with a contrary view often respond with emotions and can increase the strength of a view. Communication that enables an ability to change a view whilst maintaining their standing, beliefs, and values (rationalization) is often effective.

The scenario painted is what is often seen within bringing change and realizing transformation. Those advocating the change may believe in what they are doing, for the right motivations, and with the best of intent, but are they listening to and understanding those receiving the messages? Is the required emotional bond being formed, the change explained, and the help and support provided?

Making It Real

To have the one extreme influence the other by using those in the middle, the communication needs to form an emotional bond for it to revise a view or strengthen an existing view (Figure 3.3).

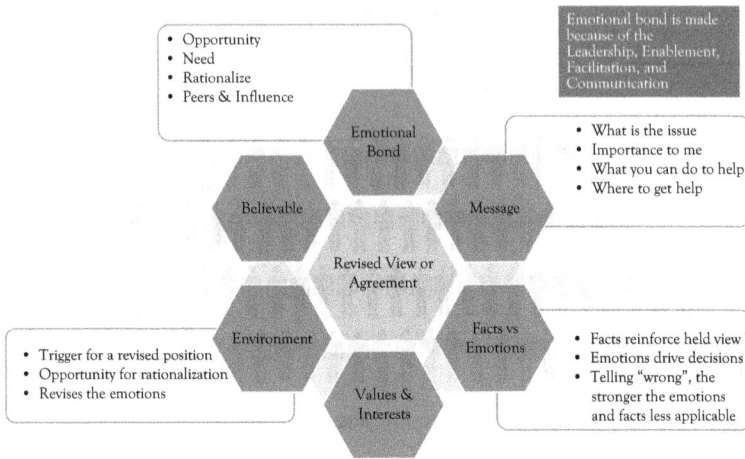

Figure 3.3 Emotional bond for revised view or agreement

This use of the influencing and changing the middle view requires:

- *Emotional Bond*—The emotional bond forms given the need, the opportunity, the ability to rationalize, and the role of Influencers and Peers.
- *Message*—The message needs to be credible, consistent, persistent, memorable, engaging, but above all, show caring. The message explains the issue, the importance, what you need to do so that you do not feel overwhelmed or useless, and where to get help and support.
- *Believable*—The message is believable when the source is credible with the Interests and Values are aligned. Those of one political persuasion get reinforcement of their views from those of similar views (interests) and values around them, leading to an intensification of their view. Those of opposing view are less credible and believable because the values and interests are seen as contrary and the message is seen to be alienating and isolating. Messages that repeatedly tell you "that what you think and believe is wrong" or "that you are less because of your view" or "you are seen as uncaring because of your view" are counterproductive. A message of care and empathy is engaging.
- *Facts vs. Emotions*—People often respond emotionally and make decisions based on emotions. Trying to use facts

to change an emotional decision is often ineffective. The more the facts tell someone "they are wrong," the more the emotions come into the mix. Messaging and communication need that emotional bond with the facts to strengthen the emotional bond.

- *Environment*—A stimulus for change, whether incremental through peer pressure or via a rapid change in their environment, can also help bring agreement and revised positions.
- *Values and Interests*—Where the message is aligned to our Interests and Values, the message is more engaging, has credibility, ties to your emotions, and is more believable.

This use of the influencing and changing the middle view is how change is realized because they do the influencing and messaging as part of the emergent behavior.

Further Details

- Leadership Needs to Form the Emotional Bond – People respond to leadership that forms the emotional bond (see Chapter 6 Section "Crafting and Shaping the Emergent Behavior").
- Video—Mirror Message—Managing Projection in Sustainable Change (https://youtu.be/TIo5fANPQ7I).
- Video—Weekly Mirror Message—The Logline in Change (https://youtu.be/uPrYY3zwF0Y).
- Video—Problem Solving Together for Our Future: Sharing Skills and Expertise—Communicating in Times of Change (https://youtu.be/tWYe51BH34c).

Communicating to Form Bonds

To Get the Most

The need for tailored communications with consistency and persistency is nothing new. Messaging the what is the issue, what is the impact, what to do to help yourself, and where to get support is also well established.

The challenge within communicating change is gaining the attention and forming the emotional bond for the required actions. Messaging is often about changing views for which there is no one simple approach to achieving. Rather it is a multitude of approaches with an adaptive and responsive technique that is required.

Setting the Example

Messaging to change views is complex, nuanced, and changes over time and with circumstance. Consider two diverse groups with contrary views (Figure 3.4). Group 1 may be aligned, but an emotional bond for action is still required for ongoing support and engagement. Where the views of Group 2 are to be revised so that an engagement occurs and transformation can be enabled, a series of approaches are needed and include:

- Working to form a common emotional bond.
- Establishing shared Interests and Values.
- Aligning aspirations.

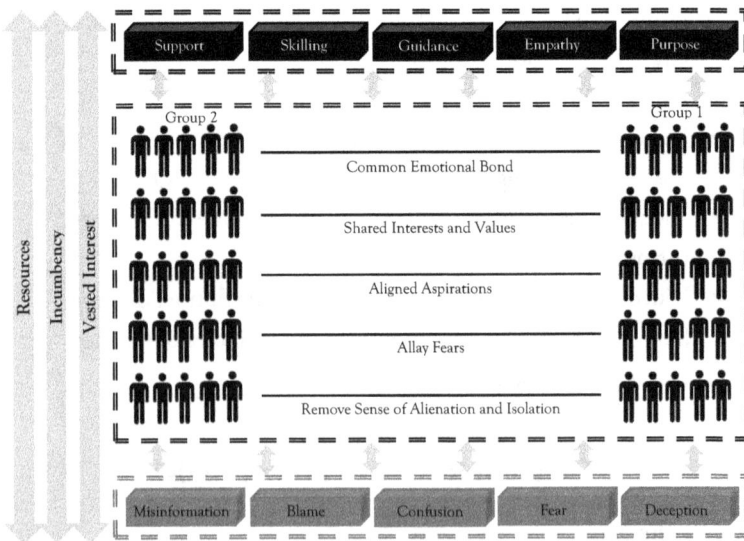

Figure 3.4 Changing a view with emotional bond

- Seeking to allay fears.
- Removing the sense of alienation and isolation.

Even if both groups in this example are positive in their desire to engage with each other, the communication may take time, it may need to evolve and adapt, and issues of trust may exist. Through providing Support, Assistance with Skilling, trying to Guide and share expertise, show Empathy, and form a common Purpose, an agreement and alignment between groups can be achieved.

Both groups may inadvertently or be seen to provide Misinformation, create Blame and Confusion which may lead to Fear and a sense of Deception. The tools of Misinformation, Blame, Confusion, Fear, and Deception can also be used to reinforce a status quo or to entrench positions and to divide efforts. Misinformation, Blame, Confusion, Fear, and Deception can be used to masquerade as Support, Skilling, Guidance, Empathy, and Purpose.

For views to change, the communication has to overcome Incumbency, has to meet the challenge of Vested Interests, and requires Resources. Incumbent Vested Interests that are well funded may use Misinformation, Blame, Confusion, Fear, and Deception to promote their view or keep their position of power and influence. Overcoming this requires Resources, an alignment of other Vested Interests, and the provision of Support, Skilling, Guidance, Empathy, and sense of Purpose to enable the communication between groups. None of this is easy to achieve. The more contrary the views and the more people to align, the greater the challenge. Tools like social networking that reinforce a view and the absence of fact checking contribute to the complexity, but communication that forms the emotional bond can bring change.

Making It Real

Counteracting negative communication and bringing groups together requires leadership and is often harder to achieve. Yet it is by coming together (not agreeing on everything but alignment of interests and values) that success is achieved. Communication is an adaptive and responsive approach that includes consistency and persistency, credibility, the emotional bond, and the shared Interests and Values. Being the change you wish to see and treating others as you would wish to be treated are key elements. Bringing the groups together requires (Figure 3.5):

- *Change in Outcomes*—Bringing groups together, changing views, and coming to consensus require a change in the outcomes expected. This needs a change in motivation (reason) and a change in skills. Skilling is the ability to do while training is how to do. We may not have the skills to change what we do and the outcomes we expect of ourselves. This is why Support, Skilling, Guidance, Empathy, and Purpose bring the Emotional Bond, Align Aspirations, Allay Fears, Remove the Sense of Alienation and Isolation, and Share Interests and Values.
- *Change in Behaviors*—Getting the required outcomes often needs a change in behaviors, for example, losing weight by going to the gym and better diets. The change in behavior comes from the influence of Peers and a change in expectation of people, both external and form within. The expectation change from within is the most important and comes through confidence, self-pride, ownership, and empowerment. Changing behaviors requires motivation and skilling, which depends upon Support, Guidance, Empathy, and Purpose.

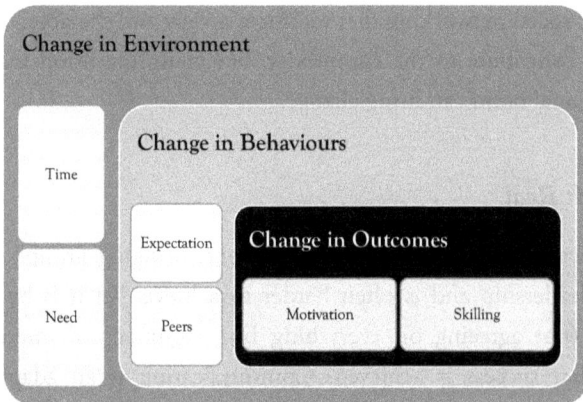

Figure 3.5 Change the environment and instill the behaviors to realize the outcomes

- *Change in Environment*—Changes in behaviors come from a change in environment. A supporting and nurturing environment encourages pride, ownership, and empowerment. Changing the environment to one of retribution, revenge, and fear instills bad behaviors and poor outcomes. Changes in the environment take time and result from the need.

Bringing people together requires leadership to change the environment, to instill the behaviors, to drive the outcomes. This requires overcoming incumbency and vested interests, but takes resources and time requiring an adaptive and responsive approach. Being the change you wish to see and treating others as you would wish to be treated are key because it brings the support, skilling, guidance, empathy, and purpose required. This creates the necessary emotional bond, the shared Interests and Values, the aligned aspirations, allaying fears, and removing the sense of alienation and isolation. It is through this combination that groups are brought together for the betterment of all.

Further Details

- Video—Weekly Mirror Message – Conversation as the Barometer of Change (https://youtu.be/1UNHyzDfKwI)
- Video—Weekly Mirror Message—Sustainable Change is Actions and Words https://youtu.be/PfpRJPpuEBQ).
- Video—Problem Solving Together for Our Future: Sharing Skills and Expertise—Communicating to Form Bonds (https://youtu.be/EZFLNtKY14k).

Working with the Nefarious

To Get the Most

The factors discussed in messaging of AMEDLI (Ambiguity Management, Messaging, Empowered Emotional Ownership, Decision Making, Leadership, Interest and Values aligned) and AMEDLI overall that are used for realizing change and the crafting and shaping of an emergent behavior for betterment are the same influencers in nefarious messaging.

These same influences can be used to create and sustain a nefarious emergent behavior or transform an emergent behavior from betterment to nefarious. Conversely, these same influencers can be used to change the nefarious to betterment. It is what we choose to do with these influencers that defines us.

Setting the Example

From deliberate sabotage, to criminal activities, to self-seeking vested interests, or just wanting to disrupt because one can, we know that people do bad things for a range of reasons and motivations. Good people have their environment changed, revise their behaviors to respond and survive; an outcome of bad or criminal activities may result. The actions of those around them reinforce their actions and a spiral sets in. Decline begets decline as growth begets growth. Good people in bad environments can change when their environment is changed, and we can see revised behaviors with good outcomes achieved. The same influencers of behaviors in messaging used for nurturing and the supportive environments (Figure 3.6) can also be brought to form the nefarious emergent behavior.

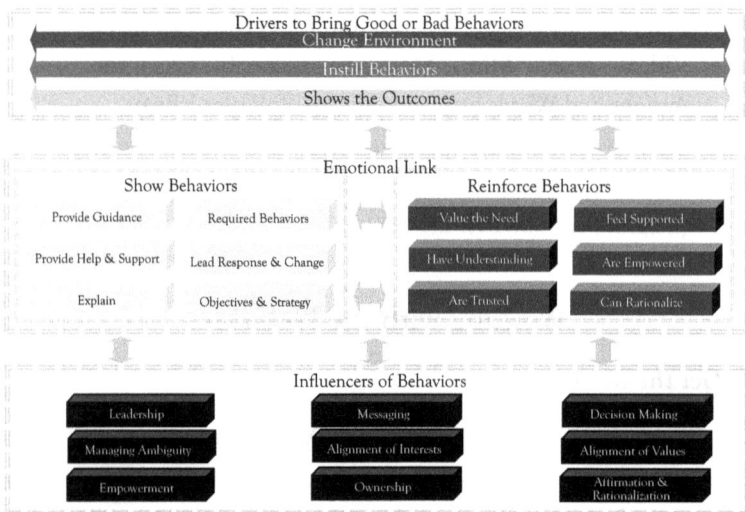

Figure 3.6 Managing the nefarious

This includes:

- *Drivers*—Change an environment for the worse, and nefarious outcomes can result. Those wishing to keep and sustain positive messages are impacted by the negative, and over time, the nature of the messaging changes. Where bad behaviors are rewarded, the messaging tends to reflect this. It is hard to message to the contrary.
- *Emotional Link*—The emotional link from messaging can be used to show the behaviors or reinforce the behaviors sought.
- *Influencers*—The messaging also influences the behaviors as much as it is driven by the behaviors.

Making It Real

There is no simple solution, no one size fits all approach, and no magic wand or silver bullet to work with and to manage the nefarious. It takes consistency and persistency, with time, effort, and resources to bring change. It starts with leadership (the empowered individuals) who seek to change the environment, influence the behaviors of others around them, and show the outcomes required. The leadership needs to be the change they wish to see and treat others as they themselves would be treated (Figure 3.7). We work with those that can be persuaded and we put efforts into the key People of Influence that can adopt and adapt.

Although the emergent behavior is the focus, we still need to address the individuals including:

- Affirmation and rationalization through rewards and benefits seen.
- Help and support.
- Training (the how to do) and skilling (the ability to do) to enable them to do the How To.
- People of Influence playing an important role.

Again, this use of emergent behavior is difficult. If it was easy, the need for it would seldom exist. Challenges and frustrations will occur.

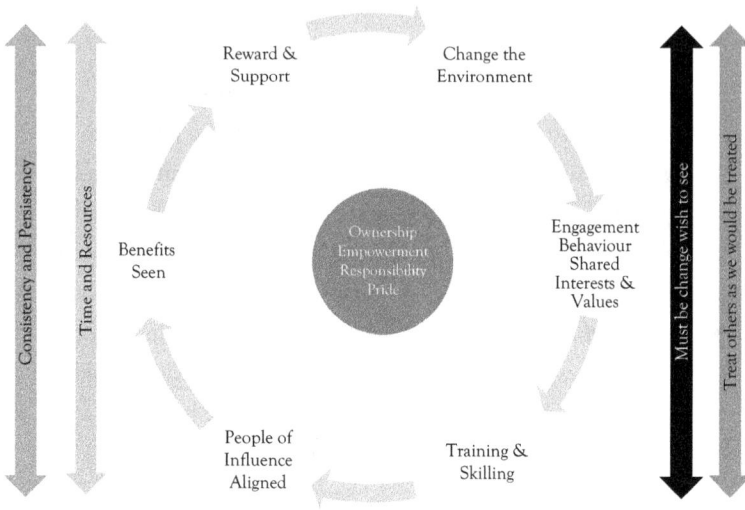

Figure 3.7 Aligning the nefarious

Setbacks and reworks are the norm. Yet, for those seeking change or even seeking betterment for themselves and their loved ones, the question is "what is the alternative?" We know the importance to us. We know how to achieve. We know that it works. Despite the perceptions otherwise, good actions by motivated people wanting to do right prevails.

Further Details

- Video—Problem Solving Together for Our Future: Sharing Skills and Expertise—Working with the Nefarious (https:// youtu.be/f7jvzEGrEog).
- Video—Strategy and Leadership to Influence Environment & Behaviours to Realise Operations (https://youtu.be/ eoCa20XRIwg).
- Video—Weekly Mirror Message—The Story of an Individual (https://youtu.be/xxHgmdiQmjg).
- Video—Weekly Mirror Message—Preventative and Response to Undermining (https://youtu.be/RcaJNeRKwnA).

The Mantra

To Get the Most

Realizing sustainable change is based summarized as *"I do good work, change is coming, help me with the change, and I can do more."* This mantra is important in forming the emotional bond and is therefore integral to messaging. In particular:

- *I do good work*—Recognizes the work so far. Shows what works. We like to be recognized for what we have done.
- *Change is coming*—Advising what is happening, why, and the impacts to align interests and values.
- *Help me with the change*—Creates the confidence, provides assurance, and strengthens the engagement.
- *I can do more*—Influence those around and reinforce the motivation to do more.

Setting the example in a crisis like a flood, we tell people "what is coming," "how it will impact them," "what they need to do," and "where to get help and support." We do this so that people can help themselves and those around them because it is the right thing to do. We also get the emergent behavior of preparation, response, and rebuild.

Setting the Example

A losing sports team that does not wish to change remains a losing team. The team knows they are losing, often want to better themselves, but may need help to make the change. To bring change, we need to know what we do well, where to improve and why, how to change, and provide help and support. From this, the change will occur, we will better ourselves and influence and help those around us, because it is in our interest to do so. "I do good work, change is coming, help me with the change, and I can do more" (Figure 3.8) is a mantra for change. Where services are provided, internal or external, with this mantra people can see that you care about them, know that you are credible, and respond accordingly.

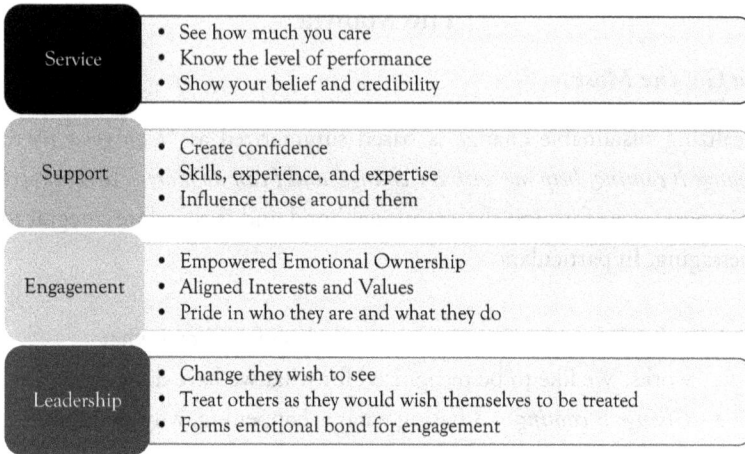

Figure 3.8 A mantra for change

If skills and expertise are shared, we can respond and better ourselves. It creates confidence and influences those around you. Change comes through empowered emotional ownership by individuals, whose interests and values are aligned, and who have pride in who they are and what they do. Recognizing the good work they do, explaining what is happening and why, providing help and support, and enabling them to do more meets the emotional engagement required.

As a leader, having a team that meets the mantra is what is required because it forms the emotional bond for engagement. As a leader you need to be this mantra so that the team sees it, and the team believes it to have confidence in the leadership and the change.

Making It Real

The mantra *"I do good work, change is coming, help me with the change, and I can do more"* is made real through the influence of leadership. The main approach is to use the mantra as a guide for messaging, for the actions of leadership, and for crafting and shaping the emergent behavior. It is a matter of leadership deciding to use the approach.

Further Details

- Video—Weekly Mirror Message—"I do Good Work, Change is Coming, Help Me with the Change, and I can do More" (https://youtu.be/qTxCGA2W0R0).

Next Steps

Messaging is part of the crafting and shaping of an emergent behavior just as messaging is part of the emergent behavior. Developing the capacity and capability for messaging and its adoption and adaption is similar to that for the other emergent behaviors. This includes:

- Leadership—Understanding the role played by messaging and the messaging being "that leadership is the change they wish to see and that treat others as they themselves would be treated".
- Emotional Bond—The consistent and persistent use of messaging that attracts attention and forms the emotional bond.
- Use of the Middle View—To persuade, change views, and to get people to change what they do is nuanced. Those that agree are motivated and the messaging reaffirms. The skill with the messaging is about influencing those in the middle, whose view can be changed and have them motivated. Those of the middle view will influence those with the contrary view.

CHAPTER 4

Empowered Emotional Ownership

Change comes from the emergent behavior of empowered individuals

Summary

Realizing and sustaining change comes from doing things differently and from an empowered emergent behavior with ownership. All of these are emotionally driven responses which require rationalization. The simple motivations of "fear and greed" or the "moving towards and away from" are manifestations form a range of complex emotions which includes: the sense of ownership, a feeling of empowerment, being trusted and respected, as well as feeling valued and appreciated, alongside self-esteem and self-worth. This chapter looks at crafting and shaping of the emergent behavior required and how it is the actions of empowered individuals (driven by emotional choices and actions) who bring sustainable change.

Key Learnings

Key learnings from this chapter include:

- Emergent behaviors are key to bringing change and transformation, but emergent behaviors take time to form and are nuanced.
- Emergent behavior comes from the actions and decisions of individuals who are empowered with ownership forming a resulting emotional response. Emergent behaviors are crafted and shaped with skilling (ability to do) and expertise.

- Leadership is required to form emergent behaviors, to sustain, and for capacity and capability building. Applied pragmatically, with incremental strengthening, leadership enables the emergent behaviors which the empowered individuals with ownership deliver.
- Rationalization of emotions is part of the emergent behavior crafting and shaping because the empowered individual with ownership needs to be able to rationalize their decisions and actions.
- Working with the known and the familiar is part of the empowered emotional ownership within emergent behaviors because we are more comfortable with the known and the familiar. There is a reinforcement of our views, perceptions, and our current understanding. The known and the familiar makes us feel valued, respected, and appreciated, as well as providing us with self-esteem and self-worth.

Introduction

Both Ambiguity Management and Messaging use emergent behavior across individuals, groups (teams), or organizations for realizing change. While other aspects like Decision Making and Leadership are also emergent behaviors, the recurring theme for realizing change is the role of people and the emotional response. From the "change the environment, instill the behaviors, to achieve the outcomes," through to the personal motivations of doing things differently, the emotional aspects are there. The emotions are based on the sense of ownership and empowerment (i.e., an alignment of interest and values) which are all part of being trusted and respected, as well as feeling valued and appreciated, alongside self-esteem and self-worth. From these the emergent behaviors can be formed.

Empowered Emotional Ownership (the E in AMEDLI) is what needs to be created for achieving change and transformation. This can be done by individuals acting on their own and for their own needs, but it is helped by Messaging and Leadership. Ambiguity Management is part of what comes from ownership of issues, the sense of pride in who you are and what you do,

Consider a business that is restructuring following underperformance of the previous leadership:

- Having Empowered Emotional Ownership—To achieve the change, the new leader needs to bring people round to support the approach, share the vision, and have them engaged to do the required work.
- Emotional Rationalization—Those involved in the change need to rationalize what they are doing, the impacts, and what it means to them going forward. This ability to rationalize is part of achieving change and needs to be supported and accommodated.
- The Known and Familiar—People start with the known and familiar and are part of how they manage change and start to do things differently. This is seen in how people respond to their engagement in making changes. Look no further than COVID-19, and how people want to go back to the way things were and how the change is disruptive and uncomforting.
- If Only—This is a common part of change and needs to be managed. This comes to the fore with hindsight (e.g., "if only we had done this"). "If Only" is part of the rationalization process and working with the "Known and Familiar." This is seen from conversations around training, to process, to job roles and career paths.
- Confidence in the Change—Enabling the change requires confidence in the change. Support is achieved when the change is seen as beneficial and succeeding.

If all of this sounds familiar, it is. From business changes to managing the COVID-19 response, to the sports team, empowered emotional ownership is required. This chapter works on the crafting and shaping of the emergent behavior required and how it is the actions of empowered individuals driven by emotional choices and actions, because of the sense of ownership for their Interests and Values, which brings sustainable change. The same applies within digital transformation, where the overall emergent behavior for change around the technology is required.

The topics covered include the overall emergent behavior and the use of rationalization within our actions and choices. Use of the familiar and known within our empowered emotional ownership is also explored. Some next steps are identified.

Having Empowered Emotional Ownership

To Get the Most

Change comes through us as empowered individuals who have ownership and who are supported. Our response is emotionally driven which can be rationalized and affirmed. Collectively, we as individuals form an emergent behavior to deliver the required outcomes in response to changes in our environment. An emergent behavior to make the change and the emergent behavior required from the change are crafted and shaped (they may be different). From an emergent behavior for Ambiguity Management or the messaging to form emotional bonds, the collective behavior brings results.

Setting the Example

When we are trusted and empowered:

- Most of us do the right thing.
- We help others.
- Change comes from an emotional response that is rationalized and affirmed.
- We form an emergent behavior to do things different from the ground up with help and support.

This emotional response when we are empowered and trusted to form the emergent behavior is the key to achieving sustainable change and transformation. We see this in the turning around of a sports team to win a championship. In the team we respond to the need for change based on emotion when:

- We value the need for change.
- We feel supported.

- We understand what is required, why, what we can do, and where to get help and support.
- We feel empowered.
- We have ownership and are trusted.
- We can rationalize and have affirmation.

The change in the performance of the sports team comes through us as empowered individuals who have ownership and who are supported. Our response is emotionally driven which can be rationalized and affirmed. Collectively, we as individuals form an emergent behavior to deliver the required outcomes in response to changes in our environment (e.g., the sports team brings in new players and a new coach). The same is seen within changes in our lives and within business (Figure 4.1). The short training session on a new process often seen within business transformation is about training and not business transformation.

To bring the change we take advantage of the opportunities for change:

- *Incremental*—The ongoing performance improvement (e.g., the drills practice for skilling and training for the sports team).

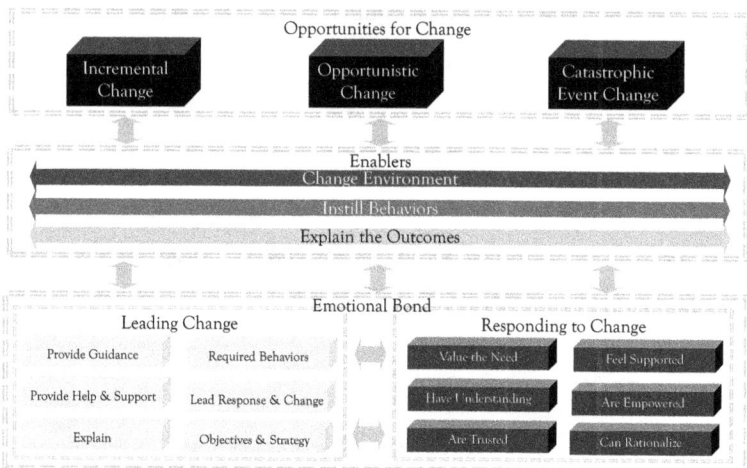

Figure 4.1 The emergent behavior through an empowered emotional response

- *Opportunistic*—Using events to bring change (e.g., injured players give new players opportunities in the sports team).
- *Catastrophic Event*—Using major event to bring change (e.g., the replacement of a CEO in a business after sustained underperformance). Real catastrophic events like global pandemics are also the opportunities for change.

With the changes in the environment comes the instilling of behaviors, to realize the required outcomes. For those leading change and/or the response to change:

- Leadership showing the right behaviors by being the change they wish to see and treating others as they would wish to be treated.
- Leadership in explaining what is happening, why, the impacts, what we need to do, and where we can get help and support.
- Leadership in where to go and how to get there (objectives and strategies). While this needs to be motivational and aspirational, it also has to be achievable, even if it is in incremental steps. The unobtainable and the unrealistic are demotivating.
- Leadership in the response required and adapting to the changes in the response as required.
- Leadership in providing guidance.
- Leadership in providing help and support.

Although leadership that understands the emotional needs of change helps, it is the response of empowered individuals to better ourselves which brings the outcomes. If the sports team is not prepared to make changes, then the turnaround seldom occurs.

Making It Real

Making the emergent behavior real takes time, skilling, and leadership. Working with what capacities and capabilities are to hand and the resources available, the process starts with leadership bringing the change they wish to see and treating others as they would be treated.

The leadership recognizes the importance of the emergent behavior and prioritizes its crafting and shaping. Making the use of skilling (ability to do) as opportunities present, as well as working on the emotional response, and enabling ownership and empowerment, the emergent behavior is strengthened. Inclusion of a process for improvement with affirmation and rationalization of efforts, the emergent behavior begets itself. Making it real is nuanced and the requirement changes over time in response to the environment.

Further Details

- Video—Weekly Mirror Message—Managing People Shutdown (https://youtu.be/m_PsC1gObd8).
- Video—Weekly Mirror Message—The Role of the Individual (https://youtu.be/7ZzKoFwtPiw).
- Video—Strategy and Leadership to Influence Environment & Behaviours to Realise Operations (https://youtu.be/eoCa20XRIwg).
- Video—Problem Solving Together for Our Future: Sharing Skills and Expertise—Empowered Emotional Emergent Behaviour (https://youtu.be/YodrsFr83JM).

Emotional Rationalization

To Get the Most

Our actions are often emotionally driven but rationalized through logic. It is this rationalization of our emotional decisions which justifies decisions and actions. The rationalization is part of the crafting and shaping the emergent behavior as well as being within our motivations and affirmations. Rationalization is therefore important in change management and transformation.

Setting the Example

Business transformation and change management is about the emergent behavior through the emotional bond formed to do things differently. It is the emotional bond that brings the motivation for the emergent behavior, which is reinforced through rationalization and affirmation. An emergent behavior is not easy to achieve, and a simple one size fits all approach seldom works. It is the integrated and multitude of styles and actions that brings the resulting emergent behavior (Figure 4.2) through:

- *Where we are heading*—For change to succeed, we need to know where we are heading. This is more than the settings of objectives and strategy, and is about:
  - Knowing the direction and having it shared so that we can unite and align efforts.
  - The direction needs to meet our shared Interests and Values so we can go in that direction and do the required actions as part of the emergent behavior. You only have to look at the lockdown protesters around COVID-19 in different countries to see the importance of shared interests and values.
  - Having clear obtainable goals, even if it is done in stages, and even if they are revised. The unrealistic and

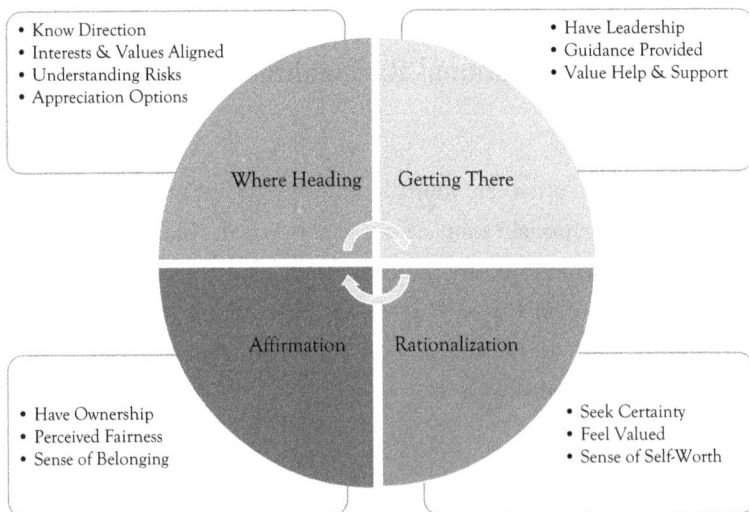

Figure 4.2 Emergent behavior through rationalized emotional bond

unobtainable is demotivating, with the emotional bond being negative rather than positive.

- ○ Where there is an understanding of the risks and an appreciation of the options, we can make the difficult choices and accept the hard circumstances. When you have lost your job prospects and are struggling for home, water, and food, your view on risks and why you are being asked to do things is very different.

- *How to get there*—Knowing where we are going is complimented by the how to get there. With a sense of what the end looks like comes the what to do to achieve. Getting there then benefits from:
  - ○ Leadership that is the change required and treats others as they would be treated is necessary.
  - ○ Having the required guidance provided. The guidance provides clarity whilst enabling us to make the decisions most appropriate.
  - ○ Help and support so that we can help ourselves.

- *Rationalization*—It is the ability to rationalize decisions and actions which reinforces the motivations and strengthens the emotional bond. We draw strength through the ability to rationalize. Rationalization is influenced by leadership, guidance, and the help and support available. The obtainable can be rationalized, while the rationalization of the unobtainable is having interests and values which are not aligned, and the emotional bond is missing or negative. Our rationalization comes through:
  - ○ Having certainty and being able to rationalize at some level of certainty even in an environment of uncertainty. It is the small relatable certainty that is of value.
  - ○ The feeling of being valued and that what we are doing is of importance and appreciated because it motivates us.
  - ○ A sense of self-worth and a knowing of our value.

- *Affirmation*—To persist with the necessary actions in an overall emergent behavior, especially in times of adversity, affirmation of our actions and decisions is required.

Affirmation is related to rationalization and comes from:

- ○ Having a sense of ownership.
- ○ A perception of fairness (aligns with shared interests and values).
- ○ The feeling of belonging for support and a source of reinforcement.

The emergent behavior and the rationalization are about an overall approach which requires nuance and varies with situation, with the resources to hand, and over time. Mistakes will be made when undergoing transformation, shared interest and values may not always align, and vested interests often compete. This is the challenge of bringing change. The emergent behavior is formed when we have the emotional bond with the required affirmation and rationalization to achieve.

Making It Real

Enabling the emergent behavior is similar to that mentioned previously, but it is the rationalization aspect that is required. Rationalization requires:

- Time—Time for the process to occur.
- Affirmation—Messaging from leadership and in the change to affirm the efforts, and decisions and actions.
- Leadership—Leadership that incorporates the rationalization of the emergent behavior into what they do and into those they lead. The affirmation required differs and is about an alignment of interests and values.

Further Details

- Logic and Emotions—Decisions are often based on the emotional response and justified by logic, a rationalization (see Chapter 5).
- Actions of Individuals—It is the actions of individuals that form emergent behaviors through alignment of interests and values (see Chapter 7).

- Video—Weekly Mirror Message—Managing People Shutdown (https://youtu.be/m_PsC1gObd8).
- Video—Problem Solving Together for Our Future: Sharing Skills and Expertise—Emotional Rationalisation (https://youtu.be/ONJJXFIsTMc).

The Known and the Familiar

To Get the Most

Part of the emergent behavior, the rationalization, and the Empowered Emotional Ownership is the working with the known. We are more comfortable with the known and the familiar. It reinforces our views, perceptions, and our current understanding. The known and the familiar makes us feel valued, respected, and appreciated; as well as providing us with self-esteem and self-worth. As we work with what we have, the known and the familiar takes us on the journey (the Journey Model), brings out the best in us, and has us do things better. It is the known and the familiar which helps with empowered emotional ownership.

Setting the Example

Most of us are more comfortable with the known and the familiar. That which reinforces our views, perceptions, and our current understanding is often more valued than the contrary. This is because that which makes us feel valued, respected, and appreciated provides us with self-esteem and self-worth, whilst that which challenges, confronts, or threatens us can bring self-doubt, uncertainty, and insecurity. Therefore, we tend to do what we know. We are inclined to keep working with the familiar. We stick with what we are accustomed to. It is how we use the known and the familiar that we bring change. Through the use of the proven, new ideas are encouraged, and adapted and adopted. We are trusted and empowered to innovate. We are enabled to take ownership (Figure 4.3).

Even with the best of efforts and intent within change management, mistakes are made and more may occur, which is to be expected. Beyond minimizing the mistakes, it is the speed and nature of the response to mistakes which is important. Now, we may seek the quick win, or the

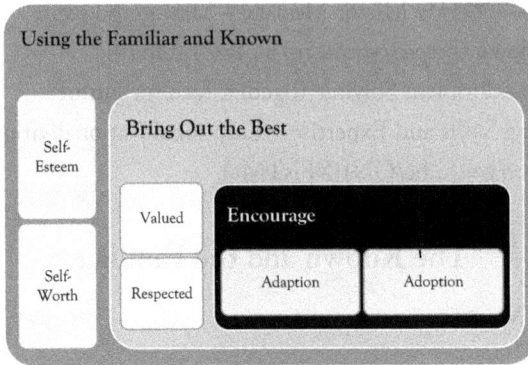

Figure 4.3 Using the known and the familiar

new solution that just delivers, without the need for the proven and the systematic hard work. It is the use of the Known and the Familiar which sustains efforts and is used in the remediation. These same principles of using the familiar and known to work with what we have and bring out the best in us apply whether managing the response to rapid changes in technology or when seeking operational efficiencies or bringing organizational change in adjustment to the new norm.

Making It Real

Using the known and the familiar within change is about a decision to use this approach and then working with it. Rather than seeking a magic wand or a silver bullet and pushing this as the way, the conversation and messaging is:

- We know this works, let's extend the approach.
- This seems like a good idea, let's try this and see if it works.
- What do we need to do? Can we do it? Who will do it? What help will we need?
- Affirmation, confirmation, and rationalization of effort.

Then pragmatically adopt, incrementally apply, and develop as skills and experience is built up. Even if the outcome is not as expected, it is the skills and experience developed that can also be of value.

Further Details

- Mentoring—Using respected people of influence to help and mentor eases the transition (see Chapter 7 Section "Feedback which Motivates by Showing Caring").
- Amount and Rate of Change—Managing the amount and rate of change supports the use of the known and familiar (see Chapter 6 Section "Amount and Pace of Change").
- Video—Problem Solving Together for Our Future: Sharing Skills and Expertise—Empowered Emotional Emergent Behaviour (https://youtu.be/YodrsFr83JM).
- Video—Problem Solving Together for Our Future: Sharing Skills and Expertise—The Known and the Familiar (https://youtu.be/SqnUmxeyy_E).

The If Only

To Get the Most

Achieving change is based on the realities to hand and working with what we have to be the change we wish to see. Where change is dependent upon the "If Only," experience shows that such change is unsustainable because of the misalignment of interests and values as well as the empowered emotional ownership: Why is change full of "If only they did this," "If only we had that," "If only we could do this," "If only they did it this way," "If only they understood" going to succeed?

Setting the Example

Bringing change is littered with the "If only," but the reality of bringing change is that you work with what you have. That is all you have. Wishing for other things will not change what there is on the ground and you do not know that the result will be any better. Bringing change is working with what is there and making the most of it (Figure 4.4). Should "If Only" bring change, then it would be a matter of budget and resources, and just wishing with being back to the panacea and the silver bullet or the magic wand. The losing sports team would just win.

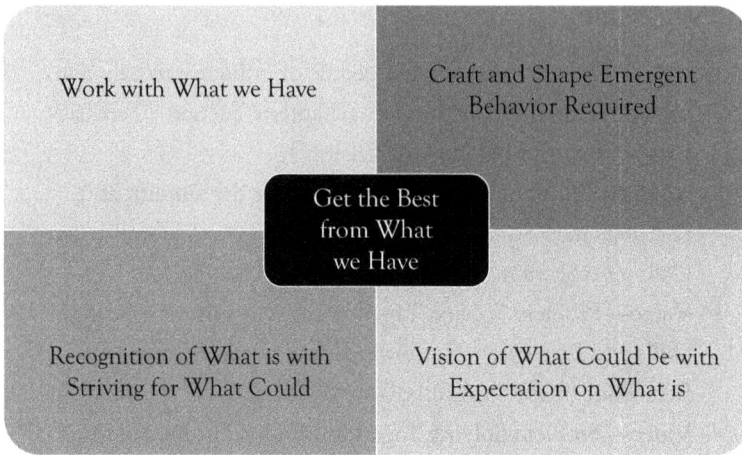

Figure 4.4 If Only—Got the Best from what we have

The realities and practicalities of change is more than the "If Only" and comes from having people do things differently. Working with what we have, the action of individuals having empowered ownership forms an emergent behavior which needs to be crafted and shaped. Leadership needs the vision and to share it, whilst a vision is aspirational, a vision needs to be achievable, even if it is in incremental steps, in an overall journey. It is in this way that the Empowered Emotional Ownership is formed with Interests and Values aligned.

Bringing change is a recognition of what has been achieved and that it is better than before: an acceptance of pragmatics and practicalities which is tempered with the desire to improve.

Making It Real

Avoiding the "If Only" approach to change starts with leadership where there is a recognition of working with what we have, building capacities and capabilities, sharing the vision, and working to that vision with recognition and rationalization of what has been obtained. The focus for leadership is on working with what is to hand and getting the best from what we have through the consistent and persistent application of proven practices. Worse than being an "If Only" change, is having leadership say that "If Only we had got the best from what we had."

Further Details

- Proven Practices—Change comes from the consistent and persistent application of proven principles (see Chapter 1 Section "Applying Proven Principles").
- Leadership—"If Only" change is a sign of poor change and leadership (see Chapter 6).
- Video—Weekly Mirror Message—"If Only" (https://youtu.be/bPyrLggpppk).

Confidence in the Change Enables the Change

To Get the Most

Confidence, if not a belief, in the change is required from the stakeholders for the change to be achieved. With confidence we can overcome any reluctancy, doubt, uncertainty, or change fatigue and create the Empowered Emotional Ownership required for the emergent behavior.

Setting the Example

Changes comes from an emergent behavior of empowered individuals with aligned Interests and Values, who have ownership, because of the pride in who they are and what they do. Having confidence in the change enables the change and requires individuals to have (Figure 4.5):

- *Confidence in Process*—This occurs when the change is credible, the interests and values are aligned, and the change is achievable, even if it is in stages and a journey.
- *Confidence in Leadership*—Leadership needs to be the change they wish to see and treat others as they themselves would wish to be treated. Leadership is about making decisions, providing guidance, and taking people on the journey.
- *Confidence in Decisions*—Decisions need to be made, understood, and well implemented. A pragmatic adoption and adaption to varying circumstances is required. Combined, this creates confidence in decision making.

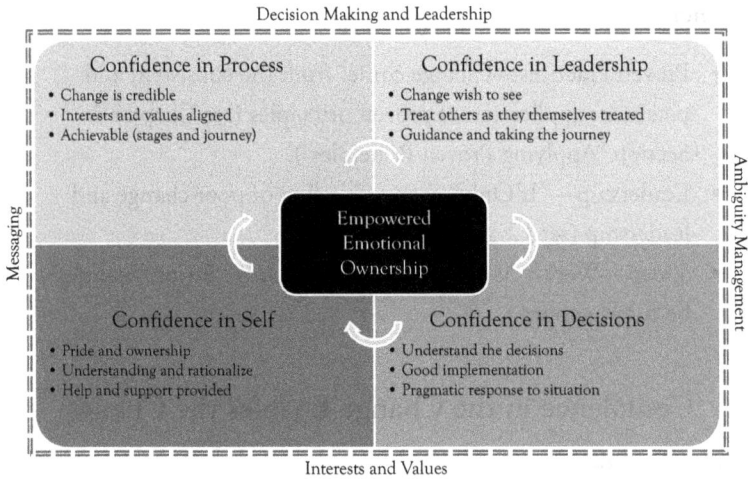

Figure 4.5 *Confidence in the change enables the change*

- *Confidence in Self*—Above all, we need to believe in our capacities and capabilities, our skills and expertise, and in our ability to achieve the change. Confidence in the process, the leadership, and decisions is required, but without belief in ourselves to make the change, the change seldom occurs. We need help and support. We need understanding and the ability to rationalize. We need the pride in who we are and what we are doing to bring the ownership, and from this the motivation to achieve.

Making It Real

Creating confidence comes from the leadership and people of influence and starts with the leadership. Leadership creates confidence in the process and in the decisions made. From this comes confidence in the self. It is the self-confidence of those in the change that is required for the emergent behavior from the Empowered Emotional Ownership of the individuals. The confidence comes by relating the change so that the interests and values are aligned. This requires leadership to recognize the need for creating confidence, the importance in the change process, and taking active measures to sustain the change. Leadership takes advantage of opportunities along the way to build support and structures to adopt and adapt.

Further Details

- Leadership—Leadership creates confidence in the process and in the decisions made (see Chapter 6).
- Working with what we have—Change is done with what we have and getting the best from them, and this is done by creating confidence (see Chapter 1 Section "Applying Proven Principles").
- Video—Weekly Mirror Message—Confidence in the Change Enables the Change (https://youtu.be/7anMim39IzU).

Next Steps

Crafting and shaping emergent behaviors, the building of capacities and capabilities, and the ongoing adaption and adoption of emergent behaviors is seen within our lives. From the parents coaching children's sports or other teams, to the military leadership, through to team leads at work, we see emergent behaviors and the efforts made to achieve. The same is with change and business transformation. All of it starts with the leadership that values the emergent behaviors and the role which emergent behaviors play. The leadership is more than management or the executive; it is the People of Influence and those around who set the example. The leadership is the change they wish to see and treats others as they would be treated.

With an acceptance by leadership, the emergent behaviors become a priority and occur incrementally and pragmatically as skills and expertise are developed. From the valuing of emergent behaviors by leadership, those involved can then form and use the emergent behaviors across the operations. This pragmatic, practical, iterative implementation is done by using what works:

- We know this works, let's extend the approach.
- This seems like a good idea, let's try this and see if it works.
- What do we need to do? Can we do it? Who will do it? What help will we need?
- Affirmation, confirmation, and rationalization of effort.

CHAPTER 5

Decision Making

Decision making for guidance and direction
is only as good as implementation

Summary

Decision making is the management of ambiguity to provide guidance and direction to others so that they know what to do and are empowered to implement. Decision making can be difficult and there is often a reluctance to make decisions with a tendency to wait for others to decide. Making a decision is a matter of following a process with the required rationalization and management of ambiguity. A decision achieves the required outcomes because of the implementation and the necessary response to changes as needed. The decision to form an emergent behavior and the decision making within the emergent behavior as part of change management is considered in this chapter.

Key Learnings

Key learnings from this chapter include:

- Decision making is the management of ambiguity to provide guidance and direction to others so that they know what to do and are empowered to implement.
- Decision making is often about the least-worse option. Decisions that address "to be seen addressing an issue" or "playing the person instead of the issue" leave the issues there which still need to be addressed.
- True costed business cases are the basis for better decision making. Having quality business cases that are more than "adjusting details so that it looks good on paper to get the

tick" is part of successful decision making and realizing sustainable change.

- Decision making around technology-driven change needs to include the business integration and the ICT Operations and Services, rather than just the technology considerations.
- A decision achieves the required outcomes because of the implementation and the necessary response to changes as needed.

Introduction

Decision Making occurs at all levels and is integral to our lives. Decision making is the management of ambiguity to provide guidance and direction to others so that they know what to do and are empowered to implement. The decision making becomes harder, as more people are involved, the greater the complexity, and the higher the risks. A delayed decision is a decision. Indecision or a decision to not decide is a decision with a cost associated and an implementation to manage. Some decisions are made quickly or with quick decisions required, while others may take time. Making a decision is a matter of following a process with the required rationalization and management of ambiguity. Any process is only as good as those that pragmatically use the decision-making process with information for the required outcome. A decision achieves the required outcomes because of the implementation and the necessary response to changes as needed.

Decision Making (the D in AMEDLI) is aligned with Leadership, but requires Ambiguity Management, Messaging, and Empowered Emotional Ownership with the resulting emergent behaviors. Decision making is part of leadership but with an emergent behavior of empowered ownership for decision making across the stakeholders involved within the change or transformation (e.g., play-by-play decisions of those in a sports team or a military unit).

Consider the sports team installing a new coach:

- Making Decisions—The leadership needs to make a series of decisions. Many may be unpopular (e.g., a player being stood down).

- Influences within Decision Making—The leadership needs to factor in many considerations in making a decision. The more factors, the more critical decision, the greater the impacts, the harder the decision often is.
- Least-Worse Option—The decision is often the best of a series of bad options. A team needs to rebuild its player base. As a result, there is a need to accept that it will lose for a while. At what point is this trade-off a problem.
- Business Cases—The business case for recruiting a new player is required. The new player could prove to be a bad purchase or is injured and unable to play.
- Technology—Technology plays a role in the rebuild of the team, but technology alone will not rebuild the team.

This short example shows only part of the decisions required to change the sports team. In digital transformation where it is the replacement of a technology system or the use of artificial intelligence, many more decisions in the change process are required which necessitate the capacity and capability building of decision making. This chapter focuses on decision making within the crafting and shaping of emergent behaviors and its role within these behaviors. The making of decisions and influences within decision making are covered, together with decision making often being the choice of least-worse options. Other aspects of decision making including use of a better business case and the decisions around technology change are also covered. Some next steps are identified. Leadership aspects of decision making are covered subsequently.

Making Decisions

To Get the Most

From the routine to the strategic, bringing change requires decision making by all parties at different times. Leaders are expected to make decisions, with the decisions being right and properly implemented. Decisions around messaging, skilling, scheduling, operational, and getting people to do things differently are also required within change. Decision making can be difficult and there is often a reluctance to make decisions. There is also a tendency to wait for others to decide, especially where decisions are unclear, ambiguity around responsibilities exist, and the implementation of a decision remains a major issue. Criticism of a decision (a delayed decision or indecision) is part of decision making. Therefore, making decisions is an integral part of change and transformation and is an emergent behavior required which needs to be crafted and shaped for successful change.

Setting the Example

Despite the use of processes and supporting analysis, decision making is often an emotional decision that is rationalized by logic based on the view, skills, and expertise of those making the decision. Decision making requires the management of ambiguity, and the ability to implement a decision impacts upon decision making (Figure 5.1).

Decision Making can occur when the outcome can be rationalized. Rationalization is achieved through:

- Inclusion of and respecting a diversity of view. Avoids the problems of group think and falling to "one party is all knowing."
- Taking an evidence-based approach to an informed view. This includes skills and expertise of those involved.

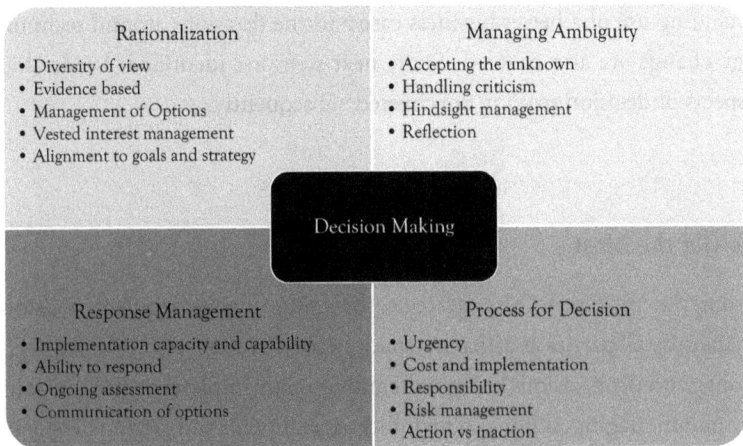

Rationalization
- Diversity of view
- Evidence based
- Management of Options
- Vested interest management
- Alignment to goals and strategy

Managing Ambiguity
- Accepting the unknown
- Handling criticism
- Hindsight management
- Reflection

Decision Making

Response Management
- Implementation capacity and capability
- Ability to respond
- Ongoing assessment
- Communication of options

Process for Decision
- Urgency
- Cost and implementation
- Responsibility
- Risk management
- Action vs inaction

Figure 5.1 Decision making is harder as with increase in the number of people involved, greater the complexity, and higher the risk

- The management of options. Whilst knowing everything around all the options is impractical, accommodating options and alternatives is required.
- Decision making aligned to goals and strategy helps.
- Recognizing and managing vested interests.

Decision making requires the management of ambiguity. Decisions need to be made with incomplete and contradicting information. Decision can play out differently to what is intended and the outcomes from decisions can change. Ambiguity can bring doubt, uncertainty, and a reluctance to decide. Ambiguity Management is key to decision making and requires:

- An acceptance of the unknown and accommodation of the unknown within the decision-making process.
- Recognition that decisions will be criticized, even the absence of decisions, and whether successful or not. Handling criticism through communication of the options and the reason for a selected path is part of the management of ambiguity.
- The ability to reflect, consider, and revise is part of the management of ambiguity. Reflection includes the balance of internal and external factors and the elimination of options to influence the timing of a decision.
- Whilst we may think a decision will play out in a particular way, it is only hindsight that tells. The effectiveness of alternatives is not proven because of hindsight. Management of ambiguity requires acceptance and management of hindsight.

Rationalization and ambiguity management form part of a process for decision making along with:

- Clarity of responsibility as to who is the decision maker, responsibility on implementation, responsibility for outcomes. We often seek a party to blame and multiple parties are blamed for adverse outcomes. It is the clarity of responsibility which aids decision making.

- Management of urgency. Sometimes a decision may seem important and so is considered urgent, yet there is still time to reflect and then make a decision. An urgent decision still requires a process with the rationalization and management of ambiguity.
- Cost. Consideration of the cost is part of the decision-making process. The cost considerations include the cost of acting, the cost of waiting, the cost of the status quo, the cost to implement, and the cost of risk.
- Implementation. The difficulty of implementation is a consideration for making a decision. The easy option may have a cost.
- The process for decision making considers the cost and benefits of action as well as the cost and benefits of deferred action and keeping the status quo. There is a cost and impacts of inaction as well as action that are considered within the decision-making process.

The decision-making process with rationalization and ambiguity management is only a process. The process is only as good as those electing to follow the process and the information they have. Whether it is a good decision or a bad decision, the right decision or the wrong decision, any decision is only as good as its implementation and its variation in response as circumstances change. Having the correct response management is also part of the decision making as it influences both the decisions made and the success of the outcomes from the decision. Response management includes:

- The capacity and capability to implement a decision. The success of a good decision comes from the effectiveness of the implementation.
- The success of a decision comes from the ongoing monitoring to determine changes in response as required.

- The ability to respond to changes include making a good decision better or mitigating a decision that turns out to be a bad decision or the wrong decision.
- The implementation of a decision or the changes in response required depends upon the ability to communicate the decision as well as the options and why the decision is the preferred solution.

Making the right decision or a wrong one is a matter of a process for the decision making with the required rationalization and management of ambiguity. A process is only as good as those that pragmatically use the process with information for the required outcome. A right decision becomes a good decision because of the required implementation and response management. A right decision badly implemented and with little response to change becomes a bad decision. The wrong decision with poor implementation and little response to changes remains a bad decision, but a wrong decision can be made better with the required changes.

Making It Real

Decision Making is an emergent behavior required for successful change management and depends upon the other emergent behaviors of:

- *Ambiguity Management*—Decisions are often made on incomplete information, with nuances, and the impacts of the decision may be unknown with unforeseen consequences.
- *Messaging*—The messaging of the information for a decision, the messaging for making the decision, and the messaging of the decision for implementation are part of decision making.
- *Empowered Emotional Ownership*—From decisions made to support vested interests or the emotions involved in a decision, emotions are a part of decision making. Where there is a sense of ownership, better decisions tend to result. Businesses require decentralized decision making which requires empowerment,

- *Leadership*—A critical leadership function is decision making. Those with better leadership skills tend to make better decisions.
- *Interests and Values*—The alignment of interests and values impacts decisions made (e.g., making a decision to support a vested interest or for self-promotion).

Forming the emergent behavior for decision making is itself a decision by leadership to prioritize and then implement through skilling and the right management framework for decisions.

Further Details

- Proven Principles—The consistent and persistent use of proven principles helps with decision making (see Chapter 1 Section "Applying Proven Principles").
- Least-Worse Option—Decision making is often the choice between least-worse options (see Section "Least-Worse Option and Alternative Decision Making" of this chapter).
- Leadership is About Making Decisions—Decision making is a key leadership responsibility, but it is the implementation that matters more (see Chapter 6).
- Video—Problem Solving Together for Our Future: Sharing Skills and Expertise—Decision Making (https://youtu.be/ m2Y7S3-OHsg).

Influences within Decision Making

To Get the Most

If decision making was easy, the decisions would be readily made and implemented. The reality is that decision making is often complex and nuanced. Decisions often need to be made in the absence of complete information and without knowing how they will play out. Sometimes, deciding not to act and to maintain the status quo is the required decision rather than bringing change. Knowing when to make a decision and act, or when to wait, can be ambiguous.

As a coach of a sports team, making the decisions to change tactics or substitute players in the middle of a game may not work out as planned. There are a series of considerations and constraints already impacting a decision, and the help provided in making decisions may be limited. Conversely, deciding to revise the training regime or the support staff may be of less urgency, may be implemented over time, more options may be available, with wider support in making the decision. Similarly, across business and in bringing change and transformation.

It is the emergent behavior around the capacity and capability to make decisions and manage the influences within the making of decisions that are needed for successful change and transformation.

Setting the Example

Using a decision to continue a business as a worked example, the management of the influencers within decision making are considered (Figure 5.2). This includes the assumptions, the dependencies, the risks, and how they relate to an overall strategy as well as shape that strategy.

- *Assumptions*—The choice to restore business is driven by need, but is also underpinned by a series of assumptions, including

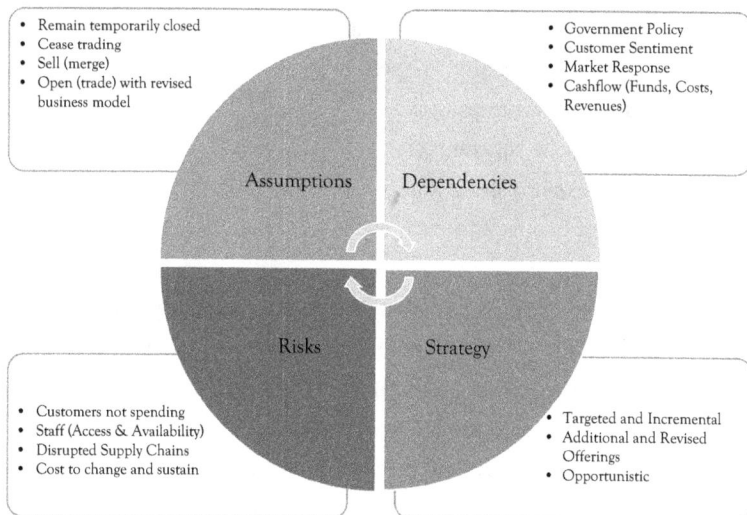

- Remain temporarily closed
- Cease trading
- Sell (merge)
- Open (trade) with revised business model

- Government Policy
- Customer Sentiment
- Market Response
- Cashflow (Funds, Costs, Revenues)

Assumptions   Dependencies

Risks   Strategy

- Customers not spending
- Staff (Access & Availability)
- Disrupted Supply Chains
- Cost to change and sustain

- Targeted and Incremental
- Additional and Revised Offerings
- Opportunistic

Figure 5.2 Business restoration: helping with decision making

what the business will look like and what is best for the
business. Does it:

- ○ Remain closed temporarily?
- ○ Cease trading?
- ○ Sell off the business or its assets or merge?
- ○ Open and/or trade with a revised business model?

- *Dependencies*—Restoration of the business depends upon
  many things including:
  - ○ Government policy, for example, continued restrictions and
    social distancing needs.
  - ○ The sentiment of customers, for example, do they feel safe
    and is it an essential or luxury service?
  - ○ The response of markets, from the availability of products
    to the funding available; a business decision is dependent
    upon what is occurring in markets, for example, border
    restrictions on the number of tourists.
  - ○ Cash flow and the revenue, costs, and available funds.
- *Strategy*—The strategy for the restoration of the business.
  The strategy needs to be clearly defined, quantifiable, and
  understood, so that activities can be aligned. For example,
  the risks in the American meat industry and the impact upon
  food supply provide an opportunity for Australian producers.
- *Risk Management*—There are many risks to opening the
  business and to keeping it open including:
  - ○ Changes in assumptions.
  - ○ Variations in dependencies.
  - ○ Customers not spending.
  - ○ Safety of people and staff.
  - ○ Disruption to supply chains.
  - ○ Cost to change a business and to sustain the business.

These are not easy decisions; there are many more risks, assumptions,
and dependencies. The business environment will change, revisions to
decisions will need to occur, and we do not know how many of these will
play out.

Making It Real

Within the capacity and capability building of the decision-making emergent behavior is the skilling of expertise in the influencers and the facilitation of the use of influencers within decision making. Clearly many routine decisions will continue to be made pragmatically and quickly. Rather it is about using influencers within the bigger decisions and the ones that take time to make. Approaches to take include:

- Ensuring a business case includes assumptions, dependencies, risks, and alignment to strategy.
- Having leadership practice these in the actions they do and the decisions they take.
- Use of check lists when making decisions for ensuring that due process is followed, for example, disclosure of conflicts of interests or showing alignment to strategy or showing how the decision addresses the issue.
- Role-based scenario training at the time of role changes and refresher training.

Over time, the influencers will become part of wider decision making and the emergent behavior.

Further Details

- Process for Decision Making—A process for decision making brings value to the decision-making process (see Section "Making Decisions" of this chapter).
- Better Business Cases—Use of better business cases within decision making (see Section "Better Business Cases" of this chapter).
- Video—Weekly Mirror Message—Balance of Influences to Revise Decisions (https://youtu.be/0ODvci-W9do).
- Video—Problem Solving Together for Our Future: Sharing Skills and Expertise—Help with Decision Making (https://youtu.be/odGlNmuI9uM).

Least-Worse Option and Alternative Decision Making

To Get the Most

For the routine and many operational decisions, the options can be clear because the way forward and what needs to occur is seen. As the decisions become more complex and the nuance increases, making a decision is often a matter of selecting the least-worse option. The least-worse option is often about a decision that is respected, even if it is not popular. After choosing a least-worse option, the issues of implementation with adoption and adaption to circumstances remain. Accepting and working with the least-worse option, including the resulting criticism, is part of realizing change and of the decision-making emergent behavior required.

Setting the Example

In setting the example for the use of least-worse option, decision making (Figure 5.3) within change is the acceptance that least-worse option decision making may be the only option, even if it is a decision not to act. Beyond the influencers (see Chapter 3), a decision that manages the issues is often better. Decisions made "to be seen addressing an issue" (e.g., management of an aircraft accident rather than the media coverage) of the accident or "playing the person instead of the issue" (e.g., arguing between politicians when an economy is in recession)

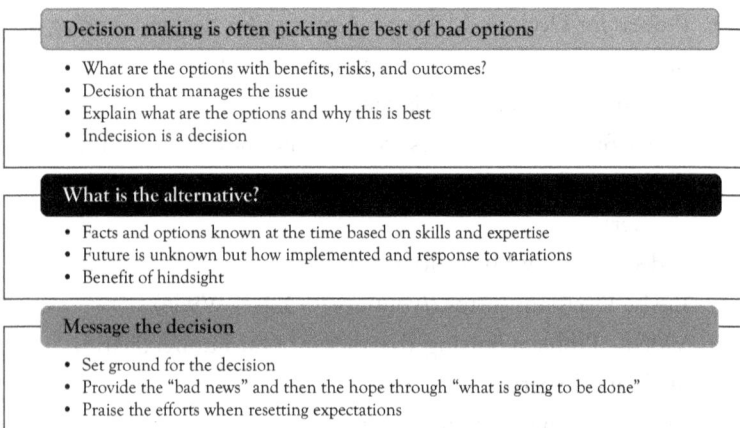

Decision making is often picking the best of bad options

- What are the options with benefits, risks, and outcomes?
- Decision that manages the issue
- Explain what are the options and why this is best
- Indecision is a decision

What is the alternative?

- Facts and options known at the time based on skills and expertise
- Future is unknown but how implemented and response to variations
- Benefit of hindsight

Message the decision

- Set ground for the decision
- Provide the "bad news" and then the hope through "what is going to be done"
- Praise the efforts when resetting expectations

Figure 5.3 Least-worse option and what is the alternative?

may provide short-term rewards, but the issue is still there and could be getting worse.

The pragmatics and practicality of implementation are a consideration in making a decision, and a decision that is unable to be implemented will struggle. This is nuanced and complexed; there needs to be a recognition of the coupling of the decision making with the implementation:

- Any decision is only as good as the implementation and the adoption and adaption as circumstances change.
- Explaining what the decision is and why it is the best of the options helps people understand and support the decision; even if it is not liked, it is respected.
- Deciding not to act is a decision, whether it is an active decision, a deferred decision, or just neglect. While no action or deferred decision may be the required response, the decision still needs to be managed as the situation unfolds. Neglecting a decision has a cost and impacts.

A decision will be subject to criticism at the time of making in terms of implementation, time of decision, and better alternatives. With the benefit of hindsight, criticism of the decision can intensify. When the least-worse option is used and addresses the issue (rather than "being seen" or "playing the person"), the use of "What is the alternative?" can help. "What is the alternative?" is used in setting expectations, messaging, and the emotional rationalization of the decision makers, the implementers, and those impacted. We make decisions based on the facts known at the time with skills and expertise to hand. The future is unknown, and the success is dependent upon the implementation and the adoption and adaption as circumstances change.

To the critics of "What is the alternative?" it is a matter of calling out the critics and holding them to account. When the critics reply it's "not my job or responsibility" or some variation of that, then where is the accountability that went with this abdication because we all have responsibilities? In addition, it is about "What are we doing about it?" (i.e., the management of the implementation and response) that is of greater concern.

Any decision needs to be messaged. Sometimes the surprise factor is required by some stakeholders, but overall, setting the ground for the decision by custom messaging is used to manage expectations. Where the decision is difficult, explain the options and why. Consider explaining what is happening, the impacts, what is required, and where to get help and support. With difficult decisions, provide the bad news to set the expectation but then bring the hope through "what we can do to help ourselves" and "what is being done to help us." Remember to praise the efforts of those involved, rather than yourself. Should the impacts be less than expected or some measure not required, then it was the good work done by those involved. Should more efforts be required, then the expectation is set and the efforts to date have stopped it being worse.

Making It Real

In many ways, least-worse option decision making lies in the options provided within the decision making. The process for decision making and the influencers are still applicable. Making it real is nuanced and is in the willingness of those involved to make the decision. Through a broad-based capacity and capability building of the emergent behavior, confidence comes, and the acceptance of least-worse option decision making follows. This is strengthened by skilling and the actions of leadership.

Further Details

- Proven Principles—Least-worse option decision making depends upon proven business principles pragmatically applied (see Chapter 1 Section "Applying Proven Principles").
- Communicating a Decision—A decision is only as good as an implementation and this requires messaging with an emotional bond (see Chapter 3).
- Video—Weekly Mirror Message—Least Worse Option and Alternative Decision Making (https://youtu.be/ JdNEvAp9XGA).

Better Business Cases

To Get the Most

A business case is frequently used in decision making and within change and transformation. From the simple bullet points discussed to more formal documents in an extended review and budgeting process, a business case is more than a point in time decision for an action. A business case is the basis for a range of decisions, planning, actions, responses, and coordination of effort. Having quality business cases that are more than "adjusting details so that it looks good on paper to get the tick" is part of successful decision making and realizing sustainable change.

Setting the Example

A good business case clearly and succinctly answers the questions: What are we doing? Why are we doing it? Who is doing it? Who owns what? What is the cost? What will stop it? (Figure 5.4).

Business cases are part of decision making and are the basis for successful implementation. Business cases are often difficult to get right because while we know the required details at the end, we often do not

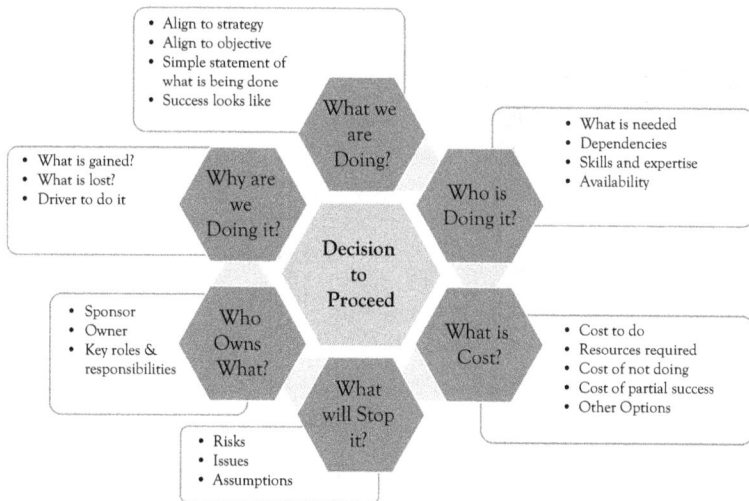

Figure 5.4 Better business cases

know these at the start. Yet there are fundamentals in a business case that can get lost with corresponding impacts, for example, cost overruns. An effective business case addresses:

- *What are we doing?*—A simple statement on what is being done so that we can relate it to overall objectives and strategy, know what success looks like, and align the effort.
- *Why are we doing it?*—A simple understanding of why we are doing it and the gains and/or losses to be had.
- *Who is doing it?*—If we know who is doing it, we can manage the outcomes.
- *Who owns what?*—Without clear ownership, a lack of accountability and responsibility can result.
- *What is the cost?*—What is the cost to do and/or not do with contingencies?
- *What will stop it?*—A simple understanding of what could stop it from occurring.

A good business case answers these questions clearly and succinctly because it is a point for good decision making, both to proceed and for ongoing referral. A good business case answers these questions clearly and succinctly because it is a tool for the emergent behavior of ownership, empowerment, interests, and values. A good business case answers these questions clearly and succinctly because it enables:

- Ambiguity Management.
- Messaging.
- Decision Making.
- Empowered Emotional Ownership.
- Leadership.
- Interests and Values.

A good business case answers these questions clearly and succinctly, forming the basis for a range of decisions, planning, actions, responses, and coordination of effort.

Making It Real

Improving business cases requires a range of approaches depending upon the current approach used. Considerations include:

- Templates—Changes to templates to reflect the messaging and information required.
- Skilling and Training—Provision of skilling on the use of business cases and how to create them.
- Process—A process for assuring the quality of business cases, including the use of true costings and true costed projects. This makes a business case an ongoing decision making document.
- Leadership—Decision Making aligned to needs and strategy with rigor of process.
- Incremental—Adoption across areas of business and operations incrementally with pragmatic adoption.
- Funding—Tying of funding to the process and decisions with accountability for outcomes.

Implementing these is often a change project in its own right. It is the desire of leadership to have the required accountability and to make the change (i.e., interest and values alignment, which is a significant factor in implementation).

Further Details

- Business Cases are Part of Project Management—Better business cases are part of good project management practices (see Chapter 8 Section "Project Management").
- Use of Recipes—Recipes can be used for creating and using better business cases (see Chapter 8 Section "Recipes").
- Skilling and Training—Making use of skilling and training for adoption of business cases (see Chapter 7 Section "Skilling and Training").

- Video—Problem Solving Together for Our Future: Sharing Skills and Expertise—Better Business Cases for Success (https://youtu.be/a7wPCcDb7jU).

Not the Technology, It's the Business

To Get the Most

Technology is transforming societies and business with operational changes around technology being a prominent business activity. Critical to the changes around technology is the need to address ICT Operations and Services as well as the integration of technology into the business. With the increasing rate of technology adoption and the automation of knowledge worker and other roles, the need for technology integration and support is of increasing importance. Decisions to implement change and technology require the recognition that successful change is more than the technology, and that the cost and benefit is the business integration and services.

Setting the Example

For successful change, the decision needs to be made that "it is not the technology, it is the business that is the issue." Consider the hype around blockchains where the CHESS replacement project of the Australian Stock Exchange is now scheduled for a year behind the previous delays because the focus was on the technology. The fanfare around blockchains to track meat from paddock to plate, which is undermined by the photocopying of QR codes in meat markets, and the need to keep central authorities for regulatory and compliance purposes (which undermines the purpose of distributed ledgers) are just some of the business realities of blockchains. This same technology hype around Java led to the desire to rewrite applications and almost brought bankruptcy to some financial institutions. In these cases (amongst many), the decisions made were technology centric, and the wider business integration and ICT Operations and Services were secondary.

Realizing change requires a decision around technology to include the business realities with the ICT Operations and Services as well as the integration into the business (Figure 5.5). Technology has the hardware and software itself as well as the data. Technology requires Development and Testing, Deployment, Operations, and Services, all of which uses the Shared Services of a business and uses the components of Delivery. Business Delivery of the Technology as products and services uses the Shared Services and the components of Delivery.

To realize changes around technology, all of the elements (Figure 5.5) need to be considered and are part of the business case and decision making.

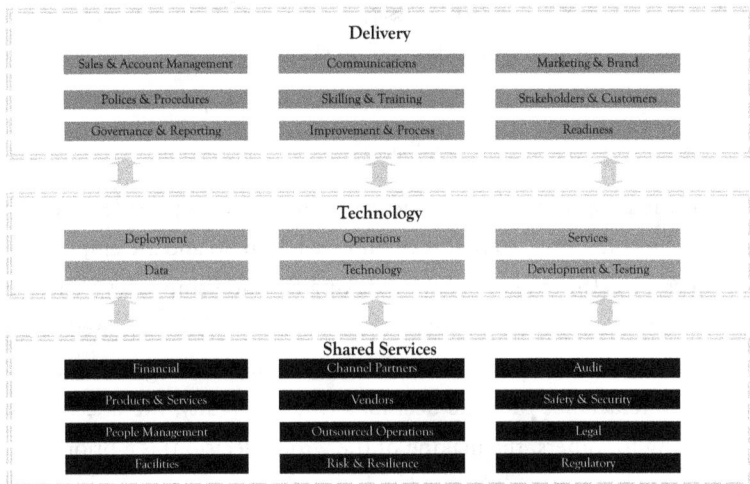

Figure 5.5 Business integration and ICT Operations and Services

Making It Real

Having decision making which includes consideration of the business integration as well as ICT Operations and Services starts with those in technology working in and understanding the business, while those in the business have exposure to the delivery of technology services and operations (i.e., cross-skilling). From this cross-skilling comes the understanding of what is required and recognition of true costs and true costed projects. This true costing is part of the business case for the change (see Section "Better Business Cases" of this chapter). All of this is dependent upon the leadership making the required decisions to work in this way and supporting the implementation.

Further Details

- Use of Technology—Adoption of technology in the business and its change (see Chapter 8 Section "Technology Adoption").
- Reference—Sherringham K., and Unhelkar, B. (2020) Crafting and Shaping Knowledge Worker Services in the Information Economy. Palgrave Macmillan Singapore 570pp (https://link.springer.com/book/10.1007/978-981-15-1224-7).
- Video—Weekly Mirror Message—Not the Technology it's the Business (https://youtu.be/uzrQePsLEg0).

Next Steps

Decision making is the management of ambiguity to provide guidance and direction to others so that they know what to do and are empowered to implement. This makes decision making by leadership a key issue and to make decision making part of an overall emergent behavior used across the realization of change and transformation. The challenge of overcoming of the reluctance to make decisions (the ambiguity, the uncertainty, the waiting for others, the making of the wrong decision) is a priority for leadership who start with being the change they wish to see and treating others as they would be treated around decision making and what is expected. Leadership to address:

- Process—A process for decision making with the required support and skilling.
- Accountability—Having the required accountability around decisions made, including aspects like true costed projects to include the business integration and any service and operational changes. This is tied to funding.
- Incremental—Adoption across areas of business and operations incrementally with pragmatic adoption.

- Impacts—Working to have those making decisions manage the impacts of the decision making. A delayed decision is a decision. Indecision or a decision to not decide is a decision with a cost associated and an implementation to manage.

Implementation is through a broad-based capacity and capability building of the emergent behavior from which confidence comes. This is strengthened by skilling and the actions of leadership.

CHAPTER 6

Leadership

Leadership needs to be the change they wish
to see and treat others as they would be

Summary

For change to be successful, leadership needs to be the change they wish to see and to treat others as they themselves would be treated. Leadership is then about decision making and providing the guidance as well as the crafting and shaping the required emergent behaviors for the actions by empowered individuals who have ownership and an emotional bond to the change. Leadership uses or changes the environment to instill the behaviors to realize the outcomes. Leadership occurs at all levels and is realized by the people of influence who impact those around them. Aspects of leadership in realizing change and transformation are explored in this chapter.

Key Learnings

Key learnings from this chapter include:

- Leadership starts with being the change you wish to see and treating others as you would wish to be treated.
- Leadership brings changes in the environment, to instill the behaviors to form the required emergent behaviors, to achieve the outcomes.
- Leadership should be able to answer the question "what makes you think you can get people to change what they do?" or at the least, answer "why do you think your change will work?"

- Leadership provides the vision, which is aspirational, but needs to be achievable, even if it is in stages, through a journey of change.
- Leadership is about making decisions and providing guidance for those implementing change to have the empowered ownership and emotional bond to achieve.

Introduction

Leadership is required to make changes of themselves, just as leadership is required during the changes. Leadership is an emergent behavior that is crafted and shaped with skilling and experience. Leadership occurs at all levels and is not just the actions of management. Rather it is done by all People of Influence who can impact those around them. Leadership starts with being the change you wish to see and treating others as you would wish to be treated. Leadership brings changes in the environment, to instill the behaviors to form the required emergent behaviors, to achieve the outcomes. Leadership is managing risk and juggling the gain against the status quo. Leadership is about managing both the reactive and the proactive alongside operations. Leadership aligns the combination of drivers and opportunity for change to help overcome the resistance to Change.

Leadership (the L in AMEDLI) requires Ambiguity Management, Messaging, Empowered Emotional Ownership, and Decision Making. Leadership brings Interests and Values alignment to form an overall approach to realizing change. Crafting and shaping the leadership emergent behavior is implemented through a broad-based capacity and capability building of the emergent behavior from which confidence comes.

Consider the implementation of a data analytics solution that automates routine reporting as part of a digital transformation, where leadership has many issues to address within the change:

- Drivers and Opportunities—Leadership uses opportunities and drivers for change to get the business case approved and to implement the solution.
- Changing What we Do—Leadership needs to be able to answer why the change will work. Without being able to do

this, remediation may be required with extra cost and more people involved in both reporting and remediation.

- Assurance—Leadership needs to assure the change and the success of the change.
- Project Management—Implementing the data analytics solution may be achieved via a project of work. Project management skills and expertise are required for the change.
- Moving Forward—Leadership needs to take the first steps and bring the change. From success comes the momentum to change. It is often easier to maintain the status quo.
- Amount and Pace of Change—A business can only sustain so much change at a given time. This will need to be managed within the project to implement the data analytics solution as well as the wider business.
- Taking People on the Journey—Leadership will need to take people on the journey. From justifying the business case, to implementation, to changing roles and responsibilities.
- Crafting and Shaping the Emergent Behaviors—The role of leadership is to craft and shape the required behaviors.

From managing the aspects of COVID-19, through business change, to the sports team; leadership is important. The use of drivers and opportunities for realizing change in leadership and why change will succeed through leadership are addressed in this chapter. The use of assurance, project and programs of work for change, and how to strengthen leadership are addressed in this chapter, together with managing the amount of and rate of change. Leadership is about taking people on the journey of change (use of the Journey Model for change), and the crafting and shaping of emergent behaviors is also covered in this chapter. Some next steps are included.

Drivers and Opportunities

To Get the Most

Leadership balances the combination of drivers with opportunity for change against the pragmatics of keeping operations going. By altering the risk and varying the balance of gain vs. the status quo, actionable change is achieved.

Setting the Example

Leadership juggles the drivers of a business (Figure 6.1) to sustain a business and to take opportunities for change. Incumbency is both a protector of a business (e.g., existing market advantage and customers) as well as a limiter on the ability to respond. Similarly, vested interest can be used to limit change and maintain the status quo just as it can be a driver of change.

Leadership uses the opportunities for Change brought by the drivers. The opportunities are the slow incremental change brought by activities like sustained process improvement. There are the opportunistic events like regulatory change that provide opportunities for change. There are also the catastrophic events which bring rapid change (e.g., COVID-19 driving online education which governments may have resisted previously). Leadership is about transformation and seeks to bring changes in the business environment, to instill the behaviors to achieve the outcomes (Transformers).

An example is a sports team that is losing (Drivers are loss of customers and revenue) changing the coach (Opportunistic change). The coach uses the Transformers. Having a new coach is a change in the environment for the team. The coach brings a new approach to the training regimes with a focus on skills which instill the winning behaviors (e.g., belief in the team because of a higher skill set and more disciplined training results). The coach has formed an emergent behavior, and through this emergent behavior achieves the outcome of a championship.

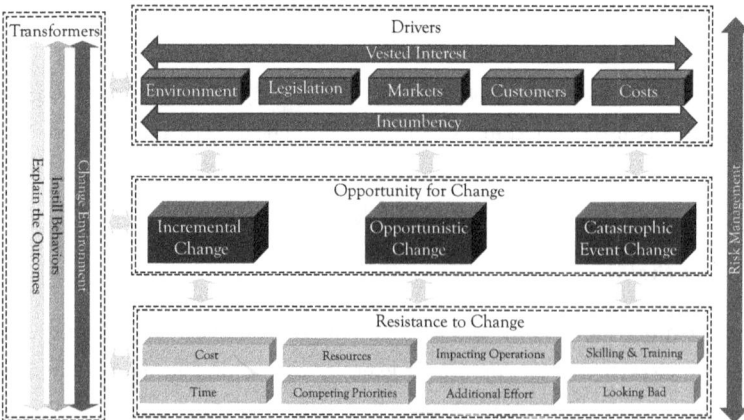

Figure 6.1 Management of the gain vs. status quo

To bring a change, leadership needs to sustain operations whilst overcoming:

- *Cost*—Making changes incurs a cost. Funds may not be available, and the promised returns may not materialize.
- *Time*—It takes time to do.
- *Resources*—These are needed to do the change.
- *Competing Priorities*—Need to manage Competing Priorities, without knowing that success will occur.
- *Impacting Operations*—Existing operations are impacted and there is a need to maintain and sustain operations.
- *Additional Effort*—Requires extra work on top of existing commitments.
- *Skilling and Training*—Skilling (the ability to do) and training (the how to do) are needed for making the changes, managing the changes, and working with the changes going forward.
- *Looking Bad*—The fear of looking bad if the change does not work, but also for looking bad if the change works when we are asked "why did we not do it sooner." Looking bad by having the proposal rejected. Factors like "I will not be listened to" or "someone else's responsibility" or "even if I try, it will make no difference" also impact the fear of looking bad.

Bringing change is about managing risk and juggling the gain against the status quo. Factors like lawsuits or loss of job may be motivating for bringing change, but these are usually reactionary responses occurring after events. Revenue prospects and market growth provide opportunities for managing change proactively, but proactive management is often difficult within the operational practicalities. Leadership is about managing both the reactive and the proactive alongside operations. Leadership manages the combination of drivers and opportunity alignment which helps overcome the Resistance to Change. By altering the risk and varying the balance of gain vs. the status quo, actionable change is achieved.

Making It Real

Managing the gain against the status quo, use of the Drivers and Opportunities with the Transformers to overcome the Resistance to change is a leadership skill. This experience often develops over time, but the skills can be instilled through a proactive management regime with mentoring and an ongoing improvement process. Leadership is about an emergent behavior with management taking an overall approach that facilitates change, empowerment, and ownership. This requires:

- Existing leadership to recognize the approach and the need.
- Leadership being the change they wish to see and treating others as they would be treated to embed the practices within their teams.
- Change selected personnel in key positions of influence so that they practice the principles which then influence those around them.
- Incremental tactical adoption through opportunities across operations.

The principles and practices mentioned in other chapters for forming an emergent behavior also apply.

Further Details

- Opportunities for Change—The drivers create opportunities to bring change, but a decision to take the opportunities is required (see Chapter 5).
- Making Change Work—Being able to take advantage of the opportunities still requires answering the basic questions (see Section "Why and How are We Going to Change What We Do" of this chapter).
- Video—Problem Solving Together for Our Future: Sharing Skills and Expertise—Drivers and Opportunities (https://youtu.be/eDjDpUnHYsU).

Why and How Are We Going to Change What We Do?

To Get the Most

One of the skills of leadership is about asking the right questions to get right answers for decision making. At the heart of leading change and transformation is "getting people to change what they do." Change takes time, is nuanced, and is about an emergent behavior. Leadership knows that there is no one size fits all approach or a silver bullet or a panacea for achieving change, making the leading questions (Who, What, Why, Where, When, and How) part of leading change.

Setting the Example

If an officer in a defense force should be able to answer the question "what makes you think you can lead those people in battle?" then those seeking to lead change and transformation should be able to answer "what makes you think you can get people to change what they do?" or at the least, answer "why do you think your change will work?" Leadership should also be able to answer some basic questions around the change they seek (see Chapter 1 Section "The Basic Questions" and Figure 6.2).

Ambiguity Management	Where it will be done?
	What traded?
Messaging	What are we doing?
	Why are we doing it?
Empowered Emotional Ownership	Who will do it?
	How long will it take?
Decision Making	What is needed?
	When do we need it?
Leadership	Why will it occur?
Interests and Values	What is cost to do it (not do it)?

Figure 6.2 Leadership questions of transformation

Making It Real

The easiest way to make the use of these questions real is for leadership to ask the questions on a consistent and persistent basis, especially as a way to realize the required outcomes from the change. Addressing the reluctance to ask the questions, the wanting to avoid the difficult questions, and those not responding are all part of the use and adoption and adaption. This starts with selected leaders deciding to use the basic questions with others using them in response to the example set (i.e., leaders are they change they wish to see and treat others as they themselves would be treated). This change is motivational and aspirational, but is also believable, so that it can be achieved, even if it is stages (e.g., the sports team winning a championship is motivational, believable, and obtainable, even if it may take a couple of seasons to achieve). This is important for confidence, self-belief, and belief in the process.

Further Details

- Basic Questions—Be able to answer the basic questions around why change will succeed (see Chapter 1 Section "The Basic Questions").
- Ability to Assure—Leadership needs to assure the change management process (see Section "The 10-Point Assurance" of this chapter).
- Managing the Journey—Making the change is about taking people in the journey of change (see Section "The Journey Model of Change" of this chapter).
- Video—Weekly Mirror Message—Why and How are We Going to Change What we Do? (https://youtu.be/ E6PQFet1GXs).

The 10-Point Assurance

To Get the Most

Related to the leading questions (see Section "Why and How are We Going to Change What We Do?" of this chapter) the questions for change (see Chapter 1 Section "The Basic Questions" and Figure 6.2) can be used as an approach for assurance of change. Through the use of the questions, managing against them, and tracking outcomes accordingly, an approach for assurance can be applied by leadership. The approach can also be used by leadership to craft and shape the emergent behaviors.

Setting the Example

A 10-point check list for assurance of transformation can used and is best considered as a pyramid built on the foundation of what we are doing and why (Figure 6.3):

- *What are we doing?*—The most important and the base of the pyramid is to know what we need to do. This is the clearly repeatable objectives to which we refer back to so that efforts can be aligned. This also provides the clarity for messaging and actions. A clear understanding of what we are doing also enables our ownership and empowerment to respond. This needs to be motivational, aspirational, credible, and believable, so that it can be achieved, even if it is in stages along the journey. This created confidence and belief that the change can be achieved.
- *Why are we doing it?*—If we know why we are doing it, we can adopt and adapt as needed. This also brings the motivation and builds the emotional bond.
- *Why will it occur?*—This relates to the "What is needed?" and looks at why something will occur or not occur. This is related

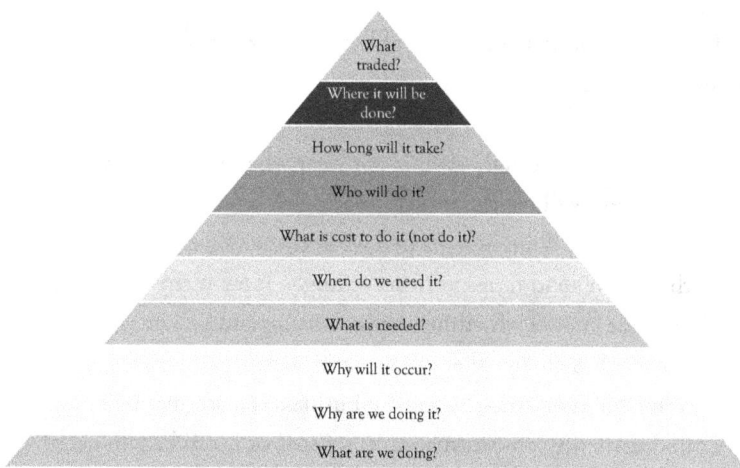

Figure 6.3 The who, why, what, where, when, how of transformation

to motivation, empowerment, ownership, and the emotional factors of Interests and Values.

- *What is needed?*—Next, we can establish what is needed to be done so as to empower us to do it.
- *When do we need it?*—This prioritizes actions and efforts as well as forming the basis for coordination.
- *What is the cost, for doing and not doing?*—The cost of action or inaction or variable scope impacts what is done and how.
- *Who will do it?*—We need to know who will do what and who has responsibility.
- *How long will it take?*—We need to know how long things will take. From this we can change effort accordingly with consideration to the other layers in the pyramid.
- *Where it will be done?*—We need to know where the expected actions are occurring like a particular team is doing well, or a given state is responding in a particular way.
- *What will be traded?*—Finally, what compromises are we prepared to make and what prioritizations result?

Each layer of the pyramid depends upon the previous layer and referral back to the "What are we doing?" and "Why are we doing it?" underpins the assurance.

For those in leadership, being able to answer the questions is part of successful change:

- What are we doing?—If it is not clear what we are doing, how do we expect business transformation to be successful?
- Why are we doing it?—When we know why we are doing things, we tend to respond accordingly. How many times have you not known why things are occurring and you are just expected to change the way we do things?
- Why will it occur?—Successful business transformation addresses why transformation is resisted or is unlikely to occur.
- What is needed?—Success in business transformation occurs when we understand what is needed.

- When do we need it?—When we know when it is needed, we can prioritize and allocate resources.
- What is the cost, for doing and not doing?—Success in business transformation comes when the costs (true costs) are known and managed. How many times have an underfunded transformation delivered poor results?
- Who will do it?—Without ownership and responsibility, there is poor accountability and weak results are seen.
- How long will it take?—Business transformation needs to be done and the benefits realized. Having realistic and sustainable deadlines helps with implementation.
- Where it will be done?—We need to know where transformation is occurring, not least for managing the workload and sustaining the business through the transformation.
- What will be traded?—Making the trade-offs to what is pragmatic and practical and achievable against the "What are we doing?"

Whether establishing, sustaining, assuring, or experiencing business transformation, success is seen when these 10-points are met.

Making It Real

Use of the 10-point assurance approach within the leadership of change starts with a decision to use the assurance. Leadership can match this assurance to AMEDLI (Figure 1.3) for wider application or use directly (Figure 6.3). From scoping the work, managing activities, reviewing outcomes, the assurance can be readily used and implemented. Use of training and incremental adoption can also be used.

Further Details

- Process Improvement—A process for improvement goes together with assurance (see Chapter 8 Section "Making Improvements").

- Project Management—Project management expertise is part of assurance (see Chapter 8 Section "Project Management").
- Video—Weekly Mirror Message—Spotting the Signs for Success in Change (https://youtu.be/A31znRW7f2c).
- Video—Problem Solving Together for Our Future: Sharing Skills and Expertise—10-Point Assurance (https://youtu.be/ CT3g8aPv09U).

Project Management and Project Managers

To Get the Most

As bringing change is a project or program of work or a series of projects and programs to change what people do and how they do it, the role of project management and project managers is part of change management and the leadership of change. Project Management is about bringing people together around a shared cause and getting the best from them to deliver. Project Managers are there to serve the project so that the empowered ownership of the work can get on and deliver.

Setting the Example

Project managing is nuanced. Specific frameworks for change are used alongside project management frameworks that use other frameworks like procurement or vendor management or stakeholder management. Within change, the type of project manager is important in leading the project and realizing the required outcomes because the leadership shown influences the project and the bringing of the change through the emergent behavior they craft and shape.

Roles

From renovating houses to running marketing campaigns, projects are part of our lives. From all of the complexities and nuances in delivering projects, or the differing approaches, or the varying sizes and complexities, the following roles are required within the leadership:

- *Sponsors*—The party that is supporting the change at the highest levels required for the change. The replacement of a coach for a sports team requires the management to support the change.

- *Owners*—The party that owns the change. The party with the vested interest to see success. This is often the one with the drive and vision of what is required and what they want to achieve. The Sponsor and Owner may be the same person or different. Project managers may fulfill the role of Owners in certain circumstances.
- *Logistics Management*—The party that manages the logistics of the activities. This is often the project manager. Those that are logistics managers are not always the best owners or the best to lead the change by example.
- *Leaders*—The leaders may be the project manager, but there needs to be one party in the project that is the leader. They show the values, be the change they wish to see, lead by example, and influence those around. Like generals in an army, those leading change require an "element of luck" with aspects coming together. As a leader of change it is not enough to be right. It is being right, at the right time, with the right people, with the right amount of money (influence).

Whether it is in one or more people, change leadership requires these skills and expertise within its projects for change.

Project Management

Project Management is about getting people to work together for a period of time to deliver an outcome. By trying to bring out the best in us, projects are delivered. Project management requires an emergent behavior to deliver the required outcomes of the work. Projects require direction and need to have decisions made so that those delivering the work are empowered and enabled to deliver.

Project Managers

Where project managers are logistics managers, the leader's role needs to be filled with by the owner or from within the project, for example, the leader of the change. Project managers need to ensure that "if I know why I am doing it, why it is important to me, what I need to do, and where to get help, then my pride in who I am and what I do sees me deliver better outcomes." To achieve this, some level of mentoring and guidance of those involved in the change is required to enable empowerment and ownership. Project managers best achieve these results by serving the needs of the project, because this is how they help people.

Making It Real

Much of this change is a formalization of governance, roles, and responsibilities, but an adoption of approach with a leadership decision to implement is required. Again, leadership is the change they wish to see and treat others as they themselves would be treated. The key element is the ownership of the work and the clarification of logistics management vs. the lead by example for the change. The emergent behavior is developed like the others, incrementally, with skilling over time.

Further Details

- Turnarounds in Change—The circumstances around a change vary, making the need for turnaround projects as part of change (see Chapter 8 Section "Turnaround").
- Projects is a core Skill—Project skills are part of change management (see Chapter 8 Section "Project Management").
- Video—Weekly Mirror Message—Project Managers and Project Management (https://youtu.be/c0D8YMk3bJE).

Moving Forward

To Get the Most

Bringing changes to leadership, whether it is executive management or senior management or people of influence, to lead transformation is also nuanced. Setting the leadership for change is integral to transformation. Within AMEDLI (Figure 1.3) the sequencing (Ambiguity Management, Messaging, Empowered Emotional Ownership, Decision

Making, Interest and values) leads to the capacity and capability building of Leadership, though some level of leadership is required initially.

Setting the Example

The emergent behavior for leadership to bring change is mainly derived from skilling but other factors impact (Figure 6.4) the crafting and shaping and the leadership in change projects and programs of work.

Starting with an idea of what is to be achieved (i.e., knowing what the outcome from the change is going to look like and how to get there), changing the leadership or the leadership to implement a change requires the management of:

- *Desire and Drive*—A desire and drive to do it. Consistency and persistency are required.
- *Fears*—The emergent behavior to overcome our fears and work with them.
- *Understanding*—An understanding of how to get there and what is going to impact.
- *Ability*—Strengthen the ability with resources, expertise, able to acquire these and to adapt as the change is made.
- *Sales*—The ability to sell to persuade and make people feel comfortable with the change.

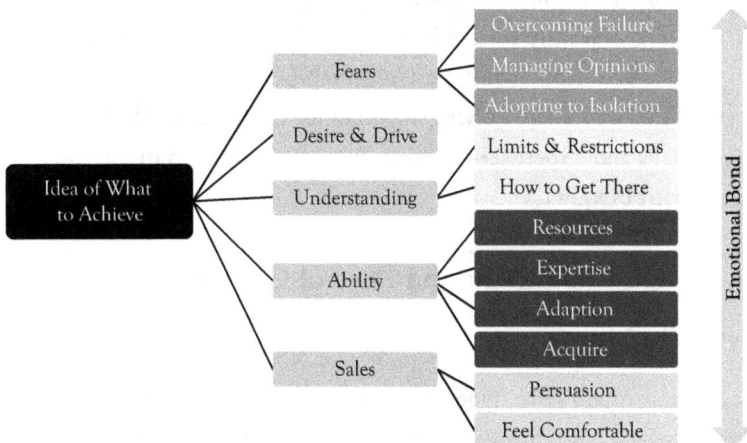

Figure 6.4 Deciding and taking the first step

All of these skills and expertise may not be present at the start nor will they all be at the level required. It is about having the basics and being able to start. The ability to grow and adopt and adapt emerges over time. Irrespectively:

- The best time to start is now.
- The fear is the missed opportunity.
- The regret is NOT having tried.

Making It Real

Using the idea of what is to be achieved and how to get there, starting and building capacities and capabilities along the way is the pragmatic and practical approach. There are risks associated with it, and the approach requires the management of ambiguity. The acceptance of mistakes is also necessary. Making it real is about the leadership wanting to work with and trusting their teams and working to craft and shape the emergent behaviors along the lines mentioned previously.

Further Details

- Role of Leadership—Although leadership crafts and shapes the emergent behaviors, the main role of leadership is to be the change they wish to see and to treat others as they themselves would be treated.
- Video—Weekly Mirror Message—Adoption and Adaption of Change (https://youtu.be/Upld4smNbQ8).
- Video—Problem Solving Together for Our Future: Sharing Skills and Expertise—Moving Forward (https://youtu.be/ NJtiPbOqljw).

Amount and Pace of Change

To Get the Most

Depending upon the type of change, the drivers, priorities, the circumstances, and the capacities and capabilities and priorities; the amount of change and pace of change varies and is a leadership issue.

This management of the amount and pace of change can also vary with time as circumstances change and as the change is realized. The skills of Ambiguity Management, Messaging, Empowered Emotional Ownership, Decision Making, and the Interests and Values are required for managing the amount and pace of change.

Setting the Example

There is only so much change that can be accepted and there is a limit to how fast the change can be done. Vary the environment, the need, and the drivers, and the amount and speed of change acceptance will adjust. Whether adoption is seen is a separate issue and there is a requirement to respond to and manage the impacts of the change (support and assistance). Managing this ability to adopt and adapt is part of leadership within change (Figure 6.5).

Using COVID-19 from the global pandemic as the example:

- *External*—The leadership is often impacted by the external factors where the drive for change originates (e.g., markets or customers, or regulatory), there is a need created for change, and the external factors often bring a change in the environment. This change in the environment leads to the

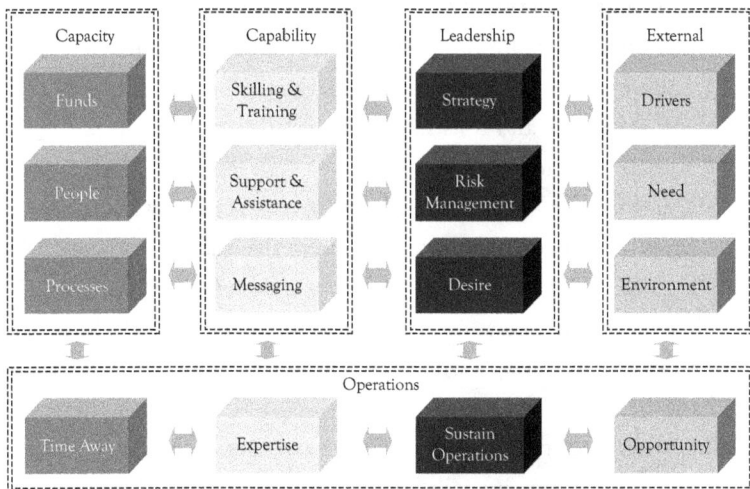

Figure 6.5 Leadership through being the change

instilling of behaviors, which brings the outcomes required. COVID-19 has been a driver for rapid change because of the need to save lives, but there have been impacts upon the economy, health, mental health, and a sense of uncertainty. Concern over the future, loss of jobs and revenue, being unable to feed families, and the risk of homelessness have come as side effects and show the need to manage the impacts and consequences of change.

- *Leadership*—COVID-19 is a driver that created a need and changed the environment to bring change. This has impacted strategy, created a desire to move fast and do things differently, and has brought risk management home. Governments that would have taken years to agree and implement online schools have been forced into change, with online schooling now being part of the education mix going forward. The risks with online schooling are being managed.
- *Capacity*—Countries with cash reserves, people with skills and expertise in pandemics, and having the required processes have tended to fair better through COVID-19. Countries that have had to develop the response capacity have a slower change. Leadership in the capacity development was also key, both before and during, and will be afterwards.
- *Capability*—The capability to respond draws on leadership and the capacity for building and strengthening. Skilling and Training to form the emergent behaviors, providing support and assistance, and consistency and persistency of messaging have all been required.
- *Operations*—COVID-19 has seen resources taken away from business operations to respond to the change, has seen development of expertise to respond, and businesses have had to sustain operations while responding to COVID-19. Opportunities have been created for some.

First-world countries with greater capacities and capabilities have often fared better than countries with lower capacities and capabilities. Where the leadership has been weak, the adoption and adaption to COVID-19 has been impacted, even if capacities and capabilities were greater.

The mirror from COVID-19 to business transformation is seen, but in addition:

- The greater the need, the more tolerance for undergoing change.
- The larger the need, the better the acceptance of change.
- The need to take people on the change.
- There is only so much change that can be accepted, for example, people reluctant to lock down.
- There is a limit to how fast the change can be done, for example, closing borders with due notice.
- There is a requirement to respond and manage to the impacts of the change (support and assistance).

Making It Real

Managing how much change can be implemented and how fast the change is adopted is nuanced, but it is a leadership function. The leadership also needs to manage the responses to the change. This is a skill and an expertise developed, but there are signs to look for:

- Level of Complaints—Complaints are expected. Where the level of complaints is increasing despite the measures to address, the complaints need to be actioned, root causes established, and remediation actioned.
- Level of Compliance—There are going to be adjustments periods and delays in take-up. Where levels of compliance (use or take-up) are plateauing at low numbers or falling, then action is required. This includes root causes established, and remediation actioned.
- Cost—Where the costs of the change are increasing well beyond what was considered and the return is not seen, then remediation is required.

- People of Influence—Listen to people of influence and their views as to what is occurring and why. Where support from people of influence is decreasing, then issues need to be addressed and their views responded to.
- Time—When the required time is not being spent on the change.
- Remediation—The time and cost on remediation and addressing the impacts is increasing for little return.

The one size fits all approach to managing the amount and rate of change is missing. This is often an intuitive call based on a range of factors. The need, the drivers, and the desire impact, but it is looking at the impacts of the change and the management of these which is required. Leadership being the change they wish to see and treating others as they would be treated is the best way to implement and manage risk.

Further Details

- Managing the Journey—The amount and pace of change is about leadership taking people on the journey of change (see Section "The Journey Model of Change" of this chapter).
- Alignment of Interests and Values—Aligning the interests and values impacts how much change can be managed and how fast (see Chapter 7).
- Video—Weekly Mirror Message—Managing Amount and Rate of Change (https://youtu.be/qT_O8wDPxzI).

The Journey Model of Change

To Get the Most

Leadership, including the People of Influence, impacts those around them. Beyond decision making and being the guide as to what is required, leadership is about taking the stakeholders along the change journey. The stakeholders have different levels of expertise and skills, varying levels of engagement, a range of roles and responsibilities, and differing alignments of Interests and Values. Each one is taken on a journey of change (the Journey Model), which varies accordingly.

Being able to form the emergent behavior and implement the change is the leadership skill.

Setting the Example

Realizing change is nuanced and is about taking people on a journey to do things differently, termed the Journey Model. Bringing change and transformation is often done through the Journey Model, because change is ongoing, is seen as a series of journeys, with rest points. The approach is to take people on the journey needed for them for the change required. The context for effective and efficient change is summarized in *"I do good work, change is coming, help me with the change, and I can do more"* (see Chapter 3). This is the journey to take people on. Leadership implementing a change or transformation often uses the following approach as part of the Journey Model (Figure 6.6):

- Organizational Squeeze—The leaders (people of influence) paint a clear picture of what is needed, explaining why,

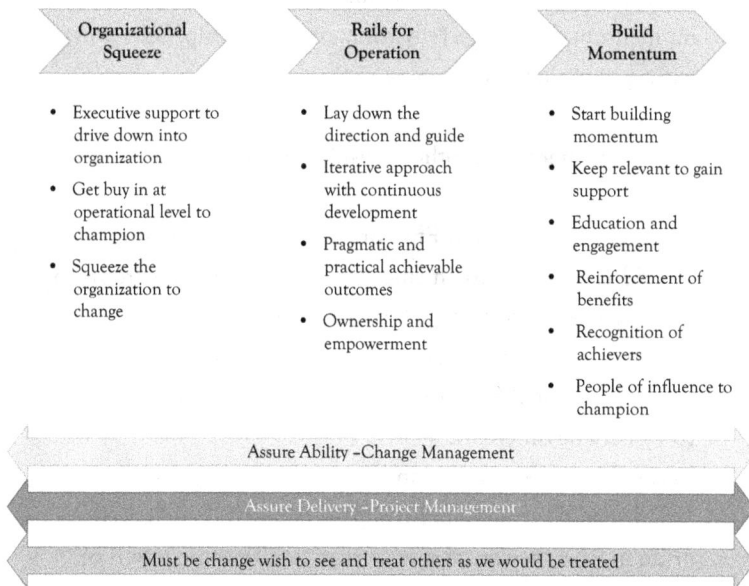

Figure 6.6 The Journey Model of change. From Sherringham, K., and B. Unhelkar. 2020. Crafting and Shaping Knowledge Worker Services in the Information Economy. Palgrave Macmillan Singapore, 570pp

and reinforce the individual benefits (not just abstract organizational benefits). The People of Influence at the operational level need to champion the changes to others. This combination of driving from the top and from the bottom puts the pressure on for achieving change.

- Rails for Operation—Sustaining the change and bringing those on the journey is about providing rails for operation for implementing change and the ongoing management of change. Changes come through the building of momentum, accepting difference in the adoption and transition, taking an iterative approach. It is building the environment and behaviors through ownership and empowerment that the journey moves along the rails provided by leadership. The change has to be good enough to get buy-in support whilst allowing people to take ownership and improve.
- Building Momentum—Change may go through stages and may be a series of starts and stops. The change is about an ongoing capacity and capability in response to the factors influencing the change. Sustaining change is about a momentum for change (environment, leadership, behaviors) with recognition and ongoing engagement.

Within the implementation, other considerations are:

- Emergent Behavior and Environment—It is the actions of individuals that forms an emergent behavior and environment for outcomes through which transformation occurs. An emergent behavior to make the change and the emergent behavior required from the change are crafted and shaped (they may be different).
- Recognition—A recognition of what works well and the "good that is currently occurring" is required. People have pride in who they are and what they do. They are proud of what they make or grow or provide. Questioning the current performance can lead to alienation of people of good will whose support is necessary in the adoption.

- Start, Build, Adopt and Adapt—Start the change, take advantage of opportunities to build support and structures to adopt and adapt along the way.
- Assistance—It is inherent within many people to want to better themselves and to want to grow and develop. What they often seek is the assistance, to be guided, and to be given the opportunity.

Making It Real

Making the change journey real starts with the leadership deciding to adopt the Journey Model and taking the first step. Then the leadership uses the journey model to implement and manage the change. Through adoption and adaption of the journey model work it to bring the change. Managing how much change can be implemented and how fast the change is adopted is nuanced, but it is a leadership function. The leadership also needs to manage the responses to the change. This is a skill and an expertise developed, but there are signs to look for:

- Level of Complaints—Complaints are expected. Where the level of complaints is increasing despite the measures to address, the complaints need to be actioned, root causes established, and remediation actioned.
- Level of Compliance—There are going to be adjustments periods and delays in take-up. Where levels of compliance (use or take-up) are plateauing at low numbers or falling, then action is required. This includes root causes established and remediation actioned.
- Cost—Where the costs of the change are increasing well beyond what was considered and the return is not seen, then remediation is required.
- People of Influence—Listen to people of influence and their views as to what is occurring and why. Where support from people of influence is decreasing, then issues need to be addressed and their views responded too.

- Time—When the required time is not being spent on the change.
- Remediation—The time and cost on remediation and addressing the impacts is increasing for little return.

The one size fits all approach to managing the amount and rate of change is missing. This is often an intuitive call based on a range of factors. The need, the drivers, and the desire impact, but it is looking at the impacts of the change and the management of these which is required. Leadership being the change they wish to see and treating others as they would be treated is the best way to implement and manage risk.

Further Details

- Video—Weekly Mirror Message—Starting the Change Journey using Opportunities to Build Along the Way (https://youtu.be/4WjqIzbHpew).
- Video—Building Capacity and Capability (https://youtu.be/-loAAPQsexk).
- Video—Weekly Mirror Message—Adoption and Adaption of Change (https://youtu.be/Upld4smNbQ8).

Crafting and Shaping the Emergent Behavior

To Get the Most

A key leadership function is to craft and shape the emergent behaviors for change. The emergent behaviors are the collective behaviors from the group, team, business area, or business (organization). The overall emergent behavior comes from the individuals with their own needs and capacities and capabilities. The overall approach is crafting and shaping of the individuals to overall outcomes. This emergent behavior is often nuanced, varies within areas of operations and with time.

Setting the Example

Crafting and shaping the emergent behaviors of both individuals and at the team, group, or business (organization) or even country levels takes time and is nuanced. An emergent behavior to make the change and the emergent behavior required from the change are crafted and shaped (they may be different). The process seldom follows a linear approach and requires multiple approaches that change over time. There is an overall approach (Figure 6.7) to building and sustaining the emergent behaviors, but it is the skills and expertise in implementation that matter.

The overall approach to the emergent behaviors is for:

- Business Need—The need for the change or transformation. The individual needs may be different to those of a group or organization, but the leadership function is to align the Interests and Values (see Chapter 7).
- Engage Stakeholders—The respective stakeholders are engaged. This engagement should be ongoing and often uses the Journey Model (see Section "The Journey Model of Change" in this chapter). Engagement includes finding out what the issues are or why things are not happening. The resources undertaking operations should know what is happening in their operations, the problems that exist, and why actions are not occurring that need to be addressed.

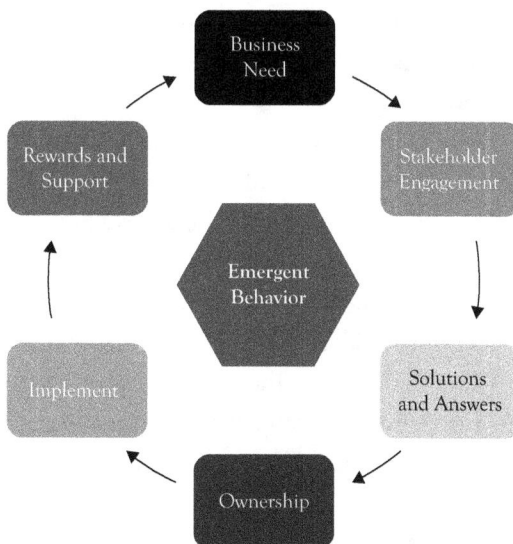

Figure 6.7 Crafting and shaping emergent behavior

The stakeholder engagement is also about laying the groundwork for change where:

- ○ Laying the groundwork takes time to develop, with the relationships often forming with time based on trust. This requires sustained engagement, strengthened by seeing success in delivery, and is often done on the basis of a judgment of the informal relationships (like a sale process and the relationship management function).
- ○ The costs and effort in laying the groundwork are often omitted within the factoring of change. This omission is partly because the value of the groundwork is often overlooked, but also because groundwork is an intangible that is hard to cost, hard to measure, and with no assured return.
- ○ Groundwork is about persistent and consistent engagement, especially with People of Influence, to build relationships, sharing of empathy, and a sense of caring.
- Solutions and Answers—The respective stakeholders often have solutions to the problems or have an approach to resolution. Often, staff are seeking recognition of the issues (by management) and to have someone address the problems.
- Ownership and Priorities—Having ownership for the outcomes is a key factor for success. There is often the need for a prioritization of solutions with staged implementation, but some changes are simple to make, and they can be readily implemented.
- Implement—With an owner and a prioritization, the agreement to implement is made and the implementation undertaken. The training (how to do) and skilling (ability to do) to support the change is required.
- Reward and Support—Changes made need to be supported ongoing. Further skilling and the effectiveness of the changes made need to be rewarded. Those involved in making the changes, especially those who identified the issues and proposed solutions, should be rewarded accordingly.

The results from the emergent behaviors then impact the business need.

Making It Real

Crafting and shaping the emergent behaviors often comes primarily from the people involved in leading and driving the change and, in particular, in the relationships they build. Beyond the expertise and the frameworks used, success often lies with the personal element. The emotions invoked from the actions of high-caliber people with integrity leading the change bring the response in others. This personal relationship and the responses to the actions of others are often intangible, but "we know it when we see it" and is an integral part of leadership. If leadership values the emergent behaviors and is prepared to make the investment in the relationship management, then change tends to succeed.

Further Details

- Video—Weekly Mirror Message – Conversation as the Barometer of Change (https://youtu.be/1UNHyzDfKwI)
- Video—Weekly Mirror Message—Managing People Shutdown (https://youtu.be/m_PsC1gObd8).
- Video—Weekly Mirror Message—Adoption and Adaption of Change (https://youtu.be/Upld4smNbQ8).
- Video—Weekly Mirror Message—The Role of the Individual (https://youtu.be/7ZzKoFwtPiw).
- Video—Weekly Mirror Message—Tangibles and Intangibles from Behaviours in Change (https://youtu.be/mLji3yTUXsg).

Next Steps

Leadership is needed to realize change. While it is the actions of individuals who are empowered with ownership and have an emotional bond, it is the leadership to make decisions and provide guidance that compliments to assure delivery. There are a series of steps leadership can take including:

- Recognize and incrementally use the balance of drivers and opportunities for change with the pragmatics of operations to sustain ongoing change and transformation. This is complimented by opportunistic change.

- When the openings occur, find ways to change the environment, to instill the behaviors to craft and shape an emergent behavior for achieving the required outcomes.
- Make use of the 10-point assurance within the management of change, from asking questions of the team to use as a guide in management across the projects and programs of work.
- Have the view of what you want to achieve and how to get there. Then share that image so that the empowered ownership with the emotional bond is formed.
- Be the change you wish to see and treat others as you would be treated.

Making these changes does not follow a recipe like training on processes, rather the change is a desire to do it.

CHAPTER 7

Interests and Values Aligned

*Aligned interest and values for empowered
emotional ownership to bring change*

Summary

Underpinning the achieving of sustainable change is the alignment of interests and values. Where a change or transformation is beneficial to those seeking the change, to those leading, to those implementing, and those experiencing the change, better results can be achieved. It is the coming together of both interests and values because this forms the emotional bond. From this emotional bond comes empowerment, ownership, the attracting of attention, motivation for sustaining, and a range of other emotions for change. Bringing the emotional bond through the alignment of interests and values within an emergent behavior is considered in this chapter.

Key Learnings

Key learnings from this chapter include:

- Successful change comes when both the interest and values are aligned across those seeking to make changes, those leading the change, those implementing changes, and those experiencing and/or responding to change.
- If the individual is engaged and motivated to achieve the change, the emergent behavior is a collection of outcomes to deliver.
- An Inferior Implementation, just being told what to do, the feeling of being ignored, and insufficient understanding, all detract from the implementation of change and the alignment

of interests and values. A reluctance to change or a resistance to change or uncertainty around change is part of the change process. These are not exceptions; rather they are the norm and an integrated part of change.

- Feedback that is supportive and motivational and shows caring helps with skilling as well as aligning interests and values.
- The decision on how to use skilling and training and its role in aligning Interests and Values and in the Empowered Emotional Ownership is a leadership responsibility.

Introduction

When there are shared interests, collaboration tends to occur. Change is about people and the emotional response from people who tend to associate with those of similar Interests and Values. When the interests and values are aligned, a greater extent of collaboration and cooperation is often seen. Successful change comes when both the interest and values are aligned across those seeking to make changes, those leading change, those implementing change, and those experiencing and/or responding to change. Interests and Values are how attention is gained, the emotional bond formed, motivation sustained, and messaging becomes effectual.

It is the role of leadership to bring people of similar but differing interests and values together to achieve the change. Look no further than the losing sports team with internal arguments: players and coaches are of differing interests and the common values of a winning team are missing. Indeed, the conflict in values or the misalignment of interests is often a root cause for change being less effective. In a digital transformation where the interests are different, those in fear for their jobs look at things differently to the technology evangelist. Techniques from the declining of meeting requests, to reprioritization of work, to seeking more details, to reallocating resources, or waiting for others can all be used to "slow" a transformation where interest and values differ.

Although Interests and Values (the I in AMEDLI) are listed last, they underpin so many other aspects for achieving change. Where the Interests and Values are aligned, it makes Ambiguity Management easier. The emotional bond of Messaging comes from the Interests and Values being realized and the alignment makes messaging more effective. Empowered Emotional Ownership is supported by the alignment of Interests and Values. Decision Making is often emotional (justified with logic) with emotional outcomes for those making a decision and those impacted by a decision. Leadership is the crafting and shaping of an emergent behavior from emotional actions where the alignment of Interests and Values enables the emergent behavior.

COVID-19 showed the importance of alignment of interests and value. Indeed, keeping people safe make the alignment inherent, but aspects like restrictions of movement also disrupted the alignment with impacts upon outcomes. COVID-19 (Weekly Mirror Message—Transformation Lessons from COVID-19—https://youtu.be/YqLFAEFCyeM) showed the importance of:

- Relate to Me—COVID-19 saw protests on restrictions of freedom used as a measure to contain the spread. This is an example of where interests and values were no longer aligned and impacted the success of the emergent behavior.
- Adoption and Adaption—COVID-19 showed that the response changed over time as more was found out about the virus. Also, when breaches in quarantine occurred, a revised response was required with decisions made.
- Feedback which Motivates—During COVID-19, leaders provided feedback to staff and citizens on what they were doing well, why it was important, and the need to sustain and/or improve the effort.
- Skilling and Training—Integral to the containment of the virus was skilling (the ability to do) and training (the how to do). From how frequently to wipe down surfaces in guidelines, to the proper wearing of face masks, to quarantine procedures, skilling and training were important. The absence of proper skilling and training led to breaches in quarantine and the spreading of the virus.

The quarantine failures that led to the spreading of the virus were characterized by guards who were not properly trained, were underpaid, were poorly managed, and were disengaged from the importance of their work and are now recorded within the COVID-19 response. Aspects of the alignment of Interests and Values are seen in this chapter, together with their underlying role within AMEDLI (Ambiguity Management, Messaging, Empower Emotional Ownership, Decision Making, Leadership, Interests and Values). The relation to the individual of change and adoption and adaption to change is covered. The right feedback as well as the skilling (ability to do) and training (how to do) within interests and values alignment is noted. Some next steps are included.

Relate to Me

To Get the Most

In crafting and shaping an emergent behavior, it is the actions and decisions of individuals with ownership and empowerment in response to emotions that are needed (Weekly Mirror Message—Individuals and the Status Quo in Sustainable Change—https://youtu.be/6bzCMmAd95I). Having pride in who we are and what we do is how the actions are achieved (i.e., an emotional response). The alignment of interests and values is how teams are formed and an emergent behavior fashioned. Any change has to be understood, meet the interests and values, and "Relate to Me." The winning sports team or the functioning of the military unit is based on shared interests and common values.

Setting the Example

Similar to the leadership being able to answer the basics around change (see Chapter 1 Section "The Basic Questions" and Figure 6.2), those undergoing change need to be able to answer similar questions (Figure 7.1). The Interests and Values come through an understanding of what is being done, why, and how it relates to the individual. Taking away the amorphous or the abstract and making it real at the individual level (e.g., you gain this, or you lose this if not done, or you can hurt this loved one) is how change is realized. If the individual is engaged and motivated to achieve the change, the emergent behavior is a collection of outcomes to deliver. The Interests and Values are influenced by the

Ambiguity Management	Where is it occurring?
	What traded?
Messaging	What we are doing and Why we are doing it?
	How you are feeling and progressing?
Empowered Emotional Ownership	What is expected of me?
	What help and support is available?
Decision Making	How do I make changes?
	When do I make changes?
Leadership	Who is showing me what is expected?
	Who understands my situation?
Interests and Values	Why are we doing this?
	What is in this for me?

Figure 7.1 Who, why, what, where, when, how alignment so "I can adopt and adapt"

Empowered Emotional Ownership as much as the Interests and Values bring the Empowered Emotional Ownership. The change is motivational and aspirational, but is also believable, so that it can be achieved, even if it is in stages (e.g., the sports team winning a championship is motivational, believable, and obtainable, even if it may take a couple of seasons to achieve). This is important for creating confidence, self-belief, and belief in the process.

Ask yourself or those around you experiencing a change if they feel better when:

- Ambiguity—The ambiguity is being managed.
- Messaging—There is clarity of messaging.
- Empowered Emotional Ownership—You feel a sense of ownership and empowerment, and you have an emotional investment in the outcome.
- Decision Making—Decisions are being made and you know what is required and where to respond.
- Leadership—Leadership is being the change they wish to see and treating you as they would be treated.
- Interests and Values—What is being asked of you aligns with your interests and values.

Making It Real

The easiest way to "relate it to me" is ask yourself if the basic questions are being answered:

- "Would you feel better if you had answers to these questions?"
- "Would those around you feel better if they had answers to these questions?"
- "Can you, who is asking others to do things differently, answer these questions to make those around you feel better?"

If not, then it needs to be addressed. Then it is about asking those who are experiencing the change "if the change relates to them?" Again, if not, actions need to be taken to achieve this. This starts with leadership being the change they wish to see and treat others as they themselves would be treated.

Further Details

- Messaging—Emotional messaging is how change is related to an individual (see Chapter 3 Section "Communicating to Form Bonds").
- Video—Weekly Mirror Message—Managing People Shutdown (https://youtu.be/m_PsC1gObd8).
- Video—Weekly Mirror Message—The Role of the Individual (https://youtu.be/7ZzKoFwtPiw).
- Video—Problem Solving Together for Our Future: Sharing Skills and Expertise—"Relating It to Me" (https://youtu.be/5Dmk0f3JJp0).

Adoption and Adaption

To Get the Most

Realizing sustainable change is nuanced. It often takes time and requires a capacity and capability building to form an emergent behavior to bring and sustain the change. A reluctance to change or a resistance to change or uncertainty around change is part of the change process. These are not exceptions; rather they are the norm and an integrated part of change.

Adopting and adapting an emergent behavior is the combination of strategy and leadership, strengthened with skilling, to influence the environment, to instill the behaviors, which gives the capacity and capability to form the emergent behavior through adaptiveness, responsiveness, and resilience.

Setting the Example

Forming an emergent behavior has its challenges; mistakes will be made and require a multitude of approaches with consistency and persistency and sustained effort. There is no one size fits all approach and there is no magic wand or silver bullet. Yet these very challenges are the reason to do it, because by helping us, we change ourselves, and we realize the required change. The success of the implementation (Figure 7.2) impacts the adoption and adaption.

The use of AMEDLI helps with an implementation (see Chapter 1 Section "AMEDLI"), but it is where the Interests and Values of individuals are missing that issues occur:

- *Inferior Implementation*—A poor implementation weakens the Empowered Emotional Ownership, and the alignment of Interests and Values is impacted.
  - Poor planning and/or preparation.
  - Inconsistent communication.

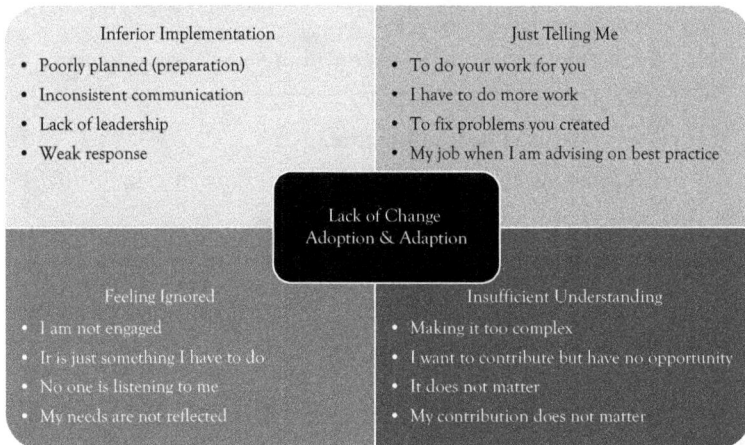

Inferior Implementation	Just Telling Me
• Poorly planned (preparation)	• To do your work for you
• Inconsistent communication	• I have to do more work
• Lack of leadership	• To fix problems you created
• Weak response	• My job when I am advising on best practice
Lack of Change Adoption & Adaption	
Feeling Ignored	Insufficient Understanding
• I am not engaged	• Making it too complex
• It is just something I have to do	• I want to contribute but have no opportunity
• No one is listening to me	• It does not matter
• My needs are not reflected	• My contribution does not matter

Figure 7.2 Overcoming to create and sustain motivation

- ○ Lack of leadership where leadership is not the change they wish to see, and leadership are not treating others as they themselves would be treated.
- ○ Weak response to variations needed.
- *Just Telling Me*—If you are just being told things, a range of emotions are created, and it builds resentment. The Interests and Values are unaligned, the emotional bond is weakened.
  - ○ I am being told by you to do your job for you.
  - ○ I have more work to do and I am busy enough as it is.
  - ○ I am fixing problems you created with your change work.
  - ○ You are telling my job and you are not listening to me.
- *Feeling Ignored*—The feeling of being ignored, or not asked, creates a feeling that they are not valued and part of the solution. Therefore, the Interests and Values are reduced with the corresponding impact upon the Empowered Emotional Ownership.
  - ○ I am not engaged and there is no point in engaging.
  - ○ It is just something I have to do.
  - ○ No one is listening to me.
  - ○ My needs are irrelevant so why bother.
- *Insufficient Understanding*—Where there is an understanding and the contribution is valued, the Empowered Emotional Ownership is formed, and the Interests and Values are aligned.
  - ○ It being made too complex.
  - ○ A sense that I am unable to contribute even though I want to help.
  - ○ A feeling that it does not matter.
  - ○ The knowing that my contribution does not matter.

It is the responsibility of leadership to work to overcome the implementation issues and to help sustain the efforts through working to align Interests and Values.

Making It Real

Two examples for the alignment of Interests and Values are presented.

Areas of Business

Businesses can adopt and adapt at many levels. From executive leadership, to managers, to team leads, or us as individuals, it is still about starting. It is about making small changes in the way we do things and to apply them consistently and persistently. An approach to try (Figure 7.3) is as follows:

- Within your work team, have a series of session for say 30 minutes over a period of time to build capacity and capability within the team.
- Pick a theme and watch one of the videos, either together or alone beforehand. Please feel free to pause and use the text in the comments.
- Within the moderated group session, identify any gaps in the team, suggest areas for improvement, look for opportunities for betterment.
- Then identify options for adoption and how you plan to implement.
- Incrementally make changes and review, responding and adapting as required.
- Seek advice from Peers and review as an individual or as a group.

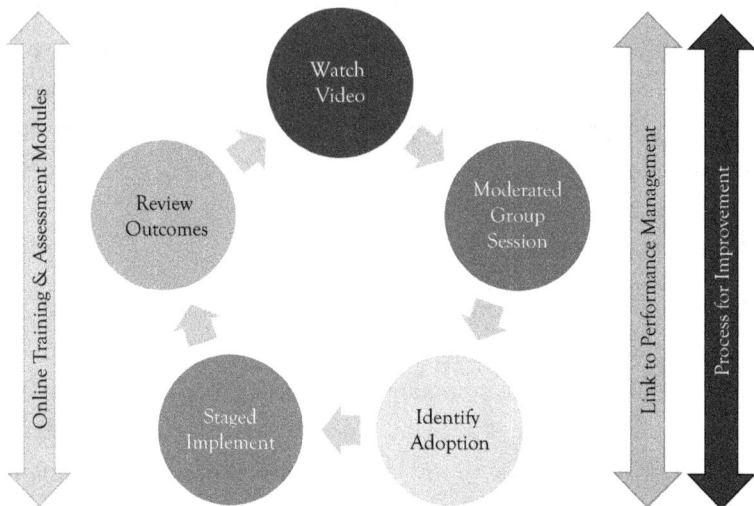

Figure 7.3 Adoption and adaption—areas of business

This can be done at the team level, or at the individual level, but also as part of a wider business area, or companywide. Other things to consider are:

- Have HR provide online training and assessment modules around the themes and developing an emergent behavior.
- Link aspects of performance management to the themes and the building of emergent behaviors by leaders.
- Provision of micro-credentials as part of training and career development.

Throughout this approach and implementation, the shared Interests and Values are central because:

- Those involved in the change are engaged and brought into the change.
- Skilling and Training are provided to enable the change.
- The support required is being provided so that people can help themselves and those around them.
- A process for betterment and sharing of experiences is included.
- A staged approach allowing capacity and capability building is provisioned.

Part of us bettering ourselves is an improvement process (see Chapter 8 Section "Making Improvements"). A business grows when it has a process for improvement. Developing the emergent behavior is a process for improvement, and a process for improvement helps develop an emergent behavior.

Courses, Accreditation, Certification

The business approach mentioned previously can be used in organizations of all types and sizes, including education and training organizations for their own business needs. Educational and training organizations can also provide courses, modules, accreditation, and certification. The themes apply to technology-based courses, business and management courses, as well as elements of these within other courses.

Consider project management. Project management is about managing people. It requires working across the silos of expertise, to bring people together to produce the required outcome. The overarching approach of AMEDLI helps with their implementation. Projects come together because of the resulting emergent behavior formed by the leadership of the project.

With project management as a context, those providing the skilling and training may undertake:

- Pick a theme and watch one of the videos. Please feel free to pause and use the text in the comments.
- In a moderated session, go through the principles, how they would be used, and the applicability to the course materials, for example, management.
- Provide group exercises (scenarios) for project work and present back.
- Have groups undertake the required work, related study, and present back based on the scenarios provided. Provide feedback and discuss the outcomes.
- Have assignments delivered for further work.

Supporting content can be provided as online modules, with the modules mixed and matched according to the course and its level (Figure 7.4). The modules within courses and the exercise and scenario approach with presenting results are part of the capacity and capability building. It leads to adaptiveness, responsiveness, and resilience which build emergent behavior for the future.

Through this approach and implementation, the shared Interests and Values are central because:

- An emergent behavior of benefit to the participants is being crafted and shaped.
- Skilling and Training are provided for the betterment of those involved.
- Support is being provided, together with details of what is needed and why.

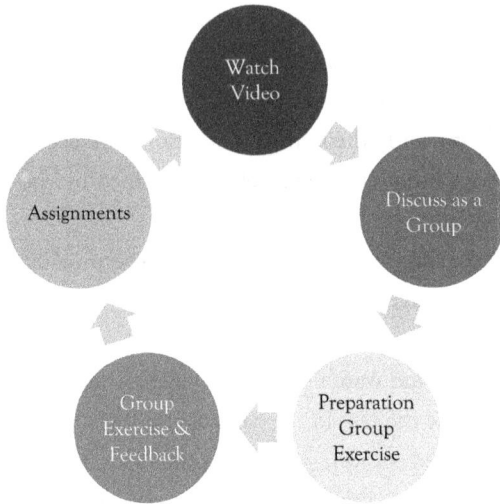

Figure 7.4 Adoption and adaption—courses, accreditation, certification

Further Details

- Messaging to Overcome—Overcoming the reluctance to change requires consistent and persistent messaging (see Chapter 3).
- Making the Journey—Any reluctance to change is part of change and it is about taking people on the journey (see Chapter 6 Section "The Journey Model of Change").
- Video—Problem Solving Together for Our Future: Sharing Skills and Expertise—Bringing and Sustaining Motivation (https://youtu.be/hoIvjCUCiqk).
- Video—Problem Solving Together for Our Future: Sharing Skills and Expertise—Adoption and Adaption (https://youtu.be/x5TdamCNOGE).

Feedback Which Motivates by Showing Caring

To Get the Most

Feedback is how we make us feel better about ourselves. Feedback is about motivation and is asking us to grow ourselves. Feedback is how we help ourselves. From pilots having colleagues fly with them providing feedback to a sports team watching recordings of a game to improve performance, feedback is part of aligning Interests and Values.

Setting the Example

Ever been ambushed by feedback? Have you had feedback weaponized against you? Have your strengths and efforts been used as a tool to run you down? Feel like you are being lectured to patronized by feedback? Do your eyes roll over when people talk about the use of feedback? Feedback is not about how much we know, but about how much we care. Feedback is how we make us feel better about ourselves. Feedback is about motivation and is asking us to grow ourselves. Feedback is how we help ourselves and is the alignment of Interests and Values (Figure 7.5).

Providing the right feedback is about finding the right place and the right time and is best done coming where there is mutual respect. Feedback may not always go right, but it is about trying and doing it for the right reasons with the right intent:

- 3-2-1—Where there is more time, try the 3-2-1 when giving feedback. Three good things. Two things to do better, done in a supporting way, with shared ideas to better. One good thing to leave feeling good about.

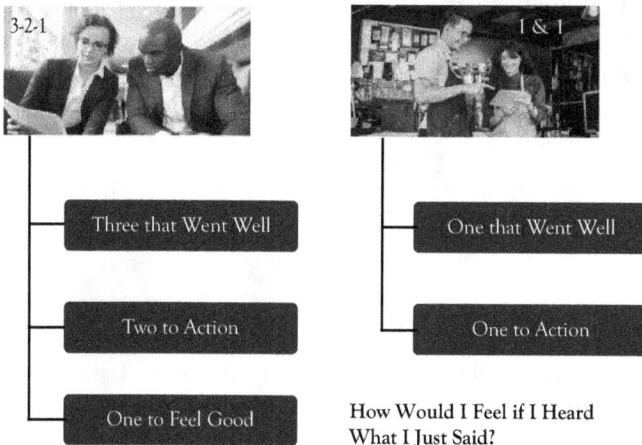

Figure 7.5 Feedback that motivates is the alignment of interests and values

- 1 & 1—Where time is shorter, try the 1 & 1 when giving feedback. One thing that went well and one thing that could have gone better, but with a suggestion of how to do it better. Share empathy and perhaps a lesson you learned through a similar mistake.

When giving feedback, take a moment to reflect upon "How Would I Feel If I Heard What I Just Said?" If you don't care about the answer, then that tells you all you need to know. If you feel bad and demotivated, then what is that telling you? If you feel good and motivated, then what is next?

Making It Real

Use feedback in a supportive and sustaining way to motivate and support. Feedback shows the alignment of Interests and Values. Feedback is something people want to do, or they don't. By providing feedback and by accepting feedback, it betters us over time. Again, it is a decision to do it and is a matter of just starting to do it in a supporting way.

Further Details

- Aligned Interests and Values—Feedback works better when interest and values are aligned (see Chapter 7).
- Rationalization—The processing of feedback requires rationalization (see Chapter 4 Section "Emotional Rationalization").
- Video—Weekly Mirror Message—Feedback That Motivates by Showing Caring (https://youtu.be/HHqV9WQfCNU).

Skilling and Training

To Get the Most

Results come from the consistent and persistent application of proven principles pragmatically. Skilling (the ability to do) and Training (the how to do) help people to adopt and adapt, provide them with the support, and make them feel empowered and emotionally engaged from which emergent behaviors are formed. Skilling and Training play an important role in the alignment of Interests and Values which underpins other capacities and capabilities for managing change.

Setting the Example

Emergent behaviors are required for bringing change and for transformation and emergent behaviors which are built through the actions of individuals having ownership, empowerment, and an emotional response. Having the Interests and Values aligned helps with skilling and training, just as skilling and training help align the Interests and Values (Figure 7.6).

Training is the how to do. Training is the procedural and the instructional, often validated by testing, and uses a role-based approach (i.e., based on a role you learn how to use certain tools and follow specific processes). Skilling helps with the training. When those doing the training feel it is of value, it is in their interest, and they see a need; the training becomes integral to the emergent behaviors.

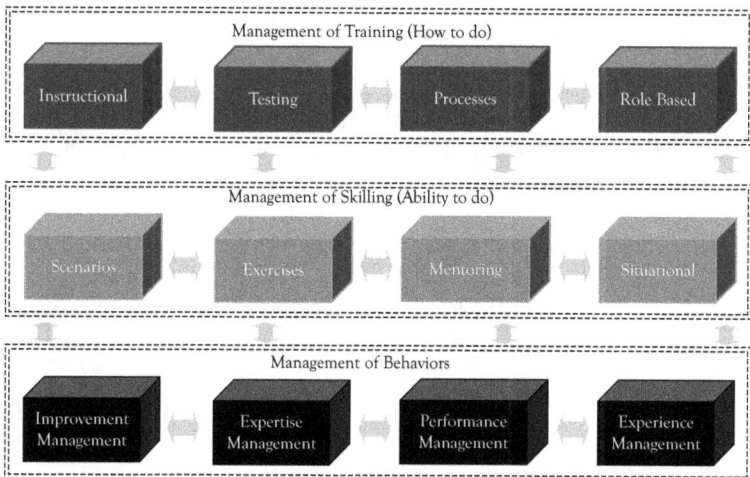

Figure 7.6 Skilling and training

Skilling is the ability to do. Often considered as the professional skills,[1] skilling is what brings confidence, ownership, and empowerment, as well as used in the alignment of interests and values. Skilling is built through the use of scenarios and exercises, especially within change, and is strengthened with mentoring (see Section "Feedback which Motivates by Showing Caring" of this chapter) and situation-based work. Skilling is at the heart of crafting and shaping emergent behaviors and is the basis of AMEDLI (see Chapter 1 Section "AMEDLI").

Within change, it is the leadership that is crafting and shaping the emergent behaviors that manages the experience of individual, the team, and the organization. The leadership also manages the performance, the expertise, and the improvements required:

- Improvement Management—The frameworks, rewards, and support for the ongoing improvement of operations.
- Performance Management—The appropriate metrics, rewards, and incentives to drive the right behaviors and environment for creating and managing the performance. It is the specific compensation that drives behaviors.
- Expertise Management—The ongoing development and management of expertise (training—how to do), with revisions to operations and processes to build capacity and capability.
- Experience Management—The ongoing development and management of professional skills (skilling—the ability to do) with ongoing capacity and capability building.

Skilling and Training are part of bringing change and transformation. The sports team uses drills and practice sessions to train the team.

---

[1] Professional skills include people management, financial management, vendor management, relationship management, strategy and planning, risk management, project management, problem solving, management of change in the business, management of ambiguity, governance, compliance management, cross-disciplinary collaboration, and communication and presentation.

The coach of the team uses sports psychology to build skills. Both the skilling and the training are managed as part of the emergent behavior.

Making It Real

There is a cost associated with skilling and training, especially the ongoing, repeat, and sustained. The business decision to include skilling and training within change and transformation resides with leadership. The decision on how to use skilling and training and their role in aligning Interests and Values and in the Empowered Emotional Ownership is also a leadership responsibility. The implementation is around:

- Skilling—Based on the roles and people involved in the situation, use of scenarios and exercises in skilling (e.g., aircraft accident to build the capacity and capability of an airlines to respond to aircraft accidents or fleet groundings). A series of exercises or scenarios are undertaken to incrementally build skills. This is complimented by mentoring as well as situation-specific skilling as required tailored to the specific needs. The decision is to develop and implement a program of skilling to develop the required capacities and capabilities across the team (group, company), recognizing the required roles within the emergent behavior with the needs of the individuals. The regime will change with time.
- Behaviors—From the skilling comes the emergent behaviors. The skilling needs to develop and strengthen the required behaviors whilst reducing those behaviors to the contrary. The use of People of Influence and mentoring to affirm the actions and behaviors is part of the regime required. Leadership identifies the behaviors required and who shows them. The gaps are identified and the required measures for development are identified.
- Review and Improvement—A process to track the developments, as well as a process for review, and improvement. The training regimes align, but the focus is on the behaviors to achieve the outcomes.

Further Details

- Testing in Skilling and Training—Testing plays a role in skilling and training (see Chapter 8 Section "Testing").
- Empowered Emotional Ownership—Training and skilling help create the emergent behaviors of individuals with empowered emotional ownership (see Chapter 4).
- Video—Weekly Mirror Message—The Panacea of Skilling and Training (https://youtu.be/3yKK431LL1U).

Next Steps

Aligning interests and values does not follow a simple recipe because people are complex, the circumstances vary, and the situations change over time. There are a series of steps though:

- Leadership takes a series of messages to ensure that the change relates to those implementing and experiencing the change.
- Leadership undertakes a range of activities to sustain motivation and include people within the change.
- The use of positive and supportive mentoring.
- The use of skilling and training within an emergent behavior.

Whilst these are nuanced and take time to develop and realize, it is a decision of leadership to use these proven pragmatic practices.

CHAPTER 8

On the Ground

Pragmatics and practicalities of emergent
behaviors through proven actions

Summary

Beyond the crafting and shaping of behaviors for the actions of empowered individuals, it is the actions on the ground with proven practices pragmatically applied consistently and persistently that bring results. Leadership is also tasked with growing the skills and expertise in these on-the-ground areas as part of bringing change. This chapter outlines some of the on-the-ground expertise for adopting and adapting to change.

Key Learnings

Key learnings from this chapter include:

- Skills and expertise built for the change have ongoing business benefits alongside that of a capacity and capability for adoption and adaption. The skills and expertise come from the consistent and persistent application of proven principles that are used within business operations as part of realizing change.
- A recipe-based approach is part of the tools for realizing change.
- Turnaround skills and expertise is part of managing change. This includes the leadership to accept the need for and role of turnarounds in change.
- A process for improvement is integral to crafting and shaping the emergent behaviors for change and the

emergent behaviors are required for the use of a process for improvement.

- Multiple frameworks are needed to deliver change or transformation, and not just a change management framework. The interdependencies across the frameworks need to be managed.
- It is the understanding of what is needed to have people change what and how they do things which is required within the project management of change projects. A special focus on the end-to-end across the silos of operations approach is also necessary within the management of change projects.

Introduction

An emergent behavior for bringing change comes through the actions of individuals with that emotional bond. Even with the alignment of Interests and Values or the Empowered Emotional Ownership, it is the actions on the ground that bring change. It is the scaling up of the proven practices and their consistent and persistent application to the situation as it evolves which brings the required changes. These proven practices support the components of AMEDLI (see Chapter 1 Section "AMEDLI"), and the skills and expertise built for the change have ongoing business benefits alongside that of a capacity and capability for adoption and adaption.

A selection of "on-the-ground proven practices" are presented in this chapter for assisting with the capacity and capability building of emergent behaviors. The use of "Recipes" for operational aspects and skilling is discussed together with the use of turnarounds and a process for improvement. Technology adoption, project management, the wider use of testing in change, the use of multiple frameworks in change, and some next steps are also included.

Recipes

To Get the Most

Within change, we look for the "how to." The "how to" can be considered a series of recipes that people can follow and use which enables and empowers (i.e., helps to align interests and values). We use recipes because they help gives us security and certainty. Recipes enable us to get where we need to be faster and at lower cost. Recipes provide the help and guidance we seek. What recipes we create and how we use them is our choice.

Setting the Example

Audience–Task–Recipe: Who are we doing it for (Audience), what are we doing (Task), and how we do it (Recipe). Recipes provide what we need to do, how to do it, tools for use, tips, and other information (Figure 8.1). The recipes can be applied and customized as needed.

Across the world, millions of people make thousands of varieties of bread every day for a range of uses in a consistent way because of recipes. Recipes combine the process, the steps, what is needed, the tools, and the practices and provide context. Recipes provide us with the "how to":

- Recipes show us what we want to achieve.
- Recipes combine the steps, with the ingredients (information needed), as well as the tools and best practice tips.
- Recipes can be customized to meet our needs.
- Recipes are easily shared.
- Recipes provide a convenient way to transfer expertise effectively and quickly.

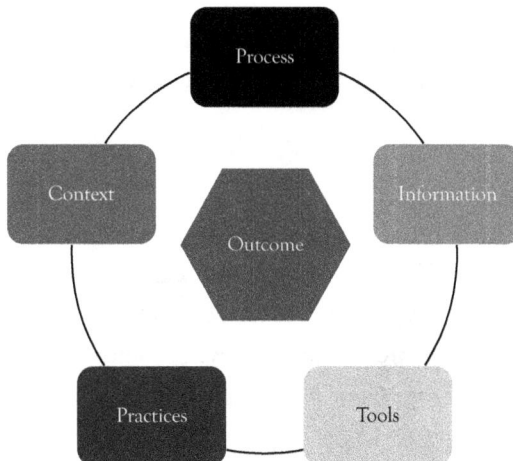

Figure 8.1 Audience–Task–Recipe: Who is it for, what we want to do, how to do it

We use recipes because they help gives us security and certainty. Recipes enable us to get where we need to be faster and at lower cost. Recipes provide the help and guidance we seek. A recipe-based approach is part of the tools for realizing change. Through the use of recipes, we share information and assure outcomes. Recipes provide the approach for achieving the emergent behavior required. For a sports team, the purpose of preset plays and the use of drills to practice these plays is a recipe and the use of the recipe in a given situation delivers a required outcome.

Making It Real

There are several main aspects to a recipe-based approach as part of the tools for realizing change:

- Leadership—Deciding to use and support.
- Development of recipes—Taking the Audience–Task–Recipe approach, development of role-based recipes for the aspects of the change required, for example, revised process.
- Implementation—The consistent and persistent use of recipes within training and operations.
- Customization—The pragmatic customization of recipes to meet needs and evolving circumstances or bettering the recipes as experience is achieved.

Again, it is a matter of starting and building the expertise with time and to pragmatically adapt and adopt with progressive incremental use.

Further Details

- Recipes in Skilling and Training—Recipes help in skilling and training (see Chapter 7 Section "Skills and Training").
- Proven Practices—The use of recipes is proven across business and society and are part of the proven business principles that bring change (see Chapter 1 Section "Applying Proven Principles").

- Video—Problem Solving Together for Our Future: Sharing Skills and Expertise—Recipes (https://youtu.be/NJzXHupiMOQ).

Turnaround

To Get the Most

Implementing change and transformation is often a series of projects or programs of work (see Chapter 6 Section "Project Management and Project Managers") to bring the change and build the capacities and capabilities required for ongoing process improvement (see Section "Making Improvements" of this chapter). The success of Decision Making and of the change lies in the implementation and responding as circumstances change (see Chapter 5). Improving change, remediating change, and responding to revised change implementation are about the application of proven project management practices and the established turnaround principles. As with other turnarounds, leadership accepting the need for a turnaround, then making the decisions required, and then undertaking the required work is needed. This makes turnaround part of leadership and decision making and a core competency for realizing change.

Setting the Example

With turnarounds, leadership needs to recognize problems, overcome reluctancy to address, avoid resisting making decisions, and resist allowing things to drift. Turnarounds seek to constrain increased costs, slippage, and adverse outcomes. In any change, the good is seen, but mistakes also occur along with the less successful. It is the willingness of leadership to respond which is key. A reluctance to change a response, or to revise an approach, or to focus on perceptions rather than addressing issues, or to be seen to be doing something rather than resolving root cause, all impact the implementation of change. It is the leadership across all levels of a business which turns around a project in response to change in drivers (Figure 8.2).

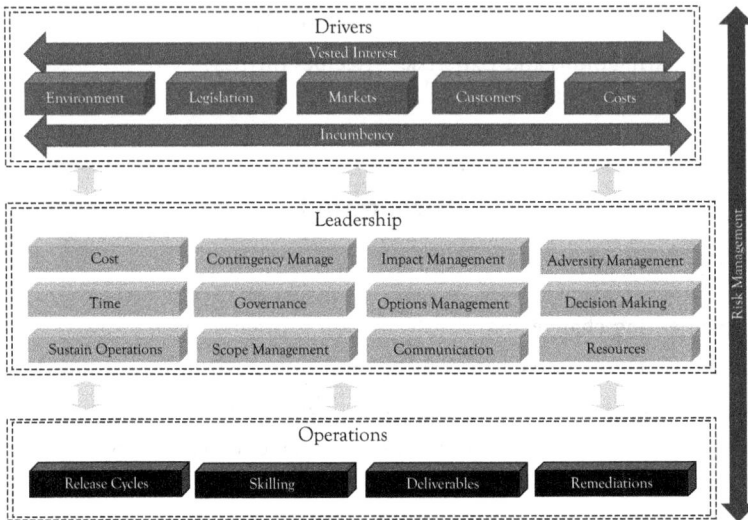

Figure 8.2 Turnarounds—we know how, but what is the desire?

Project turnarounds require:

- *Decision Making*—The willingness, ability, and acceptance of the making of decisions. Decisions are needed to accept a turnaround, to implement the turnaround, to manage the turnaround, and to address the business integration and adoption. Decision making is critical alongside Adversity Management.
- *Adversity Management*—Acceptance and management of adversity. From adverse publicity, challenging existing decision makers, vested interests, to sustained criticism, turnarounds require the acceptance of adversity by leadership and stakeholders. Within a turnaround situation, outcomes may get worse before they get better because measures take time to work and the momentum of events in flight. Adversity management is more than expectations management and communications. Adversity management is the willingness and preparedness for sustained criticism from multiple directions.

- *Impact Management*—Being able to manage the impacts of the turnaround and adopting and adapting to the changing environment.
- *Options Management*—The management of the options. From deciding to cancel, to changing the outcomes, to revising the approach, or continuing as is, the options throughout a turnaround need to be managed.
- *Contingency Management*—The preparation of, use of, and adaption and adoption of contingencies. Like our response to COVID-19, in a turnaround, it is not always known as to what will work or how effective an option is. Therefore, contingencies are required.
- *Governance*—Revisions to leadership, governance, and how a project is managed are often integral to a turnaround. COVID-19 has shown us that governance changes, for example, National Cabinets across the tiers of government, are required. COVID-19 has reinforced the need for leadership to be the change they wish to see and to treat others as they themselves would be treated.
- *Scope Management*—The ongoing definition of and response to variations in scope. This includes the scope of the turnaround, variations to original scope, and the ongoing revision of outcomes as required.
- *Resources*—Management of the resources for the project, the additional work of the turnaround, as well as ongoing operations.
- *Time*—To implement a turnaround takes time. Even the decision to stop a project has impacts that take time to work through. Within turnarounds, there needs to be an acceptance of time and that things may get worse before they get better.
- *Cost*—Management of the cost for the project, the additional cost for the work of the turnaround, as well as ongoing operations.
- *Communication*—Effective communication across the turnaround as to what is happening, why, what needs to be

done, and what is the benefit. All of the communications
need to form that emotional bond.
- *Sustain Operations*—Business operations to be sustained
  alongside the project and the turnaround.

Alongside sustaining regular business operations, there is a need
within operations to manage the deliverables, undertake the required
skilling, manage the incremental releases from the turnaround and/or the
project, as well as work through any remediations required. The turnaround of a business and the sports team under new management
are examples of turnarounds that can be overlaid against the drivers,
leadership, and operations.

Making It Real

Using turnarounds within change and transformation is part of the
multitude approach required for achieving the required outcomes and
emergent behaviors. This is also part of the use of different frameworks
necessary (beside the more familiar use of ADKAR). Adopting and adapting the turnaround practices and principles into change projects is similar
to that for the implementation of project management and the building
of skills and expertise:

- Leadership—Deciding to use and support.
- Criteria—Agreeing criteria for what constitutes the need for
  a turnaround. Rather than the specific one size fits all, the
  criteria are flexible based on both individual and accumulative
  outcomes.
- Skilling—The required skilling across key People of Influence
  to instill the wider capacities and capabilities. This includes
  the Project Managers (Program Managers, Portfolio
  Managers) as well as the Change Managers and those leading
  the change.
- Implementation—The deployment of the tools and required
  processes.
- Behaviors—Inducing a behavior that reports when things are
  wrong, as well as encouraging ownership and accountability.

Further Details

- Project Management and Project Managers—Project management is part of leadership and decision making in change, and project managers serve the change project (see Chapter 6 Section "Project Management and Project Managers").
- Video—Weekly Mirror Message—Adoption and Adaption of Change (https://youtu.be/Upld4smNbQ8).
- Video—Problem Solving Together for Our Future: Sharing Skills and Expertise—Turnarounds (https://youtu.be/nb9CBCEwBNQ).
- Video—Weekly Mirror Message—Spotting the Signs for Success in Change (https://youtu.be/A31znRW7f2c).

Making Improvements

To Get the Most

Change is about getting people to do things differently and is a crafting and shaping of the emergent behaviors. While change is often done as a series of projects based on the opportunities (Figure 4.1 and Figure 6.1), it is the ongoing use of the revised practices and operations that is the success of the change. As the business environment is changing, an ongoing improvement process is required. An emergent behavior is needed to adopt and value an ongoing process for improvement, while a process for improvement is part of forming an emergent behavior.

Setting the Example

An inherent desire to better ourselves and our families and loved ones exists. We play sport and aspire to improve. We train and skill ourselves to advance. Making improvements and a process for improvement is intrinsic to our lives. An ongoing review of a response to change and the pragmatic adoption and adaption to circumstance is integral to the success of implementing change (i.e., a process for improvement). Any improvement process need not be complex, but that it must be owned and actioned at source, meeting the needs, and with shared Interests and Values (Figure 8.3).

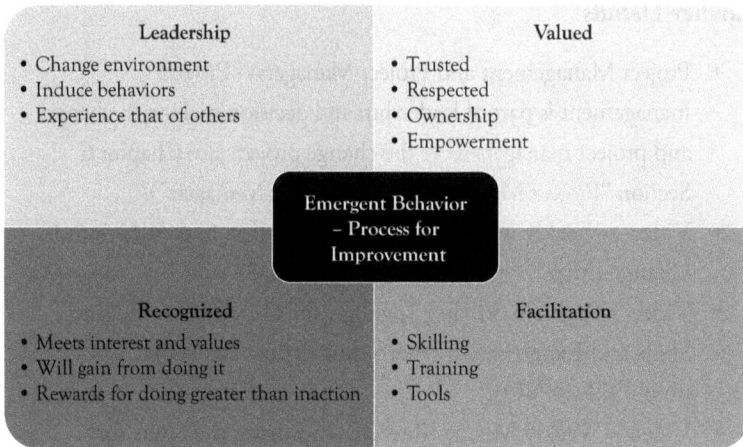

Figure 8.3 Form emergent behavior through process for improvement and use process for improvement to form emergent behavior

Where businesses have process improvement, challenges are often seen with the process:

- Being a box ticking exercise rather than behavioral driven based on interest and values.
- Viewed as not worth it or not valued, "I will not be listened to."
- Considered to be too hard or someone else's responsibility, "even if I try, it will make no difference."

An emergent behavior is needed to adopt and value ongoing process improvement, while a process for improvement is part of forming an emergent behavior. The emergent behavior requires:

- *Leadership*—The leaderships are the change they wish to see and treat others as they themselves would be treated. The leadership brings changes to the environment and instills behaviors. The leadership needs to experience what others do (i.e., "work at the coal face" and "talk to the source").
- *Being Valued*—Where we are trusted, respected, have ownership and empowerment.
- *Being Recognized*—Where it meets our interest and values, we will gain from doing it, and the rewards for doing something

difficult and possibly unpopular are greater than the rewards
of inaction.

- *Facilitation*—The skilling (ability to do), the training (how to
do), with the required tools so that we can help ourselves to
improve.

A process for improvement is part of the review and development of
a sports team. A process for improvement (Figure 8.4) is required across
change projects (programs or portfolios) as well as within areas of business
operations. It is through the emergent behavior that both opportunistic
and incremental changes (Figure 4.1 and Figure 6.1) are achieved.

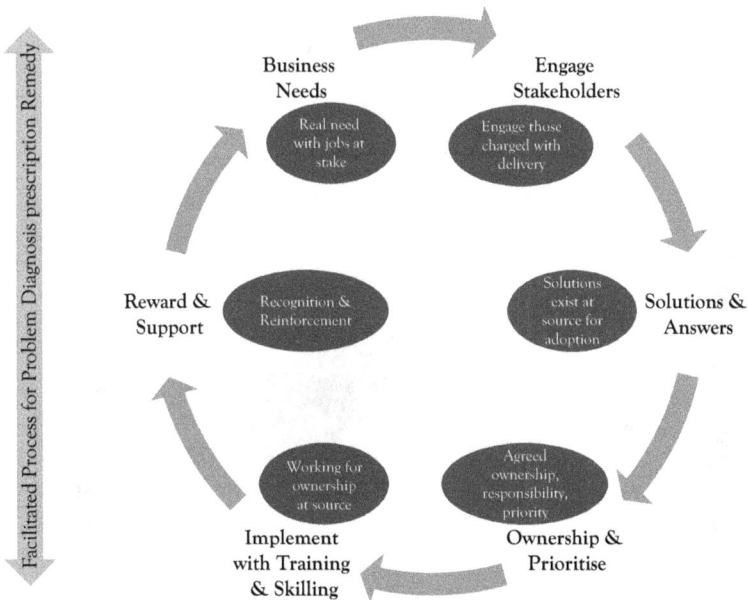

*Figure 8.4 Process for improvement. From Sherringham, K., and
B. Unhelkar. 2020. Crafting and Shaping Knowledge Worker Services
in the Information Economy. Palgrave Macmillan Singapore 570pp*

Making It Real

While having a process for improvement is a common business practice,
a process for improvement that is consistently and persistently used to
achieve actual outcomes is often harder to implement and to sustain.

Experience shows that "quick wins" are achieved with the focus then being lost, and/or the pragmatic operational demands override. Leveraging a process for improvement as part of change and then using it as part of the ongoing change is a way to help with the adoption and adaption and for business improvement.

An improvement process (Figure 8.5) starts with those in routine operations deciding they want to do this, allocating the time, and being prepared to accept that issues will be identified that may make others feel uncomfortable. Together, issues are identified, and priorities worked through with management. The priorities are implemented with Skilling and Training for adoption and those involved are rewarded. This approach needs to be cascaded through operations. Support and mentoring are part of the implementation.

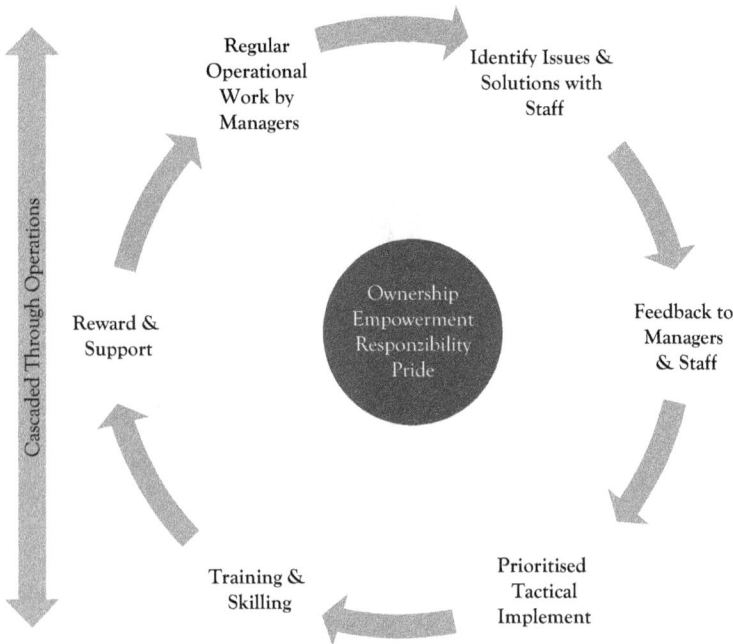

Figure 8.5 Implementing process for improvement. From Sherringham, K., and B. Unhelkar. 2020. Crafting and Shaping Knowledge Worker Services in the Information Economy. Palgrave Macmillan Singapore 570pp

Further Details

- Emergent Behavior—A process for improvement helps build the emergent behaviors (see Chapter 4 Section "Having Empowered Emotional Ownership").
- Confidence and Engagement—Using the process for improvement as a way to form the emotional bond and create confidence and engagement (see Chapter 7 Section Relate to Me").
- Video—Process for Improvement (https://youtu.be/ w7oTnVXOeW0).
- Video—Problem Solving Together for Our Future: Sharing Skills and Expertise—Making Improvements (https://youtu. be/9NZZGC9wtVM).

Frameworks

To Get the Most

Multiple frameworks are needed to deliver change or transformation, and not just a change management framework. Leadership of change and transformation manages the multiple frameworks required, brings the adoption and adaption of the frameworks to meet the business need and manages the interdependencies across the frameworks. A business has many moving parts that interact with each other and with external parties. Businesses of all types and sizes use proven business practices and principles across their operations, with many using standard frameworks to help with the management. Product Management is an example of one area of business where multiple frameworks are used including those for research, review, analysis, development, testing, pricing, and marketing, vendor management, and customer management. The frameworks rely on each other with interdependencies to be managed, just like the business operations. Bringing change or transformation impacts multiple areas of operations with impacts to be managed. Change requires the use of multiple frameworks with impacts beyond the immediate areas.

Setting the Example

Managing change for an area of business may require project management to plan and coordinate. The change makes use of shared services like financial management or ICT Operations and Services which need to be provisioned to support the change. Vendors may be required for the change or the change impacts vendors. People changes may also be needed. Areas of business like process changes may be required or services and products revised (Figure 8.6).

Specifically, multiple frameworks are needed to deliver change or transformation, and not just a change management framework (e.g., ADKAR). The interdependencies across the frameworks need to be managed. When the emergent behaviors for realizing and sustaining change are considered alongside the operational needs, then the use of multiple frameworks is further seen. Leadership of change and transformation manages the multiple frameworks required, whilst adopting and adapting the frameworks to meet the business need.

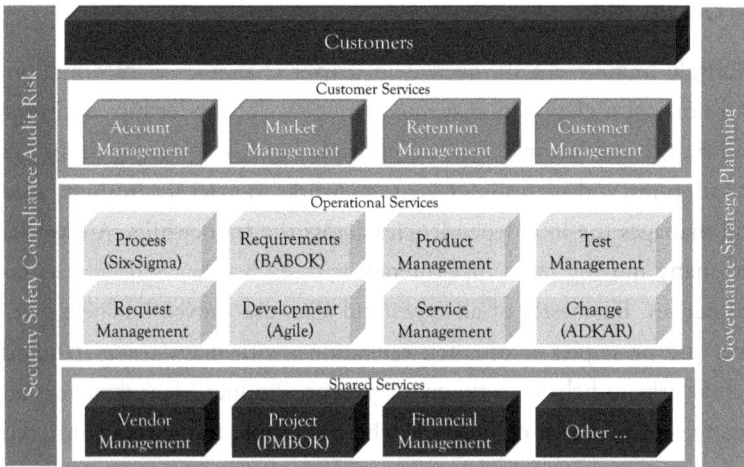

Figure 8.6 Sample frameworks across an organization. Modified from Sherringham, K., and B. Unhelkar. 2020. Crafting and Shaping Knowledge Worker Services in the Information Economy. *Palgrave Macmillan Singapore 570pp*

Making It Real

Making use of multiple frameworks for achieving change with adoption and adaption is a leadership function. The process starts with recognizing that bringing change is not just the matter of a change management framework and using that framework. Specifically, leadership needs to:

- Manage the use of frameworks.
- Instill the use of frameworks across operations while enabling their adoption and adaption.
- Have change managers and those leading change understand the use of multiple frameworks rather than just the change management framework approach.
- Foster and develop the emergent behaviors to use the various frameworks.

Further Details

- Emergent Behavior—Frameworks play a role in crafting and shaping emergent behaviors (see Chapter 6 Section "Crafting and Shaping the Emergent Behavior").
- Project Management—The delivery of projects requires multiple frameworks pragmatically applied (see Section "Project Management" of this chapter).
- Video—Weekly Mirror Message—More Than Awareness, Desire, Knowledge, Ability, Reinforcement (https://youtu.be/keT5e6Lytmk).
- Video—Multiple Frameworks to Deliver Outcomes (https://youtu.be/4ueGWtpS0wM).

Technology Adoption

To Get the Most

Technology is often a key part of change and transformation. From the use of technology to help with the change (e.g., data analytics for identifying training) or changes to operations around technology (e.g., automation of promotional messages based on customer preferences), technology is often manifested through the drivers for change (see Figure 6.1). This manifestation of technology in the drivers for change, in the need to address the ICT Service and Operations as well as the business integration (Figure 5.5), makes technology adoption a critical part of change management. Being able to adopt and adapt the technology is a leadership function within change management.

Setting the Example

Technology can be quickly integrated into business operations and services. Examples include working from home and the use of conferencing, to home-based education, to applications that track locations of people to help with workforce management. Some lessons for digital transformation, as well as general change and transformation, to consider include:

- The Ease of Change—Having people work from home using conferencing is a comparatively easy change because:
  - Technology is often already deployed to businesses.
  - Users are familiar with it.
  - Requires small process changes.
  - Limited ICT Operations and Services changes are necessary.
- The Support for Change—Having education conducted from home could be supported because:
  - Older students have the skills and expertise to educate online.
  - Younger children were supported by their parents.
  - Education institutions often had the technology and were supported to make the required changes.
  - Limited ICT Operations and Services changes were required.
- The Process Could Change—Knowledge worker services can be readily relocated. Contrast this with those in manufacturing or processing plants, working in shops, delivering goods, or frontline services where the process is much harder to change.

Business pragmatics impact the adoption of technology and continue to apply (Figure 8.7). When a response to Opportunities is made, the

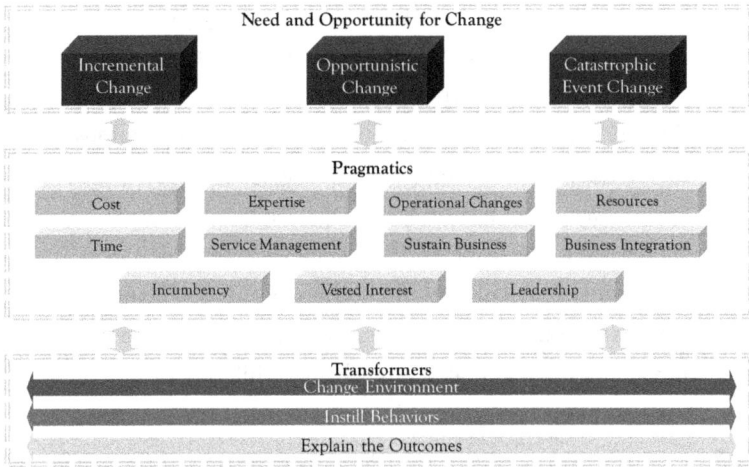

Figure 8.7 Practical pragmatic adoption and adaption

pragmatics come to bear on the adoption and adaption of technology together with the transformers:

The opportunities are the incremental change, the opportunistic change, and the catastrophic event-driven change which impact the business pragmatics. The Transformers to change of the environment, instilling the behaviors, and explaining the outcomes are impacted by the pragmatics of business. The pragmatics of sustaining business while adopting and adapting the technology include:

- *Cost*—The cost of making the change and supporting.
- *Time*—Time away from business operations to implement and support. Also, the time it takes to implement.
- *Resources*—Availability of resources for the implementation, especially business resources.
- *Expertise*—Having the right expertise and having it available.
- *Service Management*—Changes to service management to support the technology, both business service management and ICT Operations and Services.
- *Operational Changes*—Making the required operational changes around technology with the processes, policies, procedures, and governance.

- *Sustain Business*—To sustain the business through transformation including cash flow, service management, risk management, and other operational aspects.
- *Business Integration*—Taking the time to change operations and services to integrate into the business.
- *Incumbency*—Incumbent technology is established and known, even the problems. Replacing technology is a risk management exercise with the technology at least being the same as the existing, and preferably better. This risk-based approach as well as making the change while sustaining business often favors incumbency.
- *Vested Interest*—The diverse needs and drivers to be managed. For some, keeping the status quo is preferred.
- *Leadership*—The required leadership to bring results, make the changes, and integrate technology into the business and ICT Operations and Services.

Technology adoption and adaption is about managing these complexities and nuances.

Making It Real

Technology adoption is nuanced, requiring leadership, risk management, and operational change whilst sustaining operations. Alongside the technology are the business integration and the ICT Operations and Services. The adoption and adaption of technology occurs at all levels with the required Skilling and Training. It is a leadership decision around investments and use. The speed with which the take-up can occur with the investments returned impact upon the decisions around technology. Again, leadership is the change they wish to see treat others as they themselves would be treated.

Further Details

- Reference—Sherringham, K., and Unhelkar, B. (2016a) "Service Management in Big Data", Proceedings of the System Design and Process Science (SDPS2016) conference, 4-6 Dec, 2016, Orlando, FL, USA.

- Reference—Sherringham, K., and Unhelkar, B. (2016b) "Human Capital Capacity and Capability for Big Data", Proceedings of the System Design and Process Science (SDPS2016) conference, 4-6 Dec, 2016, Orlando, FL, USA.
- Video—Problem Solving Together for Our Future: Sharing Skills and Expertise—Technology Adoption (https://youtu. be/qh7LLgwDVxw).

Project Management

To Get the Most

Bringing change, even within ongoing operations, is a series of projects (programs or portfolios) of work. The initial change is often managed as a defined piece of work, and then the outcomes from improvements (see Section "Making Improvements" of this chapter) are implemented as projects whilst operations continue. This makes project management expertise a core competency across the business (Figure 2.9) and part of the frameworks used for delivering change (see Section "Frameworks" of this chapter).

Setting the Example

Whether it is the project management of construction, management of social programs, or business change, the regular project (program and portfolio) practices apply. With the right people, the projects are delivered. Provide the right processes and information, then projects tend to run smoother. Include the right governance; and the elements for a successful project are provided (Figure 8.8).

Although people are important in all projects, people are of extra importance in change projects, because the purpose of the project is to change what people and how they do it. The main people issues relate to providing the leadership and making decisions (part of AMEDLI—see Chapter 1 Section "AMEDLI"). Managing expectations of stakeholders is required for managing people within projects. The understanding of what is required, why it is required, when it is needed, who is providing, and how it is to be provided is also necessary. Within change projects, the

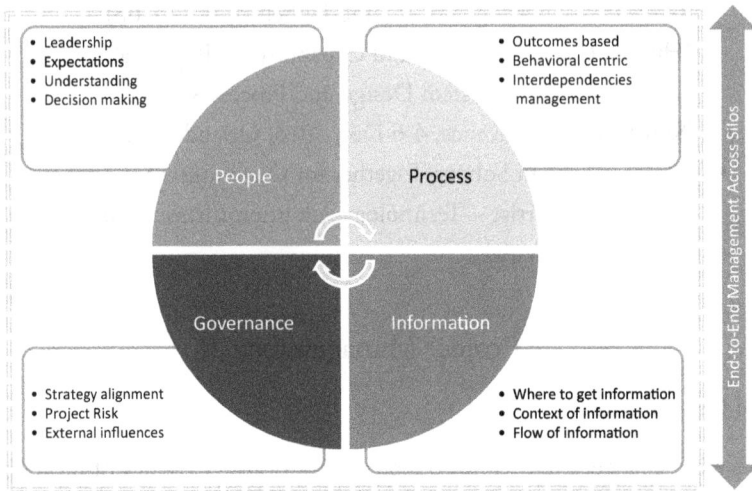

- Leadership
- Expectations
- Understanding
- Decision making

People

Process

- Outcomes based
- Behavioral centric
- Interdependencies management

Governance

Information

- Strategy alignment
- Project Risk
- External influences

- Where to get information
- Context of information
- Flow of information

End-to-End Management Across Silos

Figure 8.8 Project management in change management

understanding of ambiguity, working with nuance, and managing gray (see Chapter 2) that goes with people is required. The understanding of what brings change and the emergent behaviors required for change is necessary.

The processes for project management are known and need to exist across the stakeholders. Where change projects differ is in the nature of the processes as they are focused on the emergent behaviors of people. The processes need to be outcome based; the process is an end to a means and not an end in its own right. The processes should instill the behaviors required. The processes need to help with the management of the interdependencies within the project and the area being transformed.

Information access is part of project management, but within change projects, there are additional considerations. Knowing where to get information and from whom is often difficult in working across the silos (areas of a business) that is characteristic of change projects. Being able to see the impacts end-to-end across operations is required to manage the impacts for which information is needed across the silos. The end-to-end approach also provides context for the information that is needed for decision making. The end-to-end approach also addresses the flow of information within the project and for the stakeholders.

The last part of change projects is the governance (the management of the project). Governance is important to all projects, but for change projects, the governance especially needs to work end-to-end across the silos (areas of a business). The governance has the regular functions and responsibilities and projects, but also needs to align to strategy, because it is the strategy that is the basis for the change. By focusing end-to-end, governance can also address the external influences on the change project to manage the interdependencies. Governance also uses the end-to-end approach for managing Project Risk (see Chapter 2 Section "Project Risk") of Impact Risk, Outcome Risk, Delivery Risk, and External Risk (Figure 2.10) impacting a change project.

Making It Real

Making project (program or portfolio) management real within change and transformation can be pragmatic and tactical with a staged approach. Beyond the building of project management expertise within areas of operations, the use of multiple frameworks alongside the project management (see Section "Frameworks" of this chapter) is required. Special focus on the end-to-end across the silos of operations approach is also necessary. The emergent behaviors are an area of effort, but it is the leadership which is the must-have. The leadership needs to be the change they wish to see and treat others as they themselves would be treated because of the people aspects. It is the understanding of what is needed to have people change what and how they do things which is required within the leadership and makes change project management different from other projects.

Further Details

- Turnarounds—Part of managing change is being able to do turnarounds (see Section "Turnaround" of this chapter).
- Leadership—Leadership of change requires project management skills across the change (see Chapter 6 Section "Project Management and Project Managers").
- Video—Weekly Mirror Message—People in Project Management of Change Management (https://youtu.be/cOD8YMk3bJE).

Testing

To Get the Most

From the coach of the sports team that tests out new plays with the team in a training session or the testing of a player in a different position to the market testing of films prior to launch, testing is used across business. A range of testing types exist (Figure 8.9) that can be used in different ways according to business needs and circumstances. Testing can be used within a wider role in change management as part of the crafting and shaping of emergent behaviors.

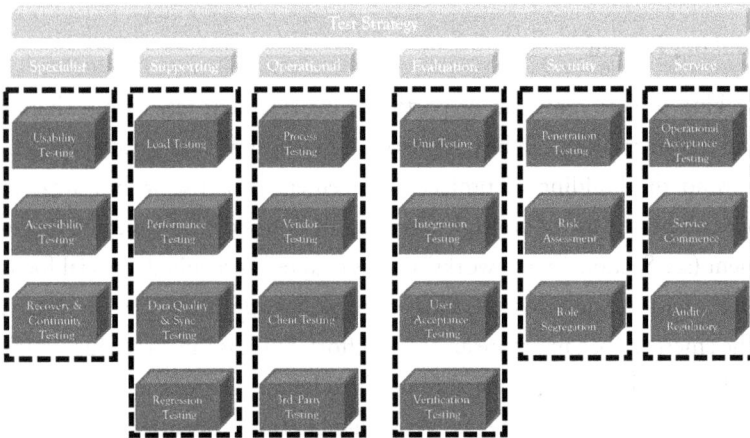

Figure 8.9 Example testing framework. From Sherringham, K., and B. Unhelkar. 2020. Crafting and Shaping Knowledge Worker Services in the Information Economy. *Palgrave Macmillan Singapore* 570pp

Setting the Example

Within change management, testing can play a wider role (Figure 8.10). Testing can be used in:

- *Requirements*—Shape the requirements through testing for iterative and staged releases as well as offering maturity. Testing can be done multiple times as well as incremental and with staged releases. It is often easier to deconstruct than to construct.

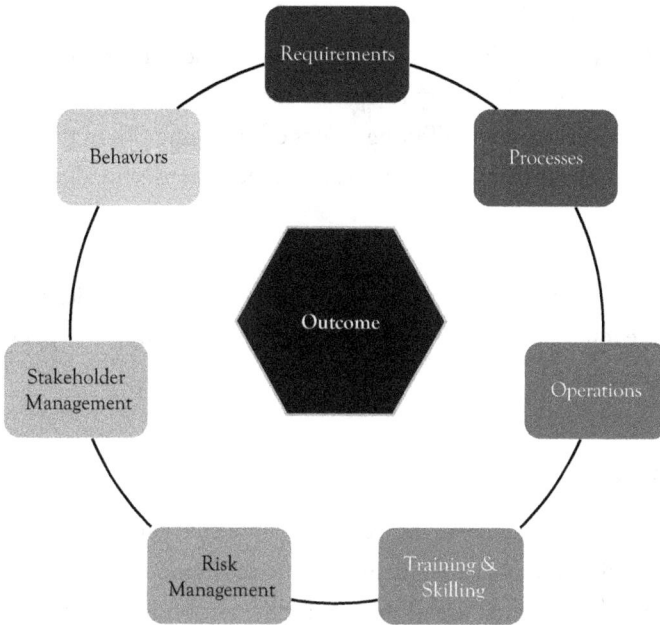

Figure 8.10 Testing within change management

- *Processes*—Assist in the development of processes (policies, procedures, standards) as well as the end-to-end flow. Testing shows how things work and with the experience gained through testing, the processes can be defined by those needing to use them.
- *Operations*—Influence the development and ongoing management of operations. By testing from an operational perspective and by testing operations with an end-to-end flow, better operations can be established.
- *Skilling and Training*—Form the basis for skilling and training. Testing enables the identification of the characteristics needed to work with the solution and the ability to provide the support.
- *Stakeholder Management*—The testing is used within the management of stakeholders to explain what is happening, the impacts, and what is being done to help them.

- *Behaviors*—Use of testing to identify individual and group behaviors required. Testing creates confidence in the solution as well as in the ability to operate and manage.
- *Risk Management*—Testing is part of managing risk in that it can be used to mitigate risks, set expectations, and identify other risks.

Testing within change includes the use of testing strategies to determine the testing to be done which can then be used within overall change management.

Making It Real

Those leading a change or the People of Influence within a change can make small revisions to existing practices to accommodate the use of testing. Small incremental use of testing in different business circumstances is the pragmatic application of testing. The major challenge to the use of testing within change management is the prioritization of testing within operations. In the adoption of technology, testing is often given a lower priority than the time for development. Even when requirements are valued and time allocated to requirements, it is often the testing that defines the requirements.

Making use of testing within change is an emergent behavior that can be done incrementally and tactically, but it is a leadership decision to use the testing approach within change management.

Further Details

- Video—Weekly Mirror Message—Testing within Change Management (https://youtu.be/QurpSctSEFs).
- Video—Changing Role of Testing within Automated Knowledge Worker Services (https://youtu. be/58r1HKKNOx0).
- Video—Testing of Automation for Knowledge Worker Services (https://youtu.be/hT_9tdKTBB8).

Closing the Gap

To Get the Most

Business change comes through the emergent behavior of individuals having empowered emotional ownership. Within a business change, common requirements are seen (Figure 8.11), and to turnaround a change (see Section "Turnaround" of this chapter) often requires:

- *Leadership*—The leadership is the change they wish to see and treat others as they themselves would be treated.
- *Messaging*—The leadership needs to be communicating what they are seeking to achieve, why, how it relates to people, to get people to talk about it; then people will include it within their roles.
- *Interests and Values*—Business change needs leadership to ensure understanding in roles and responsibilities. With all people seeing it as part of their role, to having help

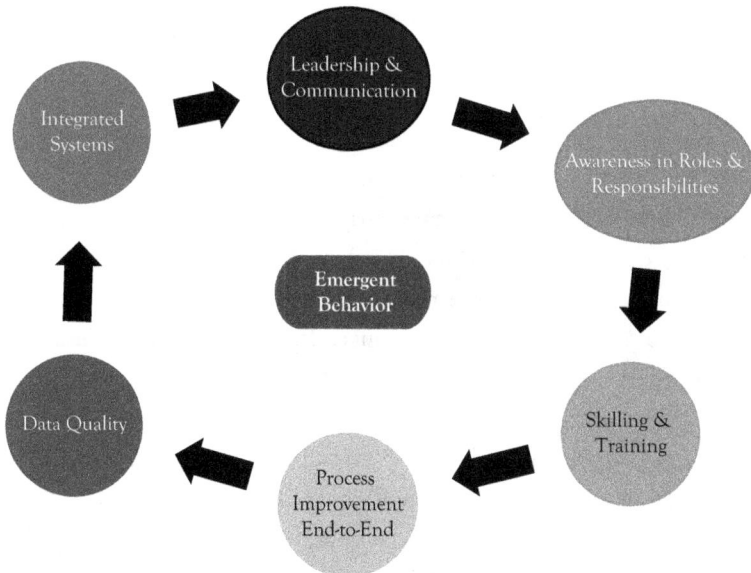

Figure 8.11 Closing the gaps in bringing business change

and support, it is the integration into roles that matters. This comes from the alignment of interests and values, which is about behaviors and requires leadership.

- *Skilling and Training*—Business change sees the leadership ensuring the skilling (the ability to do) and the training (the how to do). This is more than e-learning modules. It requires things like team-led scenario sessions and hands-on repeat as well as small incremental training.
- *Process Improvement*—Business change has leaders who see the importance of having processes operate end-to-end as the customer interacts and make the changes. This includes a cycle for process improvement.
- *Information*—Leadership addresses the quality of data and information used, provided, and managed through the processes, because it is needed for achieving business change.
- *ICT Operations and Services*—Systems are integrated end-to-end, across the silos to supply the flow of information needed.

Each of these (Figure 8.11) can be used within a wider role in change management as part of the crafting and shaping of emergent behaviors.

Setting the Example

Closing the gaps in change (Figure 8.11) is often achieved through the required behaviors. To integrate systems, resolve data quality, and improve processes, changes in behaviors are often required, for example, better leadership. To bring change, emergent behaviors are required. Emergent behaviors are an outcome of the change. Therefore, setting the example requires addressing behaviors (Figure 8.12):

- *Leadership*—The leadership is the change they wish to see and treat others as they themselves would be treated. Leadership needs to be messaging the change and be talking about the change to have people talking about the change so that they will adopt and adapt the change. The leadership needs to be communicating what they are seeking to achieve, why, how

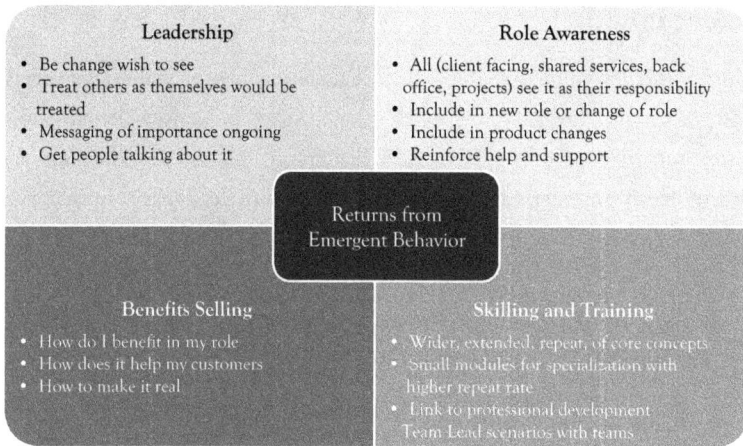

Leadership
- Be change wish to see
- Treat others as themselves would be treated
- Messaging of importance ongoing
- Get people talking about it

Role Awareness
- All (client facing, shared services, back office, projects) see it as their responsibility
- Include in new role or change of role
- Include in product changes
- Reinforce help and support

Returns from Emergent Behavior

Benefits Selling
- How do I benefit in my role
- How does it help my customers
- How to make it real

Skilling and Training
- Wider, extended, repeat, of core concepts
- Small modules for specialization with higher repeat rate
- Link to professional development
- Team Lead scenarios with teams

Figure 8.12 Better returns through emergent behaviors

it relates to people, to get people to talk about it, then people will include it within their roles.

- *Role Awareness*—Providing help and support is part of the role awareness to make the change real. Having awareness across the business with inclusion within new roles, role changes, and product and service changes is required. Those in client facing roles, supporting client facing, projects, as well as in back office roles all need awareness. The change needs to be integrated into roles with reinforcement and support.
- *Skilling and Training*—Skilling (the ability to do) and training (the how to do) are required. This includes core awareness, repeat sessions, small modules of short duration on specific areas repeated, and scenario sessions within teams tailored to business needs completed on a regular basis. When changing roles, on boarding, or moving between areas of a business, training is required. The skilling is linked to the training and career development.
- *Messaging*—The benefits of the change need to be sold and understood. This is tied to the role, to give benefits to the role.

From this combined series of actions, the emergent behaviors can be crafted and shaped.

Making It Real

Closing the gap in change, working on turnarounds, or realizing a return from other activities requires work on emergent behaviors. In addition, better returns are often seen from emergent behaviors. Making the returns from emergent behaviors real starts with leadership and makes use of other aspects of AMEDLI covering:

- Leadership—Deciding to change behaviors, prioritize behaviors, and be the behaviors.
- Messaging—Leadership communicating the change and selling the benefits, including embedding in the roles.
- Interests and Values—Alignment through skilling and training, tied to career development, with a range of reinforcement mechanisms including core awareness, repeats, scenario sessions, and short specialized awareness sessions.
- Empowered Emotional Ownership—Through role empowerment supported by skilling and training as well as the messaging.

A series of measures, in an overall integrated approach, are required.

Further Details

- Video—Weekly Mirror Message—Gaps in the Management of Business Change (https://youtu.be/-rl-2-rysYY).
- Video—Weekly Mirror Message—Returns from Emergent Behaviours in Realising Change (https://youtu.be/ QZtEXWbzJW4).
- Video—Weekly Mirror Message—Adoption and Adaption of Change (https://youtu.be/Upld4smNbQ8).

Next Steps

The on-the-ground practices for change are proven business activities that are used within a different context across the stakeholders at different levels in varying ways within change and transformation. Part of their use is the skilling and embedding for ongoing adaption and adoption, while other parts are leadership related. Key to the use is the "people of influence" who value the activities and are the mentors and motivators on the ground who use because of the benefits to them. It is the responsibility of leadership to implement and use the different activities. Incremental use and wider deployment as needs drive and as experience can be transferred is a proven approach. Provision with change projects and programs for the approaches is also advantageous.

CHAPTER 9

Bringing It Together

Start and bring people along the journey
to better themselves and those around them

Summary

"I do good work, change is coming, help me with the change, and I can do more" is at the heart of change because it encapsulates the roles of the individuals and the leadership, whilst setting the tone for empowerment, ownership, and the importance of people and their emotions. Crafting and shaping change is about working with the nuances and complexities of people and getting the best from them to do things different. Change comes from an emergent behavior by the actions of empowered individuals who have ownership with the alignment of interests and values. Change is about starting and pragmatically adopting and adapting with what is at hand to the situation at hand. Leadership needs to be the change they wish to see and treat others as they themselves would be treated.

Introduction

From building families to coaching children's teams, to leading a sporting team to a championship, to turning around businesses, through digital transformation, to bringing countries through turbulent times, proven principles exist which applied pragmatically bring change. Crafting and shaping change comes not from the magic wand or the silver bullet or the one size fits all approach, but rather it is through the consistent and persistent application of proven principles applied pragmatically to form an emergent behavior. By being the change we wish to see and treating others as we ourselves would wish to be treated, we form an emotional bond to align interests and values in those around us. From this comes Empowered Emotional Ownership of actions. Bringing change and transformation sees a changing of the environment, the instilling of behaviors, and then supporting people to bring the outcomes because of their pride in who they are and what they do. Assisting with skilling and training, providing support as well as messaging to engage and form the emotional bond, is also used. We know these proven practices and principles apply, because of our lived experiences. Making change in business or the adoption of technology is no different. This chapter pulls together the principles and practices through worked examples.

Pragmatics of Change

Realities of Change

Whether we like it or not, globalization is occurring, and jobs are being done virtually with teams across the world. Rapid changes in technology are automating industries from agriculture through to knowledge worker services. Change and business transformation is all around us. In this time of rapid change, opportunities exist, and a sense of dynamism and optimism for the future can be seen. Equally, there is uncertainty, resistance to rapid change and continual change, frustration with poorly led or weakly managed change, change fatigue, and fear about livelihoods. This ambiguity around change is more than our ability to adopt and adapt with our varying capacities and capabilities. Any hesitation, doubt, or indecision we may have is a normal part of bringing change and is often about our confidence. Our certainty in the process, our belief that it is worth it, and our trust in those leading the process are how we get the confidence.

If your eyes have rolled or are feeling a glazing over or a shiver down the spine at the thought of more change or business transformation, then this may be because of experiences with weak management and poor implementation, alongside the use of buzz words and the one size fits all panacea approach. A series of changes that have been less successful may also have been experienced and this brings doubt about the current change. Any emotions of doubt, uncertainty, and a sense of change fatigue are all valid responses.

Our lived experiences have shown us what works and what does not. From coaching a children's sports team, to lifting people out of poverty across a country, to transforming a company or a group within an organization, it is people who realize any transformation (change or process improvement). The change does not occur by some magic wand or silver bullet or panacea that will just work and produce results quickly with minimal issues. While the one size fits all approach with all the buzz words may have appeal, this is not our lived experience. From the sports team or the changes around technology at work, pragmatics tells us that it is about the consistent and persistent application of proven principles and practices over time that brings results.

We respond when leadership is the change they wish to see and treat others as they themselves would be treated. We know that when our environment is changed, we vary our behaviors, and the change results. We see teams succeed when an emergent behavior is instilled. We perceive that the actions of empowered individuals collectively form the emergent behavior. Our emotional response is triggered with the alignment of our interest and values. From this comes the ownership and pride in who we are and what we do. Then with an understanding of what needs to be done and with help provided, we can better ourselves and those around us (Weekly Mirror Message—The Story of an Individual—https://youtu.be/xxHgmdiQmjg). Knowing the proven practices and principles and their consistent and persistent application, sustainable change can be realized (Weekly Mirror Message—Concepts in the Management of Change—https://youtu.be/8uCQuChnjug).

Inherent Characteristics of Change

There are a series of characteristics of change (Weekly Mirror Message—Characteristics of Change—https://youtu.be/pSahSGDE3DU) that are inherent within it (Table 9.1), irrespective of type, situation, size, and complexities. What differs across the range of change is the emergent behaviors required, the crafting and shaping necessary, and the mixing of skills and expertise and experience. While the hands-on of how, the details, and the management of the projects for the emergent behaviors and the change differ with the variety of change, these characteristics come to the fore in managing the people aspects of change.

Table 9.1 Change characteristics and impacts

Change characteristic	Consideration	Main AMEDLI alignment
Change is about people and getting people to do things differently	Change is complex and nuanced	• Ambiguity Management • Leadership
Resistance to change, uncertainty, and managing "change fatigue" are part of realizing change	Change is emotional, and an emotional bond is needed	• Empowered Emotional Ownership • Interests and Values
The change needs to be motivational and aspirational whilst being credible and believable, so that it can be achieved, even if it is stages in the journey, because it creates confidence and self-belief	Stage the change, have the achievable so that people can feel success and rewards on the journey. Creates the confidence and motivates	• Empowered Emotional Ownership • Interests and Values
Change occurs when there is confidence in the leadership and in the change process	Absence leads to poor implementations, demotivation of people, and resistance to change	• Leadership • Decision Making
The basic questions around change and why people will change what they do need to be answered	Leadership needs to ask the basic questions and get answers and then address the issues	• Leadership • Ambiguity Management
Change does not occur by some magic wand or silver bullet or panacea that will just work and produce results quickly with minimal issues	Consistent persistent application of proven principles pragmatically applied. Leadership needs to do this	• Leadership • Ambiguity Management
The one size fits all approach with all the buzz words to change seldom delivers sustainable change	Leadership needs to avoid this and consistently and persistently apply the proven principles	• Leadership • Ambiguity Management
Mistakes are made, people respond differently, and a multitude of approaches are required which vary over time	Manage the unplanned and recognize the role of time in achieving change as well as incremental adoption and adaption	• Leadership • Messaging • Empowered Emotional Ownership
The amount and rate of change is influenced by the need and the capacity and capability to absorb the change. The greater the need, the more the change that can occur, but the impacts need to be managed	Leadership manages the amount and rate of change, but the impacts of the change need to be managed	• Leadership • Empowered Emotional Ownership

Table 9.1 (Continued)

Change characteristic	Consideration	Main AMEDLI alignment
Change the environment, instill the behaviors, and achieve the outcomes	Leadership needs to address these to bring the change and emergent behaviors	• Leadership • Empowered Emotional Ownership • Decision Making
Change comes from an overall emergent behavior	The crafting and shaping of the emergent behaviors is required, but it is done with what is to hand and adopting and adapting as required	• Leadership • Empowered Emotional Ownership
Opportunities for change include opportunistic, incremental, catastrophic	Take advantage of the opportunities for change by leadership with the capacity and capability to make change while sustaining operations	• Leadership • Ambiguity Management • Decision Making
Change is about starting and pragmatically adopting and adapting with what is at hand to the situation at hand	Change is working with what you have and how to get the most from it. It is the skill of leadership to achieve	• Ambiguity Management • Leadership • Decision Making
Change comes from the actions of empowered individuals with ownership in response to an emotional bond having pride in who they are and what they do. Interests and values are aligned	Forms the basis of successful change. Needs to align interest and values to achieve and reinforce with messaging	• Empowered Emotional Ownership • Messaging • Interests and Values
Leadership needs to be the change they wish to see and treat others as they themselves would be treated	This creates confidence in the leadership, the process, the change, and forms the emotional bond	• Leadership • Interests and Values
Decision making is part of change and a decision is only as good as the implementation and the response as circumstance change	Leadership needs to respond to the implementation as the circumstances change	• Decision Making • Managing Ambiguity • Change Management

Emotions in Change

Change is emotional. People are emotional. Bringing change is managing the emotions of people who we are asking to do things differently. Change is the contradiction between the desire to better ourselves and the unknown of uncertainty. Change is the balance between our emotions of fear and greed. Change is also the motivators of moving toward or moving away from. These emotions vary with time and also with individuals and their circumstances and needs. The sports team that is motivated to win and wants to better themselves is likely to be more responsive to changes through new training regimes and plays than the losing sports team that is infighting and doubts the leadership. Proven experience shows that change is resisted when one or more of the emotions given in Table 9.2 are experienced.

A review of Table 9.1 shows that all of the elements in AMEDLI relate to each of the change characteristics. Also, interdependencies exist between the change characteristics. Similar to the change characteristics (Table 9.1), the perceptions of change (Table 9.2) can use all of the elements in AMEDLI and the interdependencies exist (Weekly Mirror Message—Managing the Perceptions of Change—https://youtu.be/6mIC90bMA58). All of these perceptions of change contribute to uncertainty, frustration, hesitation, doubt, and indecision. Combine issues like fear about livelihoods and any existing alienation, then it is clear as to what is needed to bring change and form the emergent behaviors required.

Emotions are part of change and they need to be addressed within change management. One of the main ways to address emotions is through creating confidence in those within the change. Creating certainty in the process, our belief that it is worth it, and our trust in those leading the process help gain the confidence.

"I do good work, change is coming, help me with the change, and I can do more" is a benchmark for the emotions in change because:

- Recognition of efforts so far is there, which is part of aligning Interests and Values and forming the Emotional Bond.
- It shows the motivation is there for change.
- The recognition to do things differently is there, including the rationalization. Shows the Empowered Emotional Ownership for bringing change.

Table 9.2 Common factors in resistance to change

Perception of change	Main AMEDLI alignment
Lack of leadership, indecision, and ongoing revisions to what is required	• Leadership • Decision Making
Poor implementation and/or another poor implementation	• Leadership
Change fatigue	• Leadership • Messaging • Interests and Values
Weak engagement, including differences in understanding	• Interests and Values • Messaging
Sense of expertise not valued	• Empowered Emotional Ownership • Interests and Values
Absence of the picture as to what is occurring and why	• Leadership • Messaging
Asked to do extra work without reward	• Messaging
Seeming that it does not make sense	• Messaging
Told to do things that would not work or not make sense or there is a better way to do it	• Leadership • Messaging
Sense that no point in trying	• Interests and Values
Feeling unvalued	• Empowered Emotional Ownership • Interests and Values
Motivation is "I just have to do it"	• Empowered Emotional Ownership • Interests and Values
Lack of certainty	• Leadership • Messaging
Looking for known to help with transition	• Messaging • Empowered Emotional Ownership
Seeking help and support	• Interests and Values
Needing a sense of caring	• Empowered Emotional Ownership • Interests and Values
Basics are missing and the basic questions around the change have not been answered	• Leadership

- Identifies the need, requesting, and importance of support like skilling and training.
- The desire to do better and more is there. The Messaging is engaging and forming the emotional bond.

Sustain Operations While Making Change

Another pragmatic of change and the impacting realities is that operations need to be sustained alongside making the changes. A business needs to keep making a profit and supporting customers or a sports team needs to continue to train and play games whilst it makes changes to improve its performance. Considerations include:

- Recognizing the need to make a change.
- A desire to make the change, including the desire to do better and a willingness to improve.
- How to make the transition?
- The cost of the transition.
- The risk in making the transition vs. the risk in not making the transition.
- How to sustain services during the transition?
- The capacity and capability to make the transition, including leadership, governance, skilling, training, planning, processes, and resources.

All of these change considerations are managed alongside the cost and practicalities of operations. This is where aspects of AMEDLI are used:

- Ambiguity Management—Leadership with the skills and expertise to manage the change alongside operations, such as resourcing and cost.
- Messaging—The range of messaging required across operations and the change.
- Empowered Emotional Ownership—For both the change and in operations, creating and sustaining the empowered emotional ownership required for the emergent behaviors.

- Decision Making—Having the required decisions made, implemented, and responded to as circumstances change.
- Leadership—The leadership to make decisions, guide the change, form the emergent behaviors to make the change and the emergent behavior required from the change, all whilst leading and sustaining operations.
- Interests and Values—The alignment of interests and values to bring the change and support the additional work required while making the change.

Start, Build, Adopt and Adapt from Opportunities along the Way

Often, we know we need to make changes, but starting them can be difficult. A series of factors from "we need more details" to "the priorities are not clear" to "I don't know what you want of me" to "we don't know it will work" to "waiting for someone else to decide," all impact our willingness to start. We can only make change when we feel comfortable to start (Figure 9.1). We can gain comfort through talking to people and seeking their views on what are the issues and what needs to be done. We can start with the obvious things that we can address, even if it is done in stages and incremental (Weekly Mirror Message—Adoption and Adaption of Change—https://youtu.be/Upld4smNbQ8). Through getting results and experiences, we can get answers to the issues that lie ahead. We don't have to have everything before we start. We need to have enough to start, and to build along the way. We need confidence that we can build along the way.

Making the journey requires leadership to be the change they wish to see and to treat others as they themselves would be treated. It requires consistency and persistency with belief in what is being done, why, and that it is achievable. Making the journey is taking the opportunities, building the support and structures for the change, explaining to get the buy-in and support, and creating the ownership. From this come the emergent behaviors that vary along the journey (Weekly Mirror Message—Starting the Change Journey Using Opportunities to Build Along the Way—https://youtu.be/4WjqIzbHpew).

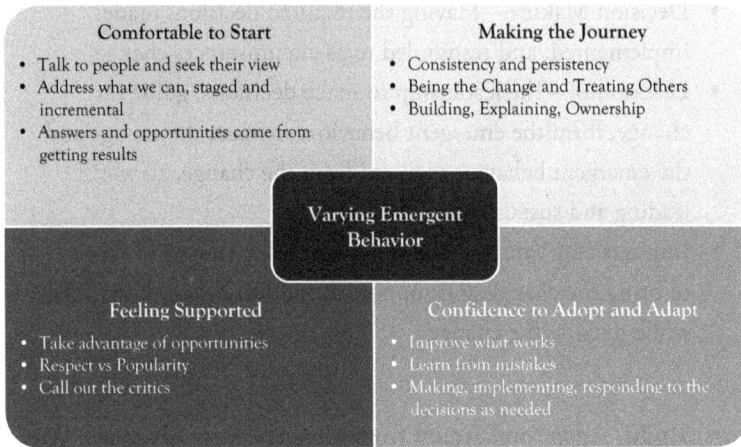

Figure 9.1 Building the support and structures from opportunities along the way

Sustaining the journey is the confidence to adopt and adapt. The confidence comes from improving what works. The learning from mistakes includes accepting that mistakes will occur, acceptance of their importance, and the management of the remediation. Sustaining the journey comes from making the required decisions, the implementation, and the response as the situation varies.

The feeling of support is needed along the journey. By taking advantage of the opportunities presented to build the support and structures for the change, confidence is instilled, belief in the change is seen, and reinforcement is achieved. The feeling of support comes from the sense of respect achieved in doing the change and from bettering ourselves. Change may not be popular, but it is the respect that brings the feeling of support. Feeling supported also comes from calling out the critics. Taking the positive from criticism and turning it into support is of value. Where the critics are raising the need for change, this is one thing, but having people who are working hard and trying to better themselves being criticized is a different thing. It is easy to criticize and deconstruct, so call out the critics and have them contribute. Where they show reluctance, that tells you all you need to know. By calling out, the critics, the respect is created.

Financial Services Example

A worked business example is used to show the different elements and components of achieving and sustaining change. The example used is the efforts by financial institutions to fight financial crime like money laundering or the funding of terrorism. This example is used because many financial institutions like banks in the United States and Europe, and Asia and Australia, have had to address the problem across their operations in multiple countries. The example starts with the drivers, shows the changing of the environment, the opportunities, the operations and technology impacts, and the need for emergent behaviors. In so doing, the overall change as well as the individual impacts can be seen. From highlighting the need for project management in achieving change or the use of multiple frameworks, the worked example should also show that bringing sustainable change is more than the magic wand or silver bullet or the one size fits all approach which just happens. The worked example shows that it is consistency and persistency in the application of proven business principles and practices applied pragmatically with responses as the situation changes which is necessary.

Background

Financial crime is mainly seen as a white-collar crime that is in the background. While the impacts may not be seen directly, the estimated annual cost of money laundering and associated crimes is around U.S.$1.4 trillion to U.S.$3.5 trillion a year with an annual compliance costs of around U.S.$180 billion in compliance. The more direct impacts are the funding of crime and terrorism, corruption of business and political leaders, and the decline in economies. Headlines around the world have seen many leading financial institutions being caught including the faking of user accounts and credit cards impacting people in their daily lives, money laundering and terrorism funding, to overcharging customers, to your funds going missing. While some cases have been specific instances, others are the result of wider issues within financial institutions. Even the executives of some of these financial institutions have come forward, apologized, are recognizing the wider behavioral issues, and are seeking to bring changes.

Financial crime is part of financial transactions. It has been there and is likely to be there as long as financial transactions are made. What changes is the scale, the complexities, the measures required, the regulatory controls, and the risks. Like having "a culture of safety in an airline" to protect passengers, people want to know their funds are safe and are going where they want them to go. This makes fighting financial crime a part of the culture of financial institutions.

Starting with the drivers for change and going through many aspects of operations and the changes adopted and adapted, the need for an emergent behavior to bring the transformation, as well as the emergent behavior required going forward, is noted. This includes:

- Respond to the drivers to bring change.
- Use of opportunities for change.
- Role of the Board in leading change.
- Role of the Executive in bringing the change and emergent behaviors.
- Resolution and application of governance.
- Technology change and its role and implementation.
- Operational change and how to achieve.
- Tactical use of regulatory gaps and audit findings for change.
- The need for project management skills and expertise and use of projects in change.
- The role of testing in change.
- The importance of skilling and training in change.
- Working with regulatory and compliance teams and their role in emergent behaviors.
- The need and use of assurance.
- Crafting and shaping the emergent behaviors for the change and ongoing.

Whether all of these or some of these aspects are required for other change, this financial crime example can be used as a road map for other changes. Using the AMEDLI overarching approach as a context is also included.

Drivers—An Emergent Behavior Response

Situation

Faced with financial crime, the financial institution is impacted by the drivers of Markets, Costs, and Regulatory (see Chapter 6 Section "Drivers and Opportunities") and Customers. Where a failing in compliance occurs, it is often the regulators that are driving the need for change, for example, adverse findings from regulators across the media. These drivers then provide the financial institution with a series of opportunities, a range of decisions to make, costs to be incurred, actions to be taken to comply and protect its brand. Through the drivers, impacts include:

- Triggering an Emergent Behavior—To resolve the issues, the financial institution has to pull together all of the required areas, work across the silos, to deliver the required the outcomes. An emergent behavior is required.
- Changing the Environment—The regulatory impacts, say, have changed the environment. Additional work is required, and things need to be done differently to meet the required outcomes.
- Revising Behavior—A range of behaviors need to be shown to meet the outcomes. From taking more care on reporting to revised risk practices, behaviors are changed.

How leadership responds, the extent of the changes, the impacts, the cost, the outcomes are all case specific. The commonality is that the drivers have changed the environment, and an emergent behavior is needed.

AMEDLI Use

Responding to the drivers would use at least the following from AMEDLI:

- Ambiguity Management—Resolving the ambiguity in what is needed, what the response is to be, managing the business impacts, and working with regulators on the response.
- Leadership—To lead the response and the change.
- Decision Making—Making decisions on what is required, funding, resources, and the response.

Take-Outs

Summary take-outs include:

- A coordinated effort to the response is required across a range of stakeholders with interdependencies and impacts to be managed.
- Emergent Behavior is required. These need to be crafted and shaped both to bring the change and for the operations going forward.
- The consistent and persistent application of proven business principles is required (see Chapter 1 Section "Applying Proven Principles").

Opportunities—Changing the Environment for Change

Situation

From the drivers come the opportunities for change (Figure 4.1). Working with the regulatory and compliance scenario, the drivers have created either opportunistic change or the need for incremental change (assuming the license to operate is not to be removed—catastrophic event). The decision for leadership is how to use this opportunity and whether they are seeking to take advantage of it for wider change. The response is likely to include regulatory management, legal impacts, working with external stakeholders, managing customers and impacts, technology changes (including data and operations), operational changes (policies, procedures, reporting, controls). Other impacts may include audit, vendors, staffing issues, and other institutions.

AMEDLI Use

Responding to the opportunities would use at least the following from AMEDLI:

- Ambiguity Management—Management of the ambiguity and nuance of the response.

- Leadership—To lead the response and the change.
- Decision Making—A range of decisions on implementation, extent of the changes, other opportunities to be taken while change is occurring, for example, a wider skilling and training regime or systems upgrades.

Take-Outs

Summary take-outs include:

- Emergent Behavior is required. These need to be crafted and shaped both to bring the change and for the operations going forward (see Chapter 4 Section "Having Empowered Emotional Ownership").
- More than the one size fits all or the magic wand or silver bullet approaches are required (see Chapter 1 Section "Applying Proven Principles").

Boards—Instilling Behaviors for Change

Situation

A larger regulatory issue would likely be a Board issue for the financial institution. The Board would be faced with a range of decisions, to which the answers may not always be known (e.g., deciding to contest a case in court). The behaviors of the Board may need changes, with replacement of responsible Directors. The decision may be made that a large program of work is needed across the business (e.g., responses to terrorism funding) or the need for major organizational change and behavioral change programs (e.g., Australian financial institutions in response to royal commission) is required. Examples have included replacement of one or more directors, replacement of one or more in the executive, divestment of assets, the need for capital raising to cover costs, and five-year behavioral changes agreement with law enforcement. The strategy of the financial institution may need to change (e.g., growth in higher sovereign risk countries changed or transformation around technology impacted).

These large-scale actions can have organization-wide change impacts and the Board needs to manage the challenges of maintaining business operations whilst bringing large-scale change. The Board is also faced with how much change and how fast, for example, timeframes set by regulators need to be managed.

Depending upon the financial institution, the regulatory requirements, and the size of the response required, a range of decisions and actions are required. It is the decisions and actions of the Board which impact the emergent behavior of the financial institution in both the response and going forward. The leaders need to be the change they wish to see and to treat others as they themselves would be treated.

AMEDLI Use

The Board's response would use at least the following from AMEDLI:

- Ambiguity Management—Management of the ambiguity and nuance of the response and to the financial institution.
- Decision Making—A range of decisions that impact the financial institution and its relationship with regulators, government, customers, and other stakeholders.
- Leadership—To lead the response and the change.

Where the larger change programs are required, the Board is also working with:

- Messaging—Consistency and persistency of messaging to stakeholders including government, regulators, customers, and markets on what is happening, why, the impacts, and how issues are being resolved. Messaging maybe that this is a new way of working, that old habits need to change, and that they are not going back to the old habits.
- Empowered Emotional Ownership—The Board is faced with managing the complex emotions across the business, including messaging to form an emotional bond, creating ownership so that the changes are made, and having empowerment to have things done in a timely way.

- Interests and Values—Where the Board needs to craft and shape the behaviors, then measures and messaging around alignment of interests and values are required.

Take-Outs

From this example, some of the take-outs are:

- Emergent Behavior across the business will be needed (see Chapter 4).
- The impacts and the benefits have to be related to the individuals to get the emergent behaviors required (see Chapter 7).
- Decisions may be the choices of least-worse options (see Chapter 5 Section "Least-Worse Option and Alternative Decision Making").

Executives—Leading Emergent Behaviors

Situation

The executive would be tasked of implementing the required changes across the business whilst sustaining business operations. The executive would at least need a 10-point assurance (see Chapter 6 Section "The 10-Point Assurance") and be able to answer the basic questions around achieving the required outcomes (see Chapter 6 Section "Why and How are We Going to Change What We Do"). Working across the silos and managing the interdependencies and interactions is required. A focus on the capacity and capability building to make the required changes, the crafting and shaping the emergent behaviors to achieve the change, and having the change create the behaviors going forward are also priorities.

Regime changes may include:

- Training and skilling.
- Revised standards, policies and procedures, and processes.
- Reporting changes.
- Technology changes.
- Information security.

- Legal impacts.
- Improved controls.
- Roles and responsibilities reviewed, including segregation of duties.
- Regulatory requirements.
- Operational changes.
- Customers, vendors, and other stakeholders impacted.
- Audit of the changes.

These are the responsibility of the executive along with making the changes, supporting the transition, the adoption and adaption to changing circumstances during the deployment, and assurance of operations moving forward.

AMEDLI Use

Clearly, all areas of AMEDLI would be used in the response. At the executive the focus is on:

- Decision Making—Making the decisions required and all of the pragmatic trade-offs to ensure implementation. This includes budgets, resources, and priorities with the balancing of keeping the business going whilst making the required changes.
- Leadership—Provide the guidance and direction for the transition.
- Messaging—Consistent and persistent messaging across the business and stakeholders to ensure alignment of interests and values as well as what is happening, why, the impacts, and how issues are being resolved.

Take-Outs

Summary take-outs include:

- Turnaround skills are required (see Chapter 8 Section "Turnaround").

- The changes would need to be implemented as projects or programs of work, and project management skills are going to be needed (see Chapter 8 Section "Project Management").
- The amount and pace of change needs to be managed (see Chapter 6 Section "Amount and Pace of Change") with the required responses.
- The business needs to be taken on the journey of change (see Chapter 6 Section "The Journey Model of Change").

Governance—Bringing Stakeholders Together

Situation

Governance changes would be required at the various levels impacted according to the situation: from governance of projects to managing the change, to revised governance with vendors, to governance of operations. From revised roles and responsibilities to skilling and training, expertise is used to achieve the required outcomes.

AMEDLI Use

For governance changes to be made and to be effective, all of the elements of AMEDLI would be used, but the main ones include:

- Ambiguity Management—Governance is about overall management of multiple stakeholders with competing interests, varying motivations, and skills and expertise to work across silos for a common outcome. This is nuanced, needs to manage the unplanned, and works with the unknown.
- Empowered Emotional Ownership—Achieving the outcomes required is from the actions of individuals who are motivated to make the required changes, with the required support.
- Interests and Values—Working to align the interests and values so that the ownership is achieved, and the emotional bond formed.

Take-Outs

Governance take-outs include:

- Multiple frameworks for managing the change are going to be required (see Chapter 8 Section "Frameworks").
- The change is going to be related to the individual to get the ownership (see Chapter 7).
- Messaging to diverse stakeholders is required (see Chapter 3).

Technology—To Support the Change and Impacted by the Change

Situation

Technology plays an important role within financial transactions and there is:

- Technology—This is the technology itself, the servers, the databases, the applications, the network, and others. Changes in these may be required in response to financial crime. From the strengthening of network security, to revised audit logs, to revised fields for data capture, a range of changes need to be implemented and tested. Audit of the changes may also be required.
- Data—The data stored in the technology. From quality of data, consistency of data, data assurance, and information security, revisions to data may be required.
- ICT Operations and Services—The support and the operations of the technology and the services provided to the business may be impacted and require changes. From revisions to role-based access, segregation of duties, to account clean-ups, password revisions, to new products and services, a range of impacts may occur.

Responding to and detecting financial crime typically sees all three of these impacted. From managing vendors, to revised legal contracts, impacted service-level agreements, and installing new equipment, technology change is required. Not only are the proven technology frameworks for activities like business analysis, development, and service management required to achieve the change, but other capacities and capabilities may be required, for example, strengthened project management or testing. New systems may be required for responding to and detecting financial crime with integration of data feeds from external parties as well as information flows to external parties. Advanced analytics tools may also be required, for example, matching of cash transaction patterns or the matching of transactions to shipping manifests.

All of these show again that change management requires multiple frameworks (see Chapter 8 Section "Frameworks") with impacts across the silos of operations to be managed. Like other areas of the business, the skilling and training as well as revised operations and extensive stakeholder management are often required.

AMEDLI Use

Depending upon the changes required, all or some of AMEDLI are required for managing technology and its changes. Particularly used are:

- Empowered Emotional Ownership—From emergent behaviors for improved ICT Operations and Services (see Chapter 8 Section "Technology Adoption") through to adoption and adaption (see Chapter 7 Section "Adoption and Adaption") requiring ownership to achieving the outcomes, bringing technology change requires Empowered Emotional Ownership.
- Leadership—Bringing the change requires leadership and emergent behavior of leadership in those across the change.
- Interests and Values—For those making the required changes, an alignment of interests and values is required.

Take-Outs

Beyond the ICT Operations and Services changes, and the take-outs mentioned previously like use of multiple frameworks and project management capacities and capabilities, the following are seen:

- Technology adoption and the wider business integration are important in change (see Chapter 8 Section "Technology Adoption" and Chapter 5 Section "Not the Technology It's the Business").
- Testing is of importance in responding and detecting financial crime changes, and not just for the technology, but also for the changes to business operations from the technology changes (see Chapter 8 Section "Testing").
- Better business cases with true costed projects are required (see Chapter 5 Section "Better Business Cases").

Processes—Emergent Behavior from Vested Interest

Situation

Bringing change in response to financial crime often requires a review of processes. The existing processes may have led to the problems, even if the required processes were not followed (this itself is a process failure). The processes need to be changed, with revisions to standards, policies, and procedures. Updated and new processes that flow end-to-end across the silos, ensuring quality of hand-off, segregation of duties, and management of exceptions can be required. The processes need to be tested, with skilling (ability to do) and training (how to do) provided. From reporting, to controls, to products and services, through regulator interaction, to customer engagement, aspects of processes are changed.

Integral to the process change is the role of the individual. When the individual has pride in who they are and what they do, has a sense of empowerment and ownership, the processes are more likely to be followed. When the processes are in the vested interest of those using them, the processes are more effective. For example, having financial crime detection as part of the valued product offering with solution selling of value-added offerings to clients is in the vested interest of the customer and the sales team. This then brings compliance and cascading impacts across the processes. Part of the emergent behavior is a process for improvement (see Chapter 8 Section "Making Improvements").

AMEDLI Use

Bringing changes to processes, designing end-to-end, integration into the business, and ongoing use see all elements of AMEDLI used. The specific use varies with the situation, role, and scope of changes required. Considerations include:

- Ambiguity Management—Nuance, complexity, and risk management are all required.
- Messaging—A diverse range of engaging messaging that forms an emotional bond is necessary for the change.
- Empowered Emotional Ownership—This is the basis for forming the emergent behavior. Relating to the individual for pragmatic adoption and adaption is a leadership priority.
- Decision Making—A range of decisions are required from the routine operation through to more complex ones around stakeholder management and business management.
- Leadership—To lead the response and the change.
- Interests and Values—The example of value-added products solution sold aligns the customer and sales team interests, which has corresponding impacts across the processes and helps achieve the required regulatory outcomes.

Take-Outs

The importance of an emergent behavior for making the changes in the ongoing operations is again seen. In addition:

- Make compliance a value-added proposition where there is vested interest in meeting, especially at the personal level. Products that help protect customers that can be solution sold as a higher value proposition are in the vested interests of the customer and the sales teams. This then impacts the other areas of the business and helps form the emergent behavior.

- Financial crime detection and compliance starts with the customer value proposition and the products and services, so that the impacts cascade through the processes and craft and shape the emergent behaviors.
- Processes need to work end-to-end across the silos and need to be tested accordingly.
- A process for improvement is required.

Operations—An Emergent Behavior to Fight Financial Crime

Situation

Much of the discussion around processes (see Section "Processes – Emergent Behavior from Vested Interest" of this chapter) applies. Operation is revised through the changes to form the emergent behavior and makes addressing financial crime the responsibility of individuals. Training across the aspects of financial crime detection and management (like Risk Management, Know Your Customer, Customer Due Diligence, Ongoing Due Diligence, Extended Due Diligence, Market Risk, Credit Risk, Anti-Money Laundering, Anti-Terrorism, Fraud, Bribery, People of Influence, Operational Risk, Liquidity Risk etc.), the tools, processes, roles and responsibilities, standards, policies, procedures, governance are required. In addition, skilling is important, because the emergent behavior needed for detection and management of financial crime requires changes in the following:

- Prioritization of importance.
- Changes in rewards and incentives.
- Ownership of actions.
- Overcoming the fear of reporting the nefarious in case their job is lost (management of whistle-blowers).
- Revisions to roles and responsibilities, including segregation of duties and assuring independence of reporting.
- Crafting and shaping the environment that values the detection and management of financial crime.

Other operational changes may include customer and stakeholder management, updates to data, refunds, and settlements. Again, the need to manage the interdependencies, work across the silos end-to-end, and the emergent behavior are needed for the change.

AMEDLI Use

Bringing changes to operations is similar to the use of AMEDLI for processes (see Section "Processes – Emergent Behavior from Vested Interest" of this chapter).

Take-Outs

The main take-out for the detection and management of financial crime is an emergent behavior from operations that sees the detection and management of financial crime as a core competency and expected function and is just part of the offerings. The emergent behavior is that detection and management of financial crime is not an afterthought or a burden that needs to be done, it is just business.

Regulatory Gaps and Quick Wins—Opportunities for Change and Showing Progress

Situation

Within the detection and management of financial crime, the three-ringed defense is common.[1] Audit findings or regulatory gaps for remediation may exist. As rules change and interpretation is revised, or technology is changed and new opportunities for financial crime arise (e.g., mergers and acquisitions and the time to adjust to revised regulatory regimes),

---

[1] In a three-ring defense, the outer ring is the ownership of issues at the business operational level. The middle ring is the overall regulatory and compliance which identifies the issues and advises on how to resolve. The inner ring is the audit, either internal or external, that identifies audit findings for resolution.

gaps in the detection and management of financial crime can occur that need remediation. Some of the audit items are readily completed and may have shorter timelines attached. These can be treated as projects (see Chapter 8 Section "Project Management") and/or as turnarounds (see Chapter 8 Section "Turnaround").

The other feature is the use of "quick wins" which are simpler short-term items to address within larger programs of work. Quick wins can be used to show progress and can be managed as projects. Together the regulatory gaps and the quick wins form a way to show progress, reinforce the achievements, and can be used to help with motivation. The quick wins and regulatory gaps are also used in painting the picture of what the outcomes from the change will look like. Leadership can use regulatory gaps and quick wins to help influence and sustain transformation.

AMEDLI Use

All of the elements of AMEDLI are used in establishing, delivering, and ongoing management of quick wins and regulatory gaps. The regulatory gaps and quick wins can also be used within AMEDLI for:

- Messaging—Use the progress from quick wins and regulatory gaps to message the change and to help with the emotional bond.
- Empowered Emotional Ownership—Make tactical use of quick wins and regulatory gaps in the crafting of emergent behaviors. Use them to influence the sense of ownership and the emotional bond in particular.
- Interests and Values—The quick wins and regulatory gaps can be used to show the alignment of interests and values to others to get the buy-in and support, and the building of momentum.

Take-Outs

The main take-out is that within overall programs for the detection and management of financial crime that bring change, regulatory gaps and quick wins can be used tactically aligned to the overall strategy to influence the required emergent behaviors whilst delivering outcomes.

Project Management—Getting the Change Implemented and Imbedded While Sustaining Operations

Situation

While making changes, the business needs to be sustained and ongoing operations managed. Bringing change is often done as a series of projects or programs or portfolios of work (Figure 2.9) with project management skills and expertise being required for change (see Chapter 8 Section "Project Management"). The change required for financial crime within financial institutions is no different. The larger the change, the more stakeholders effected; the more complex the change, the greater the risk to the business; the more need there is for rigor around project management. Small and tactical implementations which are isolated in nature can be readily done with minimal administrative overhead, but where the financial institutions need to "get off the front page," more rigor around project management is required.

The leadership of the change may need to strengthen the project management expertise as part of the emergent behaviors for the change. Often having project management expertise embedded within the areas of the business is sufficient. Working in a virtual Project Management Office (PMO) approach across the business may also be adequate. Where a greater rigor is required, the change programs may have their own PMO operations.

AMEDLI Use

Project management skills and expertise are required for the management of change and are part of the emergent behaviors required. AMEDLI is used across projects, programs, and portfolios, and especially within change:

- Ambiguity Management—Managing projects with their risks, interdependencies, scope management, and the complex stakeholder management is the management of ambiguity. By strengthening the skills and expertise of project management, the capacity and capability to manage ambiguity is also enhanced. Likewise, skilling and training on the management of ambiguity help with projects.

- Messaging—Projects require messaging. Projects that form the emotional bond are often better supported by the business when it comes to juggling priorities and resources.
- Empowered Emotional Ownership—Projects are delivered by the efforts of the project teams who have the emotional bond to the project and the need to have it delivered. Having the business do projects helps with the emergent behaviors.
- Decision Making—Project managers serve the project by providing guidance and making decisions to enable others to deliver. Projects can strengthen the decision-making expertise in an area of business and contribute to the emergent behaviors.
- Leadership—Projects provide leadership to areas of business by showing how to make changes, what the required outcomes are, and how operations are to occur.
- Interests and Values—Projects take people on the journey of change (see Chapter 6 Section "The Journey Model of Change"); through this the interests and values become aligned to craft and shape the emergent behaviors.

Take-Outs

The need for and use of projects (programs or portfolios) of work to deliver change, especially for the detection and management of financial crime, is a core competency that is required. Given that projects are nuanced, require complex stakeholder management, and cut across the silos of a business also show that:

- Project management skills and expertise are required and are an emergent behavior that is crafted and shaped.
- Bringing change requires a multitude of approaches that are adopted and adapted to need, support variations over time.

- Leadership can use projects to deliver the required changes but also to craft and shape the emergent behaviors required for the change.

Testing—Expertise and Experience for Operations

Situation

The detection, tracking, tracing, and reporting of financial crime cuts across the areas of a financial institution. One customer may have multiple products and be in one or more roles with the financial institution (e.g., a personal account, personal share trades, a business account holder). Committing a financial crime in one area has impacts in other areas (e.g., personal money laundering sees personal accounts impacted, but the employer also needs to be notified in case of impacts on that business). This requires both processes to work end-to-end across the silos (see Section "Processes – Emergent Behavior from Vested Interest" of this chapter) and the testing (see Chapter 8 Section "Testing") to be end-to-end. Testing is also used in the creating of requirements as well as in the formation of processes, policies, and procedures. Testing also helps with skilling and training and can be used in forming the emotional bond within emergent behaviors. The leadership of the change is tasked with overseeing the use of testing, the wider use of testing within the change, and the end-to-end approach of testing to assure service delivery.

AMEDLI Use

AMEDLI can be used across testing and the resulting emergent behaviors including:

- Empowered Emotional Ownership—The wider use of testing is a way to create confidence in the solutions to be used, in the change process, and in the outcomes from the change being fit for purpose. The change helps with skilling and training.
- Interests and Values—End-to-end testing across the silos of the business can assist with the alignment of interests and values of the diverse stakeholders.

- Leadership—Has the responsibility to ensure the testing, that the outcomes are fit for purpose, but can also use testing in the crafting and shaping of the emergent behaviors.

Take-Outs

The main take-outs are:

- Have testing conducted end-to-end across the silos to make sure that the solution works but also because of the wider benefits.
- Use a role-based and product-based approach to the end-to-end testing of processes and operations for the detection and management of financial crime.
- Testing is the basis for skilling and training and the embedding in operations.

Skilling and Training—Create the Confidence and the Expertise

Situation

Skilling (the ability to do) and Training (the how to do) are required as part of the change and ongoing. Beyond creating the expertise required, skilling and training that are tailored to the needs of the individual, help with making the change by showing people that they are valued with a sense of engagement and worth. To form the emergent behavior where the detection and management of financial crime is a core routine business activity that is done because of the alignment of interests and values, there needs to be an emphasis on skilling. The emergent behavior takes time to achieve.

AMEDLI Use

Skilling and Training are seen within AMEDLI mainly in:

- Empowered Emotional Ownership—Use of skilling and training to create confidence, show caring and a sense of engagement and valued. This then leads to the strengthening of the emotional bond, facilitates empowerment, and enables ownership.

- Interests and Values—Skilling and training also help with the alignment of interests and values.
- Leadership—If the role of leadership is to deliver the change, and the emergent behaviors are required for the change and ongoing, then skilling and training are a leadership priority. This includes the ongoing development of capacities and capabilities.

Take-Outs

The main take-outs are the need and prioritization of skilling and training in the emergent behaviors for change and ongoing. The wider role of skilling and training in forming the emotional bond, the empowerment and ownership, and the motivations need to be nurtured by leadership.

Regulatory—To Be the Change They Wish to See

Situation

Within a response to financial crime, there are regulatory impacts and aspects to be managed. While the actual regulatory requirements vary the overall principles discussed for the change apply. The regulatory and compliance team(s) need to be the change they wish to see. It is a leadership function that those in the regulatory and compliance practice what they ask of others and that they hold themselves to the standards (if not higher) they seek in others.

Consider their role in the three-ringed defense (see Section "Regulatory Gaps and Quick Wins – Opportunities for Change and Showing Progress" of this chapter). The service which the regulatory and compliance team(s) provide is summarized by the mantra *"I do good work, change is coming, help me with the change, and I can do more,"* where they practice this for themselves and those they service and support. In particular:

- *I do good work*—They identify the good work in the other areas of the business and use these as examples. They use the

good work to support the efforts. They do this to themselves
as well.

- *Change is coming*—Prepare for the changes, explain the
  changes, show the benefits, and influence the emergent
  behavior required.
- *Help me with the change*—Advise on solution(s), assist with
  the change, the role in skilling and training, and aspects of
  processes (standards, policies, procedures).
- *I can do more*—Continuous improvement practices
  (see Chapter 8 Section "Making Improvements").

Within a financial crime instance, the regulatory and compliance
team(s) will need to make changes to what they do and how they do
it and manage the impacts of the change. Consider where the regulator advises of a failure in reporting where reports were not provided,
or the data are incorrect. Small errors may be a case of following up to
ensure the correct reports are provided. A change in the processes within
regulatory and/or related business areas may be required which can be
done as part of business as usual. More extensive change may occur as
a project or a turnaround (see Section "Project Management – Getting
the Change Implemented and Imbedded While Sustaining Operations"
of this chapter). As the issues become more complex, or more extensive,
or greater the failings, then the program of work to remediate is varied
accordingly. Either way, the regulatory and compliance team(s) need to
change what they do and be the example for others.

AMEDLI Use

The regulatory and compliance team(s) can use AMEDLI within their
own operations and in those they support:

- Ambiguity Management—Needed in interpreting regulations,
  especially where a risk-based approach is used, and
  engagement with regulators and evolving needs.
- Messaging—The messaging to stakeholders on what is
  required, where, when, how, and why.

- Empowered Emotional Ownership—Required for forming the emergent behaviors within areas of the business as well as with the regulatory and compliance team(s).
- Decision Making—Making decisions on what is required, where, when, how, and why.
- Leadership—Providing leadership to the financial institution on the detection, tracking, tracing, and reporting of financial crime.
- Interests and Values—The alignment of interests and values within the required emergent behaviors.

Take-Outs

The main take-outs include:

- The regulatory and compliance team(s) need to change what they do within financial crime events and be the example for others.
- The regulatory and compliance team(s) provide the service and hold themselves to the mantra *"I do good work, change is coming, help me with the change, and I can do more."*
- The regulatory and compliance team(s) are important in the emergent behaviors they need and seek within operations.

Assurance—Quality of Outcomes

Situation

Related to the governance and the overall change is the need for assurance to oversee the outcomes. The assurance needs to address:

- The regulatory outcomes required for specific issues.
- The regulatory needs across the financial institution, including the emerging areas around the rapid changes in technology.
- The overall emergent behaviors across the financial institution so that the ongoing detection, tracking, tracing, reporting,

and management of financial crime occurs. This includes the approach that it is in the best interest of the financial institution to be proactive in this area.

• Assure the protection of the business, the brand, and its customers.

An emerging area for assurance is the rapid changes in technology, which bring new opportunities for financial crime as well as new ways of detection, tracking, tracing, reporting, and management of financial crime. The use of technologies like analytics, artificial intelligence, machine learning, real-time decision making changes the risk profile of a financial institution. The use of cloud services for operational knowledge worker services (like Audit as a Service or Tax as a Service or Risk Management as a Service or Operations as a Service) along with other specialist knowledge worker services (like Project Management as a Service or Testing as a Service) also changes the regulatory regimes, the risk profile of a financial institution, and the assurance frameworks used.

AMEDLI Use

While AMEDLI can be used within assurance, including the development of assurance around technology, an aspect of assurance to be developed is the use of assurance within AMEDLI. While we know the management of ambiguity when we see it, the accreditation and certification of ambiguity management, especially in different contexts and scenarios, is still maturing.

Take-Outs

Beyond the need for assurance across the detection, tracking, tracing, reporting, and management of financial crime, assurance of emerging behaviors is needed to support changes and for the ongoing emergent behaviors. In addition, assurance around the emerging technologies and the cloud services for knowledge worker services as well as automation is required.

Emergent Behavior—Bringing the Change

A recurring theme for change is the crafting and shaping of the emergent behavior for the change and ongoing (Weekly Mirror Message—Feelings in Sustainable Change-https://youtu.be/MX6N6Q3VYRI). Each individual undertakes actions, and this collectively forms the emergent behavior. Different skills, experience, and expertise are required reflecting the different roles and contributions made. It is the leadership to craft and shape the emergent behavior and then lead the adoption and adaption required. The leadership makes the decisions and provides the guidance as well as being the change they wish to see and treating others as they themselves would be treated.

The emergent behavior is what is needed for the detection, tracking, tracing, reporting, and management of financial crime within financial institutions. Having each area proactively manage financial crime, meeting their roles and responsibilities, working end-to-end with processes across the silos, ensuring the quality of hand-off are required. Having ownership of risk, proactive measures, and timely response is required. This proactive management comes from the individuals who have the emotional bond to their actions. By sharing personal stories of how individuals have helped customers and seen the benefits from it, the emotional bond is formed. From the emotional bond comes the actions and emergent behavior.

Any emergent behavior will not be perfect, mistakes will occur, new methods of crime will evolve, and it takes time to respond. Regulators will revise their needs and these changes take time to implement. Key to the emergent behaviors are:

- Leadership—The leadership of the financial institution needs to be the change they wish to see, treating others are they would treat themselves, and setting the example for others to look too. The regulatory and compliance team(s) also need to provide the leadership for the detection, tracking, tracing, and reporting of financial crime.
- Interests and Values—The alignment of interests and values. Start with the product-based and role-based approach that

makes it in the vested interest of the customer and the sales teams to detect and manage financial crime. This then impacts upon the other areas of the operations.

- Empowered Emotional Ownership—It is the actions of individuals that detect, track, trace, and report financial crime. Where there is pride in what they do, ownership, and empowerment of action, the required outcomes from financial crime management are achieved. Ongoing skilling and training are required.
- Messaging—The emotional ownership comes from messages. One of the main ways for engaging is the use of personal examples. By fighting financial crime, they have helped customers and the benefits are seen. It is through these emotional stories, where the benefits can be seen and individuals relate to it, that the emotional bond is formed. From the emotional bond comes the ownership and the actions, and through the actions comes the emergent behavior.

Technology Automation Examples

Introduction

Rapid changes in technology are transforming businesses, creating opportunities, reorganizing markets, and supporting globalization. The emergence of search and social media companies has impacted traditional media companies. Online shopping providers with automation of warehousing and logistics have contributed to the closure of shopping malls and changes in retail. Through the use of technology, healthcare services can be increasingly provided remotely (x-ray analysis conducted in one country and results returned to the patient by a doctor working in a different location to a patient at home). Schooling and education can also be provided online. The changes in technology act through the drivers of Markets, Costs, and Regulatory (see Chapter 6 Section "Drivers and Opportunities") and Customers, as well as impacting vested interest and incumbency.

Technology also brings changes to industries like agriculture and manufacturing (see Chapter 1) as well as transforming knowledge worker services. Routine operations (e.g., mortgage processing or insurance claims or the processing of invoices and payroll) are being automated as provided as services from the cloud.[2] More complex services (like Audit as a Service or Tax as a Service or Risk Management as a Service) are increasingly using technology, being offered as cloud services, and are making use of technologies like analytics, real-time decision making, machine learning, and artificial intelligence within aspects of their services. Other specialist knowledge worker services that are more face-to-face based with greater complexity of stakeholder management (like Project Management as a Service or Testing as a Service) are also being sourced as cloud services and are making greater use of automation within their offerings.

The rapid changes in technology bring (amongst others):

- Strategic risk and revisions to objectives and strategy.
- Changes to services and products and the offerings made to customers. This includes revenue and the revenue mix, with impacts upon cost base, as well as having existing customers change product and service offerings.
- Alterations to service models and operational support.
- Revised risk profile across the business.
- Adjustments to the business operations in support of the revised service models, and products and services.
- Improvements in ICT Operations and Services.
- Outsourced operations and vendor-supplied services amended.
- Managing the impacts and interdependencies in changes to the aforementioned.

---

[2] Cloud-based knowledge worker services combine infrastructure, databases, applications, frameworks, processes, and governance with reporting using best practice. Other services like resourcing, routine administration, the training (how to do), and skilling (ability to do) are also provided.

The worked example of detection and management of financial crime (see Section "Start, Build, Adopt and Adapt from Opportunities Along the Way" of this chapter) would see the aforementioned items addressed within change and in the implementation of technology. Other examples of technology change are considered.

Financial Institutions

Situation

Automation of roles and the use of technology is bringing large-scale changes to financial institutions. Digital transformation includes the provision of services online, through self-service operations, to big data and analytics in marketing and financial crime detection, or to loan approvals assessment using artificial intelligence; financial services is being transformed. While technology changes exist, the greater challenge lies in the business application and use of the technology.

Depending upon the structure, size, and offerings, financial institutions typically use shared services to support areas of the bank based on customer types (Figure 9.2) with a range of products and services provided (e.g., for Personal Banking with Cards, Loans, Transactions,

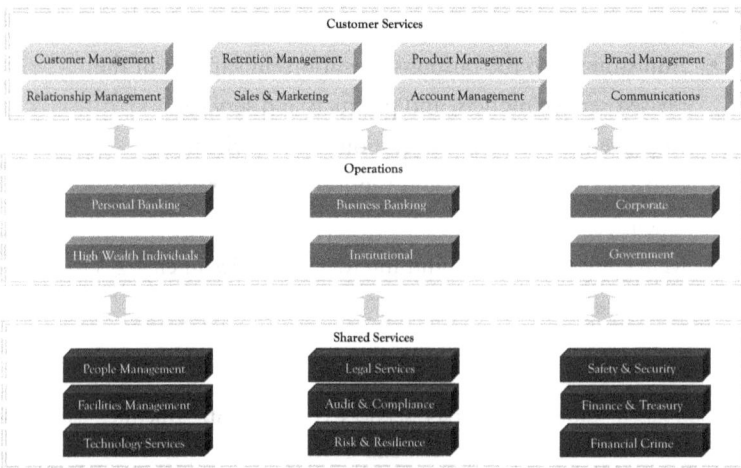

Figure 9.2 Stylized operations in a financial institution

Foreign Exchange, Mortgages, Accounts, Rewards, Managed Investments, Self-Managed Investments, and may include Superannuation and Insurances). Some of the automation around technology examples are in the following sections:

Deposit Taking Cash Transactions—Technology Changing the Opportunities

The use of ATMs (Automatic Telling Machine) for easier deposit taking of cash transactions has impacts upon the controls and reporting for the detection of money laundering. Existing reporting of number of transactions, location, amount, payee and payor details, tracking to thresholds and reporting limits apply. One example is the application of real-time analytics of deposits across an ATM network with pattern matching and trend matching against threshold limits, banking history, transaction values and volumes, geographic spread. Depending upon the jurisdiction, use of mobile device authentication alongside access authentication, the use of biometric recognition with pattern matching can be applied. The wider adoption of transaction data and user data against a transaction with wider tax records, employment history, bank account usage, criminal history, and others on real-time and post event monitoring could also be used.

While aspects of the technology are still being developed, and the feasibility of real-time validations to be resolved, the business issues to consider, to name a few, would include:

- Cost and Benefits—The cost of implementation and the benefits.
- Customer Response—Would customers be accepting of this level of real-time validation as well as post event validation.
- Privacy Management—Management of data privacy issues.
- Information Management—Access to information through data feeds, assurance of information quality, and security of information to name a few.

- Systems Changes—The implementation of the required systems and systems changes as well as ICT Operations and Services.
- Business Integration—The revision to operations to support the changes.

The technology is maturing and is driving the opportunities for the detection, tracking, tracing, and reporting of financial crime for cash deposit taking.

Cashless Payments—Technology Changing the Products and Offerings

The changes in technology such as tap and go payments from cards, mobile device-based payments, and biometric recognition-triggered payments alongside RFI (Radio Frequency Identity) tagging are also bringing changes in the need for ATMs, their location, and the features provided. With less cash required, fewer ATMs are needed with changes to the provision and servicing of ATMs as well as the transportation and management of cash. Changes in technology are also impacting cards and the information stored on the cards. The use of artificial intelligence, big data, analytics, and machine learning for payments tracking, payments authentication, and payment confirmation in both real time and after the event is of value. Depending upon the jurisdiction, the tracking of payments alongside tax records, employment history, bank account usage, and criminal history amongst others may become part of the detection, tracking, tracing, and reporting of financial crime. Other uses such as marketing and product offering may also occur.

Again, the technology is maturing, and the opportunities for change are occurring, but it is the wider business change and adoption that is often the limiter on the rate of change.

Loan Approvals—Technology Changing Risks

From cash advances, to the purchasing of equipment, to mortgaging on property or assets, loan approval is a core banking function. With technology changes, the more routine the loan process, the more it is suited to automation of the lending process. From the diversity of data feeds, the use of artificial intelligence in data validation, to pattern matching of data to criteria, predictive modeling of the ability to pay, revised asset depreciation modeling, insurance considerations, and more; the more complex loan approvals can be automated. With the automation comes a change in the risk profile for the business including:

- Technology Risk—The technology risk to the business changes. The dependency upon technology is increased and the need for assurance of service from technology is increased.
- Information Risk—The greater the use of information sources in the automated decision making, the greater the risks on the supply of information, the quality of the information, and assurance of these. The information risk of the business is changed with corresponding impacts on risk to the business.
- Vendor Risk—Increased dependency upon vendors and external parties for the supply of information and cloud services.
- Implementation Risk—The technology brings changes to operations with revised processes, policies, procedures, standards, and the need for skilling and training. Change needs to be made around the technology while operations are sustained. The risk to the business changes during the transition and in the revised operations.

Technology changes the risk profile of a business as operations are increasingly automated or provisioned from the cloud.

Sales and Marketing—Technology Changing the Engagement

The technology transformation around sales and marketing is familiar to many. Social media and search with the use of algorithms has brought transformation to the advertising industry, the media industries, and the way businesses engage with customers. The use of big data and analytics has enabled businesses to target offerings and understand the needs of customers better, with an emphasis upon predictive needs. For a financial institution the regulatory regime of what data can be matched and how is different to other business. The privacy issues, the information custodianship obligations, and the segregation of responsibilities all impact upon the adoption of technology and the change required.

The use of machine learning and artificial intelligence to track the permissions to information and its use is increasing within financial institutions. Beyond the customer application of data analytics, a suite of technologies are being used amongst others for:

- Determining the incorrect access to information in marketing operations.
- Establishing the incorrect use of information in marketing operations.
- Reporting on breaches and remediation.
- Regulatory reporting.
- Analytics on the effectiveness of campaigns.
- Analytics on the value of skilling and training and the returns.

The assurance of information, the changes to operations, the reporting, and compliance all impact the adoption of the emerging technology and the required changes.

Take-Outs

The selected examples from this section provide further guidance to the adoption and adaption to change and the need for crafting and shaping emergent behavior in support of the changes coming from technology including:

- Change is needed around technology to manage the risks for a business. As more services are automated the information risks around the quality of information, assurance of the information, supply of the information, and dependency on information increase.
- As more cloud services are used, the risks to the business change.

- Changes in technology bring new approaches for financial crime as well as for the detection, tracking, tracing, and reporting of financial crime.
- Increases in real-time monitoring, wider use of related information through pattern matching and trend matching, to impact authentication and confirmation of transactions.
- The business integration and adoption of the technology, including regulatory change, impacts the take-up of the technology and the required change.

Higher Education

Situation

Higher education and education in general are impacted by digital transformation. This includes being faced with changing their own operations around technology, including integration of the technology and the changes to products and offerings. Researching the technology and the wider business and societal issues and teaching the technology as well as the ICT Operations and Services, the wider business impacts, and other societal issues are required. Higher education also plays an advisory role to government and industry and would be expected to advise on the technology, the ICT Operations and Services, the business management, and the wider societal and economic considerations (Figure 9.3). Making these changes are likely to be incremental as the technology changes and the impacts are managed. A series of programs of work will be to realize the change.

Teaching—Technology Changing the Offerings and How

Technology is changing what is taught and how it is taught. Teaching sees a regular review of curriculum and content as a matter of routine, but the rapid changes in technology bring extra demands in keeping courses current and the use of artificial intelligence and automation in detecting fraud and plagiarism. Artificial intelligence, automation, and big data are used in assignments and training as well as the use of analytics. Those

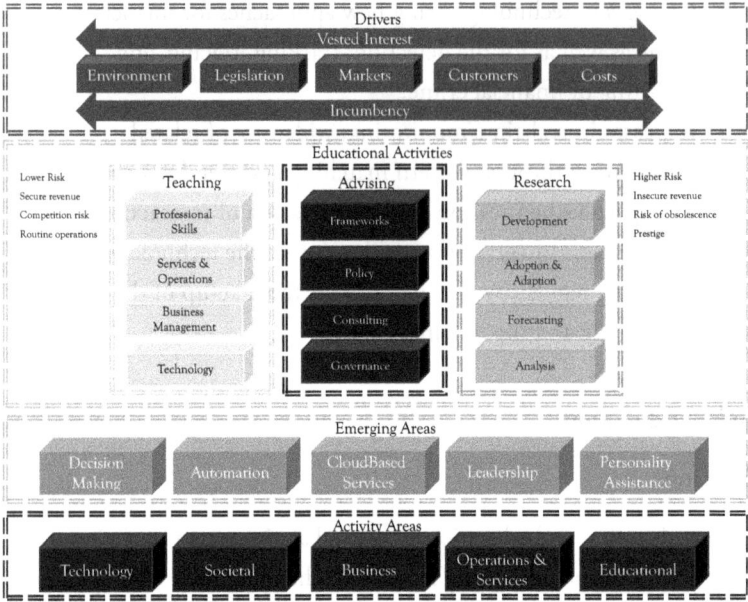

Figure 9.3 Influencing the offerings of educational institutions. From Sherringham, K., and B. Unhelkar. 2020. "Higher Education in Capacity and Capability Building for the Information Economy" In Role of ICT in Higher Education Trends, Problems, and Prospects Latwal, *eds, G.S. Sharma, K.S. Mahajan, and P, Komers. (Chapter 30, pp. 411–422). Apple Academic Press F.L. USA.*

teaching need to keep up-to-date with the technology, the ICT Operations and Services, and the business applications, as well as being able to teach using them.

From the changes in funding to revised product offerings in response to the market forces, technology is transforming teaching. Educational institutions are faced with managing this change while supporting operations.

Research—Technology Bringing Research Opportunities

The changes in technology are bringing change in how research is conducted as well as the types of research required. There is the research and development of the technology. There is the research on the application of the technology. There is the research on the business impacts and use of the technology. There is the research into the wider societal impacts of the technology. All of the research is increasingly making use of, automation, analytics, and big data as well as cloud services (e.g., on demand computing for modeling and prediction).

Again, educational institutions are faced with managing this change. From revised funding priorities, to training and skilling of staff, to management of intellectual property, and cyber security, the business integration impacts the technology adoption within research.

Advisory—Changing in Response to Technology

Educational institutions play an advisory role to government and industry on the changes in technology and the impacts of that technology. From advisory groups on standards, to accreditation and certification, to policy and funding priorities, advisory on the change around technology is required. Advisory would include amongst others:

- Revisions to objectives and strategy for companies and governments.
- Emerging opportunities and research on trends.
- Business advisory on changes to services and products and the offerings, including revenue and the customers.
- Impacts on cost base, as well as the cost of transitioning.
- Guidance on alterations to service models and operational support.
- Management of risk and making the transition.
- Skilling and Training of resources and the resourcing needs.

To provide this advisory, the educational institutions themselves need to change around the technology.

Operations—Self-Change to Be Relevant and Viable

The educational institutions need to change their own operations around technology (similar to a financial institution). This needs to be done so that the educational institution remains relevant and competitive (i.e., viable in an environment of change), but also to sustain operations while making the changes. The educational institution needs to be the change they wish to see.

Food Production

Situation

Technology has transformed food production and is ongoing through the digital transformation of operations. From high-density agriculture in warehouses with controlled environments managed by automations, to robots planting, looking after, and picking in fields, through the automation of processing plants, agriculture is a high-technology industry. Other examples are the use of satellite tracking of animals, the automated image capture of animals, and the loading onto transport triggered by an RFI tag. Beyond the advanced technology used in research of soils, land use, water management, pharmaceuticals, and more are the issues of adoption and integration of technology across the operations and supply chains (e.g., paddock to plate tracking). This technology change is set against the increasing demand for food for a growing global population and with increasing affluence bringing changes in demand for varying types of food.

Food production is broadly split into the following areas:

- Producers—Produce the food (e.g., dairy farmers or wheat growers).
- Providers—Provide support to the industry (e.g., chemicals and fertilizers or pharmaceuticals).
- Processors—Process the food into value-added products (e.g., meat processing plants or grain milling).
- Logistics—The transport and logistics management and related support (e.g., sales yards or trucking or ports).
- Services—The range of service providers involved (e.g., technology providers or equipment suppliers or veterinary or research services or consulting services).
- Sales—The Wholesale, Food outlets, and Retail operations. This would include any additional processing for specialist products.

- Government—From regulations, through quarantine, to border control, to health and hygiene standards, to transportation standards, to animal welfare practices, to infrastructure, and international trade agreements, governments play an important role within food production.

Each of these areas of food production has its own requirements and needs, meeting the differing customers and markets. With changes in technology, Producers can market to the end customer directly, and Processors can also market directly to the end customers whilst shortening their supply chains. All of these areas of food production are faced with the adoption and adaption to changes in technology and bringing change at the level of the industry sector, the organization, the individual, as well as cross-sector needs. Across the industry sectors are the interdependencies and the integrated end-to-end supply chains that share information, with the need for common standards, protocols, and frameworks. Globalization considerations also apply as well as trade agreements. Clearly, adopting and adapting to technology, coordinating, and bringing change across and within the industry are complex with competing needs and stakeholders.

Technology in Operations

Given the differing needs within the varying sectors, businesses, and stakeholders within the food production industry, any technology change is going to require cross-sector and sector leadership as well as at the company levels. It is the end-to-end management across the silos of the industry which brings it challenges (e.g., agreement on standards for information sharing and their implementation). Technology change is often done by default standards from the early adopters and the 20 percent of the industry players that typically generate the 80 percent of revenues. This 20 percent of players cooperate on implementation because their interests and values align and meet the needs of vested interest to do so. They show the Leadership, the Decision Making, and manage ambiguity of establishment and implementation. These adopters then provide the Rails for Operation (see Figure 6.6) as well as providing momentum to incrementally and progressively align the other players. This will take time, and not all players seek to align, but it is the commercial realities which will drive the cooperation and the change. Examples of the change and related technology use are seen (Table 9.3).

Table 9.3 Example change and technology in operational aspects of food production

Activity	Shared needs	Example change and technology
Animal welfare	• Real-time compliance monitoring across sector from consumer to producer including regulators • Minimum role-based sector-wide training levels with continuous assessment from cloud-based services • Integration with government systems, e.g., bio-security	If an industry does not regulate itself, the government will end up regulating it. It is better the government endorses an industry standard and that the industry is proactive. Requires agreed information sharing, real-time reporting, standards, and protocols. Integration with government systems is part of the solution. Skilling and training to support the adoption are also necessary. Requires complex stakeholder management to realize the change
Land management	• Land regeneration program with a focus on the "soil carbon sponge" to build water storage and improve animal feed and animal health while capturing carbon • Land consolidation, alternative use programs, with infrastructure, assistance, and acquisition programs • Minimum role-based sector-wide training levels with continuous assessment from cloud-based services • Real-time compliance monitoring across sector	Industry leads in land use, land regeneration, which brings wider environmental outcomes. Beneficial to producers as well as for brand and marketing to conscientious consumers. Principles apply to other stakeholders. Again, it is better the government endorses an industry standard and that the industry is proactive. Requires agreed information sharing, real-time reporting, standards, and protocols. Integration with government systems is part of the solution. Big Data, analytics, and artificial intelligence used. Skilling and training to support the adoption are also necessary. Requires complex stakeholder management to realize the change

Table 9.3 (*Continued*)

Activity	Shared needs	Example change and technology
Water and waste management	• Integrated infrastructure programs with government endorsement for recycling, reclamation, and management • Minimum role-based sector-wide training levels with continuous assessment from cloud-based services • Real-time compliance monitoring across sector	An industry-wide move to recycling and reclamation of water and waste aligned with government programs. Industry-led standards and protocols proactively managed with government endorsement. Requires agreed information sharing, real-time reporting, standards, and protocols. Integration with government systems is part of the solution. Big Data, analytics, and artificial intelligence used. Skilling and training to support the adoption are also necessary. Requires complex stakeholder management to realize the change
Free trade and market access	• Country- and industry-specific agreements	Technology changes to support the conditions of the agreements (e.g., quality assurance and end-to-end tracing)
Access to capital	• A range of activities for capital investments in the industry including technology and infrastructure, aligned with government policy and decisions	Technology changes include systems integration, data feeds, and use of analytics in a variety of ways (case specific) but leveraging industry standards and protocols

Bringing the changes (Table 9.3) would take time, complex stakeholder management, and leadership. A range of complex decisions are required; the many shades of gray in the decisions managed, nuance and ambiguity across the work, and competing interests and values are seen. The implementation would be a series of programs of work incrementally applied with capacity and capability along the way with a focus on the emergent behaviors.

Technology in Support

A range of supporting activities are also required to bring the change to the industry and for the adoption of technology (Table 9.4). These activities would be completed as programs of work across the sectors, within

Table 9.4 Example change and technology in support aspects of food production

Activity	Shared needs	Example change and technology
Research and development	• Industry-specific research and development. Priorities may include regenerative agriculture and drought resistance for climate change • Other areas include alternative proteins and pharmaceuticals • Aligned with government funding and priorities	The research adoption of technology and change is similar to the research in educational institutions (Section "Higher Education" of this chapter) and aligned with government funding. Industry-led development (the commercialization) is the consumption of cloud-based services, automation, analytics, and artificial intelligence in support of the commercialization and management. The change experience of commercialization applies
Technology	• End-to-end records for production and related information provision with role-based access and real-time access across the supply chain, including customers • Messaging exchange services and standards for information exchange integrated globally and to government systems (prioritized in Australia) • Data standards for information exchange integrated globally and to government systems (prioritized in Australia) • Real-time reporting services to industry and government for operations, compliance, and monitoring • Data analytics service for value-added products and information services to the industry and government, and for compliance purposes	A range of change programs of work to support the development, application, operation, services, and management of technology: • Information service provider—A consortia and commercial partnership, to deliver the information services needed by the industry • Cloud-based training service—Cloud-based training service for the industry with government-endorsed training standards for minimum industry compliance training, and other industry training (includes virtual reality). Includes skilling and training on the use of technology • AI and analytics—Development and commercialization of artificial intelligence and analytics for services and value-added products and information to the industry • Robotics—Development and commercialization of robotics within the industry with supporting services and operations

Table 9.4 (Continued)

Activity	Shared needs	Example change and technology
People	• Cloud-based training service for the industry • Revised minimum standards certifications, role based, across the industry, including land management, animal welfare, and technology use and adoption • Member organizations provide skilling and training to their sectors against minimum government accreditation • Mentoring support around bringing change in land management, animal welfare, water and waste management, and ICT integration and adoption	The crafting and shaping of emergent behaviors for industry change through capacity and capability building. Addresses the emotional bond for change. Align with government funding and regional support
Products and markets	Industry- and business-specific considerations	Industry- and business-specific considerations
Infrastructure	• Renewable powered desalinization as part of water and waste management • Renewables adoption across sector as part of water and waste management and government carbon programs • GPS coverage, Internet, and 5G provision and adoption	A range of industry-wide infrastructure as part of government programs to support economies, rural areas, and other infrastructure investments: Technology will vary to circumstances, but an integrated standardized approach is beneficial
Regulatory and government	• Endorsement of industry-led frameworks (animal welfare, land management, water and waste) and industry training • Systems connectivity, data standards, and information sharing with government agencies (especially bio-security) • Market access	Sustained campaigns of change to influence government policy to endorse industry-led frameworks and approaches

sectors, and businesses according to need and are in support of other activities (e.g., Research and Development is required for Water and Waste Management—Table 9.3). The technologies used would vary, but the need for an integrated end-to-end approach remains, with common standards and protocols, and business integration support.

Technology and Change

Recurring themes around the rapid changes in technology impacting businesses and change are seen including:

- Drivers—Rapid changes in technology impact a business through the drivers: Markets, Cost, Customers, and Regulatory. Rapid changes in technology impact incumbency and affect vested interests. All of this creates opportunities for change.
- Opportunities—The drivers have created the opportunities for change, but there is a need for ongoing sustained incremental change around technology through an improvement process.
- Journey Model—Adopting and adapting to changes in technology is a journey of sustained change with periods of more intense activity. The journey is the business integration with product management changes and revised products and offerings and service models. This includes revenues and the revenue mix, with impacts upon cost base, as well as having existing customers change product and service offerings. The journey is the incremental adoption and adaption sustained with leadership taking advantage of opportunities for wider change.
- Boards—The changes around technology are an issue for the Board of a business. From the objectives and strategy of the business, managing the strategic risk, to the funding, and ensuring the business is sustained are complex and require Leadership, Decision Making, and Ambiguity Management. A diversity of skills and expertise is needed (including technology, financial, legal, industry experience, customer representation, government, employees).

- Executive—The executives need to be the change they wish to see and treat others as they themselves would wish to be treated. The executives are tasked with changing the environment, instilling the behaviors, and ensuring the outcomes by crafting and shaping the emergent behavior. The business needs to be sustained around the change. The changes in the risk profile of the business around the change and the use of cloud services with artificial intelligence and automation are to be managed.
- Governance—A level of pragmatic and practical governance for the changes needs to exist. The governance should work across the silos and operate end-to-end to assure the required emergent behavior, outcomes, and business integration.
- Technology—The implementation of the technology and the ICT Operations and Services. The move is from a technology-centric view to an information service for the use of artificial intelligence, machine learning, big data, and analytics. The move is to the assurance of information supply across the disparate sources, quality of information, and the derived value-added products and services that are then used. Areas including cyber security, information security, vendor management, and risk management are of increased importance.
- ICT Operations and Services—The process changes to the ICT Operations and Services around the new technology and use of new technology in their processes. Includes revised processes that work end-to-end, policies, procedures, standards, and protocols. The governance, risk, regulatory, compliance, Audit and service models are also addressed.
- Business Integration—Beyond the technology processes are the service management changes to the business, from the changes in roles and responsibilities, through business processes, to customer management and vendor management as well as outsourced operations.

- Emergent Behavior—Technology change is an enabler of the required emergent behavior and the emergent behavior is required for the adoption and adaption of technology.

Capacity and Capability to Adopt and Adapt

The capacity and capability building for achieving sustainable change is nuanced. Recognizing the importance of people in change and sustainable change is about getting people to do things differently, the importance of emergent behaviors is seen. This applies to digital transformation as well as other change. It is through the development, nurturing, and maturing of professional skills[3] (Weekly Mirror Message—Professional Skills in Managing Change—https://youtu.be/Avp4lUDdM1U) that the ability to adopt and adapt is seen for the achievement of change (Figure 9.4).

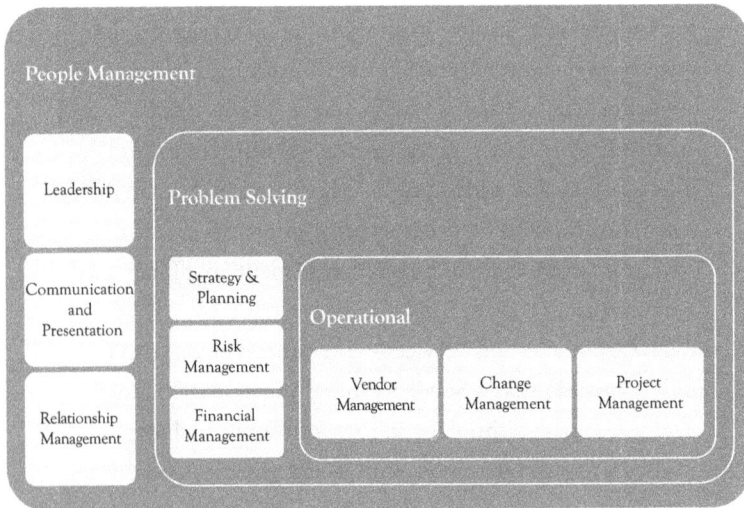

Figure 9.4 Professional skills in achieving change

---

[3] Professional skills include people management, financial management, vendor management, relationship management, strategy and planning, risk management, project management, problem solving, management of change in the business, management of ambiguity, governance, compliance management, cross-disciplinary collaboration, and communication and presentation.

With change being about people, this makes people management a primary professional skill, which includes leadership, communication, and presentation skills (messaging), as well as relationship management for managing relationship with and between people. After people management skills, it is problem solving for achieving results which is required including professional skills in strategy and planning, risk management, and financial management. After all, without funding, things seldom happen. The operational professional skills to achieve results use the people management and problem solving as well as vendor management, change management, and project management expertise and skills for the delivery of services while managing the change. All of this makes use of the overarching approach within AMEDLI.

Capacity and capability building of the professional skills and the emergent behaviors are often achieved through a multitude of approaches and through a series of programs of work which are sustained. Achieving such emergent behaviors is not easy, often takes time, and the immediate returns are seldom seen. Consider the coach of the sports team seeking an emergent behavior of a winning team by running a program of work to have the team train differently, who changes players around, and does select drills with players. Similarly for organizations, where sustained programs of work (Weekly Mirror Message—Program of Work to Craft and Shape Emergent Behaviours—https://youtu.be/Z4o1c7LIotw) using a variety of approaches is required to form emergent behaviors (Figure 9.5):

- The Board and the executive need to be the change they wish to see and treat others as they themselves would wish to be treated. From messaging to the organization with stories to form the emotional bond, through scenario sessions, specialist knowledge awareness, and others, the leadership can change their emergent behavior to influence others. Having the executive work in frontline roles is often very beneficial for understanding issues and showing leadership.
- Managers too need to set the example for their teams. From messaging the emotional stories, scenario sessions, integration to product and service and role changes, to repeat business-specific awareness, a range of measures can be used.

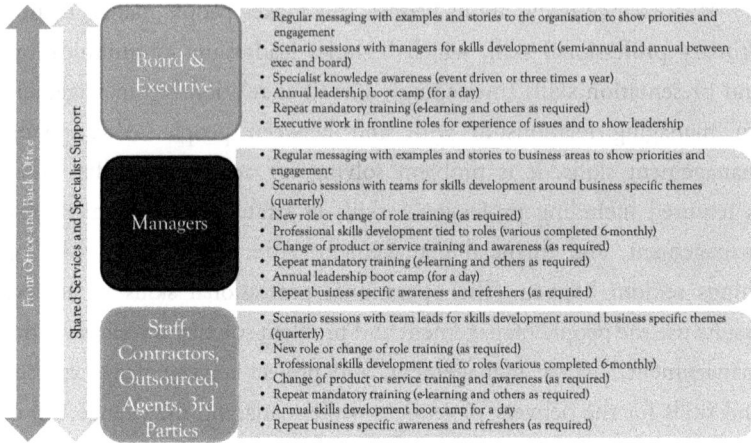

Figure 9.5 Program of work for emergent behaviors

- Staff, Contractors, and Outsourced providers, including third parties and agents, complete a range of activities including scenario sessions, role change, change product and service changes, to repeat business-specific awareness.

These apply to front office, back office, those in shared services, as well as specialized support. This combination of approaches, pragmatically applied with consistency and persistency, is how the professional skills and emergent behaviors are formed and maintained for achieving sustainable change.

Appendix A

Suggested Change Leadership Courses

Craft and Shape the leadership to form the emergent behavior

Summary

It all starts with one person with the vision and desire who influences those around the person. Through serving, influence is brought using skilling and training. Some suggested courses and study outlines are presented to craft and shape the leadership to form the emergent behaviors for change.

Introduction

Bringing and sustaining change takes time, is nuanced, and comes through the emergent behavior. It is the actions of individuals with empowerment and ownership that bring the change, but it is the capacity and capability for adaption and adoption which is required to support the change and sustain the necessary emotional bond. Skilling and training is integral to achieving change because they help provide confidence, strengthens the emotional bond, and shares skills and expertise for the emergent behavior to have people do things differently. While a way forward for selective and opportunistic capacity and capability building was mentioned previously (see Chapter 7 Section "Adoption and Adaption"), this chapter provides an additional view on the use of the shared skills and expertise for courses. Any suggested courses and content would be suitable for both room and/or remote study. While chapters are suggested, content from all chapters should be drawn as required and the supporting videos used (https://youtube.com/channel/UCz0yQvABRRd7s_llUKWhlVw). Those looking for research topics in support of change, technology adoption, or knowledge worker transformation will also find the suggested areas from the courses of benefit in identifying research opportunities. The main purpose of the suggested

QR Code for Videos

courses is to capacity and capability build for the emergent behavior for achieving the change and ongoing.

Half-Day Leadership Workshop

This half-day workshop is aimed at leadership (especially senior leadership) in organizations who are seeking to bring sustainable change within their operations. Their role is to lead the change (assure outcomes) rather than operationalize the change. This workshop would include alignment to objectives, strategies, and organizational needs. This change may be as part of a business turnaround, responses due to adverse publicity, or the need to transform operations and services around technology or regulatory-induced change or maybe mergers. The workshop is over five hours (the approach of Chapter 7 Section "Adoption and Adaption" can also be used) with hands-on exercises and group discussions (Table A.1).

Table A.1 Half-day leadership workshop

	Mapping of the chapters in this book to a Half-day leadership workshop		
Session	Workshop topic	Relevant chapters	Comments
08:00– 08:30	Objectives, Introductions and House keeping		
08:30– 09:30	Experience of leading change with what has worked and the less successful	Chapter 1 for context. Chapter 9 for pragmatics of change	Group exercises on shared experiences of leading change. Include what is expected of leaders and draw out the role of people in change

Table A.1 (Continued)

Session	Workshop topic	Relevant chapters	Comments
	Mapping of the chapters in this book to a Half-day leadership workshop		
09:30–10:45	Pragmatics and realities of change	Chapter 1 for AMEDLI and pragmatics alongside Chapter 9. Draw out leadership role from Chapters 5 and 6	Draw out the lessons learned in conversation to cover pragmatics and practicalities and relate to AMEDLI overarching approach
10:45–11:15	Break, with networking and informal discussions		
11:15–12:00	Crafting and shaping emergent behaviors	Chapters 5 and 6 for leadership and decision making. Chapters 7 and 4 for the people aspects	Role of leadership in emergent behaviors with examples and experience of participants. Relate to people aspects
12:00–12:45	Leading Change	Draw on Chapter 8 to have the realities of leading change made real	Group exercises to tie drivers, opportunities, and emergent behaviors, with experiences and lessons learned
12:45–13:00	Key Messages. Next Steps. Closure		

Based on your workplace or the course(s) you are involved with, consider the following activities as groups or individuals. Be sure to include comments and feedback within the activities.

One-Day Leading Change Workshop

This one-day workshop is aimed at those who are leading the change to make it real and operationalize, rather than assurance of outcomes. Participants may be change managers or project managers or business managers needing to bring change. Knowledge of change management approaches and/or project management frameworks is advantageous, but they are not required for this workshop. Those attending may wish to have participated in the half-day workshop for context, but this one-day workshop is standalone. The drivers and opportunities for change, for their particular circumstance, should be known to participants to help get the most from the exercises. The workshop is over nine hours (the approach of Chapter 7 Section "Adoption and Adaption" can also be used) with hands-on exercises and group discussions (Table A.2).

Table A.2 One-day leading change workshop

	Mapping of the chapters in this book to an One-day change leadership workshop		
Session	*Workshop topic*	*Relevant chapters*	*Comments*
08:00–08:30	Objectives, Introductions and House keeping		
08:30–09:30	Experience with change and what has worked and the less successful	Chapter 1 for context. Chapter 9 for pragmatics of change	Group exercises on shared experiences of change. Draw out the role of people in change and the emotional aspects
09:30–10:45	Pragmatics and realities of change	Chapter 1 for AMEDLI and pragmatics alongside Chapter 9. Draw out people and emotions using Chapters 4 and 7	Draw out the lessons learned in conversation to cover pragmatics and practicalities and relate to AMEDLI overarching approach
10:45–11:15	Break, with networking and informal discussions		
11:15–11:45	Ambiguity Management	Chapter 2	The role and importance of ambiguity management and how to build emergent behavior. Group exercises on where ambiguity management is used, and benefits gained
11:45–12:15	Messaging	Chapter 3	The role of messaging to engage and build the emotional bond. Group exercises on where emotional messaging delivered, benefits gained
12:15–13:00	Empowered Emotional Ownership	Use Chapter 4 with reference to Chapters 3, 7, and 8	Importance of individuals with empowered emotional ownership in emergent behaviors. Group exercises on how to craft and shape
13:00–14:00	Lunch, with networking and informal discussions		
14:00–14:30	Decision Making	Chapter 5	Making decisions, implementation, and response to adopt and adapt. Group exercises on emotional bond and tied to leadership

Table A.2 (Continued)

	Mapping of the chapters in this book to an One-day change leadership workshop		
Session	Workshop topic	Relevant chapters	Comments
14:30–15:00	Leadership	Chapter 6	Role of leadership in guiding, making decisions, and emergent behaviors. Group exercises on response to leadership
15:00–15:30	Break, with networking and informal discussions		
15:30–16:10	Interests and Values	Chapter 7 with use of Chapters 3 and 8	How to align interests and values to underpin the emergent behaviors. Group exercises on how to craft and shape
16:10–16:50	Adoption and Adaption of emergent behaviors	Draw on Chapters 8 and 9 to have the realities of leading change made real	Group exercises on how emergent behaviors for the change are to be shaped
16:50–17:00	Key Messages. Next Steps. Closure		

Within Courses

Courses at the master's level and/or postgraduate diploma level are suited to a range of modules from this book within the overall curriculum. This is to educate as well as capacity and capability build, especially of the leadership necessary to realize the transformations and automations.

For business administration courses:

- The half-day workshop can be used for crafting and shaping leadership. Using a theme like Chapter 9 is suggested.
- The one-day workshop can be used for teaching how to achieve change (the approach of Chapter 7 Section "Adoption and Adaption" can also be used).
- The workshops can be combined and taught over a semester, one session a week, with assignments, followed by group discussions.

Similarly, for leadership in the adoption of technology.

- The half-day workshop can be used for crafting and shaping leadership, especially with an ICT Operations and Services focus. The themes of automation of operations can be applied within the group exercises and discussions (see Chapter 5 Section " Not the Technology It's the Business" and Chapter 8 Section " Technology Adoption").
- The one-day workshop can be used for teaching how to achieve change around technology, especially the automation of operations (see Chapter 9).
- The workshops can be combined and taught over a semester, one session a week, perhaps with assignments, followed by group discussions. A technology focus can be employed.

About the Authors

Keith Sherringham, BSc (Hons), FACS, consults to executive and senior leadership in corporations and government on business strategy and planning, the business application of ICT, and business services and operational improvement, as well as delivering high-profile business turn-arounds and business transformations. Keith is a noted author and speaker on the business application of ICT and is known for his thought leadership and pragmatic strategy in areas including real-time decision making, business transformation, and standardizing the roles of knowledge workers. He peer-reviews papers and proposals for leading journals and publishing houses. He is a board director for the Australian Computer Society and has guest lectured at various universities in Australia and overseas on the impacts of changes in ICT to business. Keith is a company director, director for not-for-profits, and mentor to CEOs and boards within not-for-profits.

Bhuvan Unhelkar, BE, MDBA, MSc, PhD, is a Professor of IT at the University of South Florida; an Adjunct Professor at Western Sydney University; and an Honorary Professor at Amity University, India. He is also Founding Consultant at MethodScience and PlatiFi, with Mastery in Business Analysis & Requirements Modeling, Software Engineering, Big Data Strategies, Agile Processes, Mobile Business, and Green IT. Bhuvan is a thought-leader and a prolific author of 25 books, including *Artificial Intelligence & Business Optimization* and *The Art of Agile Practice* (CRC Press, USA). Bhuvan is Fellow of the Australian Computer Society, IEEE Senior Member, and Life Member of Computer Society of India and Baroda Management Association. He is past president of Rotary Club of Sarasota Sunrise (Florida) and multiple Paul Harris Fellow, Discovery volunteer at NSW parks and wildlife, and a previous TiE Mentor.

Index

Letters *f* and *t* after page numbers indicate figures and tables, respectively.

www.ingramcontent.com/pod-product-compliance
Lightning Source LLC
Chambersburg PA
CBHW061145220326
41599CB00025B/4366